Retreat from China

Retreat from China

British Policy in the Far East 1937–1941

NICHOLAS R. CLIFFORD

University of Washington Press

© Nicholas R. Clifford 1967
First published 1967

Library of Congress Catalog Card Number 67–12395

Printed in Great Britain
by Ebenezer Baylis and Son, Ltd.
The Trinity Press, Worcester, and London

Contents

Preface

Everything that has been written about the 1930s seems only to confirm the fact that we are still too close to the period really to understand it. Since the defeat of the Axis, it has been tempting to deal with the history of that period as a play in which, after many dangers, good finally triumphed over evil, as it had somehow been fated to do all along. What we too often fail to understand is that the problem facing the Western statesmen of the prewar world was not how to defeat the Axis in a war which would inevitably come, but how to get along with the Axis and prevent the outbreak of the war which they desperately hoped would not come. It was, quite simply, a problem of coexistence (to use a favourite word of the Japanese Foreign Office), and it meant living in the same world with countries like Hitler's Germany and Mussolini's Italy, countries which were strategically dangerous as well as morally repulsive.

Nowhere was this more true than in the Far East. Japan did not want the West to intervene in East Asian politics, and the West did not want to intervene; yet there was a limit as to how far they could ignore each other. Both sides, despite loose talk about 'inevitable' war, wanted to coexist, or felt they had to coexist, yet in the end this proved to be impossible.

Britain, particularly, wanted to stay out of oriental entanglements; she had quite enough problems at home. Few men, it appears, gave much thought to Asian problems (east of India, at any rate), and this lack of contemporary interest has been fairly well reflected by historians since then. The press of the day reported the news from China, but it took something big, like the *Panay* sinking, or the Tientsin crisis, to divert attention from Europe. The memoirs, autobiographies, and journals of the leading figures of the time, published since then, generally give East Asia only passing mention; one looks in vain through the works of men like Halifax, Vansittart, Hoare, Simon, or Amery for any treatment of the war in China. A score of important books by professional historians deal with Britain and the outbreak of the Second World War, but by and large, they restrict themselves to Europe. In the thirties, Europe's problems seemed more immediate, and more comprehensible, and it was easier to focus attention on a country like Spain, where the forces of darkness did battle with the forces of light, than on the mysterious Orient, so many thousands of miles away, where the neat categories of European political thought and ideology turned out to be so disconcertingly inappropriate.

Yet the story has its own interest, and this book is an attempt to fill a gap left by the other studies of prewar British foreign policy. More than that, it is a look at a period of four years which saw a tremendous acceleration of the Western withdrawal from Asia. Future historians may differ on whether Japan at the time represented a progressive or a reactionary force in history, but it is obvious that while events since then have not followed the course that her leaders would have chosen, it was she, more than anyone else, who paved the way for the present reconstruction of Asia, by destroying the hold which the West had built up during the centuries of Europe's expansion.

Furthermore, the point needs to be made that for most of this period, it was Britain above all among the non-Asian powers who bore the brunt of the Japanese drive. The history of these years has perhaps been written too much with an eye cocked towards the final Japanese-American negotiations which led to Pearl Harbor, and it has been easy to assume that London, occupied as it was by domestic and European troubles, played a secondary role to Washington's lead in the East. In fact, it was not until late 1940 that America emerged as the West's chief spokesman in the Orient, and before that, weak and preoccupied as she was, Britain, almost by default, had to take the lead in the West's rather uncertain efforts to stem the course of Japanese imperialism.

Consequently, in examining these years, I have chosen to emphasize certain topics while giving others perhaps less than their due. Until September 1939 much of Britain's concern was devoted to the protection of British interests in China, caught between a Chinese nationalism on the defensive, and a Japanese imperialism on the offensive. Furthermore, the emphasis lies on the period up to the fall of France, for after that Britain had no choice but to concern herself almost entirely with Europe. Then it was that slowly, and with obvious reluctance, the United States came forward to fill the gap, taking over the task of dealing with Japan in the year and a half of negotiations which have been so brilliantly described by historians such as Feis, Langer, and Gleason. After September 1939, also, the main focus of interest in Anglo-Japanese relations shifted from the defence of Western interests in China to the defence of the Empire, and this question has been dealt with at length by the official British historians of the war, who have had access to the materials which will remain closed to the rest of us for decades to come.

I have made no attempt to deal with the making of Japanese policy, and have relied heavily on the work of scholars like G. Richard Storry, F. C. Jones and Robert Butow. There remain a number of significant gaps in any study written now of this period. From our present vantage point one of the most important is the question of the relationship of the Chinese Communist movement to the making of British policy in China. What picture did the British have of Communism in China, especially after the Sian incident of 1936 and during the uneasy United Front period that followed? Practically nothing emerges from the official British documents, and it is very likely that London's ignorance of Chinese Communism matched that which Dorothy Borg tells us prevailed in Washington during these years. Finally, I have emphasized in this book the role of Anglo-American relations. They were vitally important, and because of their importance the generous information on British policy and British attitudes which is contained in the American diplomatic papers makes up to some extent for the lack of British documentation, the uninformative nature of British memoirs, and the zealous application of the fifty-year rule.

My thanks are due to a number of people who helped me in various ways while the book was in preparation: to David Owen, who saw it through its original form as a dissertation at Harvard University; to Dorothy Borg, for many talks, and for allowing me to read her *The United States and the Far Eastern Crisis of 1933–1938* in manuscript; to John K. Fairbank, Marius Jansen, G. Richard Storry, and Sir James Dodds; to L. K. Little, for much help on the matters of the Chinese Customs; to Masataka Kosaka, who scanned a number of the microfilms of the Japanese Foreign Ministry archives for me; to Lady Maze and the Librarian of the School of Oriental and African Studies at London University, for permission to use the papers of Sir Frederick Maze.

I am also indebted to the following for permission to reproduce copyright material: Faber and Faber, Ltd., and Random House, Inc., for lines from 'In Time of War' by W. H. Auden from *Journey to a War* by W. H. Auden and Christopher Isherwood; the late Joseph C. Grew and the Harvard College library for extracts from the Grew papers at the Houghton

Library; Mrs. Albert Levitt and the Harvard College Library for extracts from the Moffatt papers at the Houghton Library; the Controller of Her Majesty's Stationery Office for extracts from *Documents on British Foreign Policy, 1919–1939*; *The Journal of British Studies* for extracts from 'Britain, America and the Far East: A Failure in Cooperation' by Nicholas R. Clifford, printed in the *Journal*, November 1963; and the Director of Naval History, Washington, D.C., for permission to use the manuscript study by Captain Tracy B. Kittredge, USNR, 'United States–British Naval Cooperation, 1939–1942.'

Finally, my thanks are due to my parents, who read and criticized much of the several versions of the manuscript; and above all to my wife, who not only read the manuscript, helped the book through its various stages, helped prepare the maps, but above all bore with me patiently during my work.

Chapter I

Britain in East Asia, 1937

During the night of 7–8 July 1937 a company of Japanese infantry from Peiping, on manoeuvres near Wanping and Lukouchiao, came into contact with the troops of the Chinese 29th Army, and sometime during the hours of darkness shots were fired and fighting broke out. The Japanese commander demanded entry into Wanping in order to search for a Chinese who allegedly had fired on his troops, and when this was refused, a skirmish followed on the 8th. After the repulse of a Japanese attack, negotiations resulted in an agreement announced on 11 July, calling for a cessation of hostilities and a withdrawal by both sides. General Sung Che-yuan, the Chinese commander, did not sign it, however, and within a few days, fighting began again. From what had at first seemed to be a relatively unimportant incident, a war began, a war which unleashed the forces which would ultimately expel from China the chief protagonists: Japan, the Chinese Nationalists, and the Western powers who were drawn in, while trying to reach a settlement to protect their own position. Lukouchiao meant more than that, too; it marked a major step in the long and sometimes painful withdrawal of the West from Asia, and there is a direct line from the events of July 1937 to the transfer of power from the British Raj to a Congress government in Delhi in 1947, to the Dutch defeat in the East Indies, and to the French failure at Dien Bien Phu.[1]

It is easy enough to see this now, but it was less evident then, and this is not simply because we know what course Asia has followed in the last quarter century, or because Neville Chamberlain and his cabinet were unimaginative, parochial men who could not understand the world outside England, as their critics charged. No doubt one of the faults of the makers of the appeasement policy was that they lacked imagination, but as far as foreign affairs were concerned this was a common failing in the Britain of the 1930s. Appeasement, after all, as Lord Templewood (Sir Samuel Hoare) has said, did not mean surrender, but 'the methodical removal of the principal causes of friction in the world',[2] and it had deep roots in the pacific, nonconformist conscience of Britain. Chamberlain and Halifax, it must be remembered, were pursuing a policy which was generally popular, and which represented a majority opinion, both in the cabinet and in Britain as a whole.

Appeasement meant, among other things, an over-emphasis on fair-mindedness, a willingness to take the easy way out, and to justify it by arguing that one was only trying to see the other side's point of view. Moreover, as Mr A. J. P. Taylor has reminded us,[3] the appeasers were as much influenced by economic and social arguments as any Marxist, and if you could explain Hitler's actions by a reference to the injustices of Versailles, you could understand Japanese policy in a similar fashion. Photographs of dead civilians, lying in the streets of Canton after a Japanese air raid, made a direct appeal to the conscience, but so did the reminder that Japan's sins might in part be the fault of Britain; for had not the British contributed to Japan's unstable economy by imposing quotas on her exports to the countries of the Empire and thus forcing her to seek new markets?

Nevertheless there is no escaping the fact that Chamberlain was not the man to deal with what was in fact part of a great revolutionary movement in Asia. Nor were those men better equipped who were his principal advisers on foreign affairs in the years to come: Sir John Simon, and Sir Samuel Hoare, both of whom had been Foreign Secretaries, and Lord Halifax, who within a few months of Lukouchiao, would succeed Anthony Eden at the Foreign Office. All these men indeed had been associated with one aspect of the Asian revolution, in having to deal with India, and Halifax, as Lord Irwin, had had a considerable success as Viceroy; but then his chief antagonist—Mahatma Gandhi—was a man whose idealism Halifax could understand, and there were no Gandhis in East Asia.

The outlook of the Chamberlain government towards the Far Eastern crisis was purely defensive. There was the best possible reason for this: the force to mount any sort of an offensive was lacking. The Dominions wanted no trouble, and the situation in Europe, despite efforts at appeasement, was not likely to improve enough to allow the Admiralty to send a squadron of capital ships to Singapore. So Chamberlain played for time, trying to protect British business interests, and searching for the bright side of an increasingly dark picture. A good deal of damage was being done in China, he admitted to the House of Commons on 1 November 1938, but think of the opportunities for British capital when reconstruction began! This was the sort of unfortunate statement which came all too often from the Government benches, and it confirmed the darkest views of the Left about Tory governments; hadn't Lord Birkenhead, after all, while at the India Office a decade earlier, stated flatly that India was held by British forces, not for its own good, but for the benefit of Lancashire?[4]

Yet Chamberlain's statement was less important as an indication of any ties to the reactionary world of British finance capital than as a betrayal of the sort of optimism, too often totally unwarranted, which pervaded British policy in these years. One aspect of this was manifest in the pacific outlook of the leading members of the Government, and their conviction that all men, even Hitler, were amenable to the forces of reason; here, perhaps, the very qualities which made Halifax a great Viceroy made him a less than great Foreign Secretary. And even when it was becoming evident that Hitler might not listen to reason, this optimism encouraged the belief that Italy and Japan, if handled tactfully, might be detached from Germany, and thus deter her from going to war. Nor was this entirely unsuccessful; Japan and Italy were detached for a while, but Germany fought nevertheless.

Furthermore, Chamberlain's government showed a greater flexibility in dealing with the Orient than with Europe. This was most apparent in the number of approaches made to America which, despite their failure, showed a willingness to work for some degree of collective security. At the same time Britain was, if anything, even less ready to come to an understanding with the Soviet Union in the East than she was in Europe. At the time the Left charged that this was due to the ruling classes's fear of the leader of world revolution, the fear which led to an acceptance of Hitler's actions because he was a bulwark against Communism. Whether or not this was true in Europe, the charge is certainly less applicable to the Far East. Japan did indeed claim to be a bulwark against the red menace, but there were few in Britain who took her seriously. She had already strengthened Chinese Communism by forcing the formation of a popular front between Mao Tse-tung and Chiang Kai-shek, and in any case it was clearly Japan, and not Russia, who posed a direct threat to British interests in China, and who was beginning to point her expansion not towards Siberia and the frozen north, but towards the rich colonial lands of the south: Indochina, Malaya, the East Indies, and perhaps even—who could tell?—towards India herself.

Ever since it has been tempting for Chamberlain's critics to seek the

3

cause for all Britain's failings in these years in an analysis of the personalities and prejudices of the men of the National Government. But if the Conservatives lacked imagination and understanding, they were joined in this by a good many of the leading figures of the Left. It was not just that the Left was, for years, 'dedicated to the lunacy of collective security *without* rearming', as A. L. Rowse has written;[5] more important, perhaps, was their contribution to muddled thinking in international questions. They had a sense of vision which their opponents lacked, and could see, as did W. H. Auden when he visited Shanghai, that

> . . . the material contest that has made Hongkew
> A terror and a silence, and Chapei a howling desert
> Is but the local variant of a struggle . . .

which was being fought in different places under different names throughout the whole world. But their vision was clouded by a tendency to see life in terms of European political ideology (perhaps here they were the prisoners of the thirties' revived interest in Marxism) and when they thought of East Asia at all, they were too apt to try to fit the Sino-Japanese struggle into the categories which their studies of European social and political movements had provided. The European concepts of right and left made little sense in Japanese politics, and if Chamberlain was too hopeful in believing that he could detach Tokyo from Berlin, his opponents, knowing little of Japanese affairs, made no distinction between Germany and Japan, and damned them both as Fascist states. Name-calling was no substitute for clear thought, however. No doubt the military was the most important factor in Japan at the time, but it was neither unified, nor was it the only important factor. From 1937 through 1941 there were five different Prime Ministers in Tokyo, including men whose outlook on the questions of the day varied considerably. All this happened in a period of one man rule in Germany, Italy, and Russia; and how many changes of government were there in Britain and America? Furthermore, Japan was indeed the aggressor in a war against China, but what European parallel was there to China? A country of immense size and complexity, still not entirely sovereign, beset both by political and geographical faction, she had been undergoing a revolution for more than two decades. Her future in 1937 was uncertain; would she break up, as the Habsburg and Ottoman empires had broken up? or would she, like Russia, maintain her imperial boundaries under a revolutionary government? Chiang Kai-shek, who a few years earlier, had been chasing the Communists out of Kiangsi, even became something of a hero of the Left for a while after 1937, and it was tempting to build up a picture of a free democratic China struggling against a Fascist Japan, controlled by generals and industrialists. Yet it was not an accurate picture, and its interest lies chiefly in its betrayal of a passionate desire for clear issues, a well-marked division between right and wrong, the sort of issues which seemed to exist in Spain.

In 1937 both Left and Right in Britain shared an overwhelming desire for peace, yet each attributed to the other a lack of understanding and a lack of honesty; Stafford Cripps could call the National Government a 'pro-Fascist gang',[6] and the Tories could point to the Labour votes against rearmament, their dependence upon the frail reed of Geneva, and the compromising position of some of the intellectual wing towards the Russia of Stalin's purges. The Left had this advantage: they felt that they were leading a crusade for peace and freedom, while the National Government could no longer build on the traditional call to arms of the Conservative party—security of country, security of Empire. As rallying cries these were out of fashion in the thirties, and were unashamedly taken up only by a few Tory backbenchers, men like Winston Churchill and L. S. Amery, who passed these years in the political wilderness.

Of course there were no easy solutions, and the problems of Asia were not problems which began in the thirties. The threat to the Western domination of the continent was nothing new; it antedated Chamberlain's government by a good three decades, ever since the Japanese defeat of Russia in 1905 had sent a thrill of revolutionary enthusiasm through the young nationalists of China and India. Even then Britain had already lost her old predominance in Peking and, forced to devote most of her energies in Asia to the problems of revolution in Bengal and the Punjab, went for years without evolving anything which could be called a China policy.

Midway through the decade of the 1920s Britain's relations with China had reached their nadir. The Northern Expedition, the unification of China and the triumph of Chiang Kai-shek's Nationalist Government had been accompanied by those manifestations which have since become familiar during the emancipation of colonial and semi-colonial territories: an intense nationalism and anti-imperialism, a xenophobia mingled with anti-capitalism, and a determination to assert as soon as possible the nation's newly won independence. Britain, as the country with the largest stake in China, and the one which had done the most historically to develop China along her semi-colonial lines, bore the brunt of the anti-foreign feeling, and the climax came in the years from 1925 to 1927 with the May Thirtieth Incident in Shanghai, followed by an extraordinarily successful anti-British boycott, and the over-running, in January 1927, of the British Concession in Hankow.[7]

It was at this point that Britain, under the Foreign Secretaryship of Austen Chamberlain, entered upon a new policy, whose aim was to appease Chinese nationalism, rather than to try to thwart it by insisting on the strict maintenance of the nineteenth-century treaties. The main lines of the new approach were laid down in a memorandum of 18 December 1926, in which Britain indicated her readiness to make far-reaching concessions on the questions of the Chinese tariff, foreign control of certain Chinese revenues, and extraterritoriality. This was followed a month later by an offer to modify the treaties. Although China officially disparaged this at the time, it marked a considerable step forward, and London's prestige rose rapidly in Nanking, so that by the early 1930s Britain had become China's leading Western champion. Other factors helped: the purge of the Communists from the Kuomintang in 1927, and Chiang's apparent willingness to do away with the unequal treaties in a legal, if rapid, manner. Some of the relics of colonialism disappeared when the British concessions in Hankow, Amoy, Kiukiang, and Chinkiang were handed back, and the lease on Weihaiwei was terminated. Britain was also ready to concede China one of her most eagerly sought goals, that of tariff autonomy, but, along with a number of other powers, she refused to make an immediate surrender of extra-territorial privileges, insisting that this be a gradual process. By the time of the Manchurian crisis in September 1931, China was far from absolute independence, and Britain was far from having given up her treaty position entirely, but it was apparent that by her support for a moderate Chinese nationalism, Britain was staking her position in the East—both strategic and economic—on cooperation with an independent China.

The Japanese seizure of Manchuria was the most sensational of a number of disasters, political, economic, and natural, which shook the world in 1931, the *annus terribilis* of Toynbee's phrase. It marked a definite end to the Japanese policy of moderation towards China, the policy of the twenties, which had been associated with the name of Foreign Minister Shidehara Kijuro. In its place came a reversion to the expansionism of the sort characterized by the Twenty One Demands of 1915. Manchuria also ended Japanese cooperation with the West, and closed an era which had seen Japan at Versailles, Japan as a member of the League, and as a signatory of the chief instruments of Pacific stabilization: the Four Power Pact of 1921, the Nine Power Treaty of 1922, and the naval limitation agreements of 1922 and 1930.

Nineteen thirty-one was also the year of the 'economic blizzard', and in late summer Britain was plunged into a severe political and financial crisis. Thus when China appealed to the League of Nations, the League turned to Britain and the United States, looking for a leadership which neither country was prepared to give. America, after some hesitation, informed China and Japan on 7 January 1932 that she would recognize no changes in the situation brought about by force. This was the 'Stimson doctrine' which eventually came to mean the refusal of a number of powers to recognize the new state of Manchukuo, as Manchuria was called by its new masters. Britain, however, failed to support Washington's move, and instead issued a communiqué which sounded like a rebuff to the United States. Later, during the Shanghai fighting, when Secretary of State Henry Stimson suggested to Britain an Anglo-American invocation of Article VII of the Nine Power Treaty (calling for 'full and frank communication between the contracting powers') he felt that Foreign Minister Sir John Simon was lukewarm, and he let the matter drop. In fact, it was a British proposal of non-recognition on American lines that the League ultimately adopted on 11 March 1932, but by then Manchukuo had already been born, and the next day the Changchung government appealed to fifty-two nations for the initiation of diplomatic relations.

The importance of the failure to act at this point cannot be over-estimated. Not only was it made apparent that the democracies were unprepared to block Japan, but perhaps even more important it led many in both Britain and the United States to believe that Washington had proposed a positive plan of action against Japan, and that Simon had rejected it, preferring to give Tokyo the benefit of the doubt. Stimson's publication of *The Far Eastern Crisis* in 1936 confirmed this view among the many who read it with more enthusiasm than accuracy. It was a view popular at once with American isolationists and with the British Left, and both groups remembered it when the second great Sino-Japanese crisis arose in 1937.[8] Rightly or wrongly Simon and the new National Government emerged from the episode with a reputation for a strong pro-Japanese feeling.

On 14 February 1933 the Committee of Nineteen, which had been set up by the League to deal with the crisis, adopted a report blaming Japan for the state of affairs which had existed since 1931, recommending the establishment of a Manchuria which should try to satisfy the legitimate claims of both China and Japan, and recommending also that Manchukuo be refused recognition. Washington concurred, and agreed to serve on the League's newly established Far East Advisory Committee. No action was

B

taken however, save for the general refusal of the world to recognize Manchukuo, and early in 1933 Japan invaded and absorbed Jehol, rounding off her territorial gains. On 31 May a truce at Tangku brought the fighting temporarily to an end.

The next few years saw Japan consolidate her power in Manchukuo and her position in north China. In 1935 she bought the Chinese Eastern Railway from the Soviet Union, thus ending a potential source of conflict with Manchukuo's northern neighbour. That year she brought strong pressure to bear on China, presumably to encourage the secession of the five northern provinces, but Nanking stood firm, and all that emerged was a semi-autonomous 'Hopei-Chahar Political Council' and the outright puppet government of the 'East Hopei Autonomous Area'. To all of this there was no substantial objection by the outside world. There were, however, indications of an expansion of aid to China, both by the League and by individual nations. A special committee was established to study cooperation between Geneva and Nanking; in 1933 Washington granted China $50,000,000 in credits, and the same year saw the mission of General von Seeckt, the creator of the new German army, and the consequent expansion of German military aid.

Partly as a result of such moves, in April 1934 the Japanese Foreign Office spokesman, Amau Eiji, announced that China should not avail herself of the aid of any country other than Japan, and that Tokyo would oppose the furnishing of China with war materials or with funds for political use. In other words, aid to China which was unauthorized by Japan was to be considered a menace to the peace of East Asia. The Amau statement was thus a sort of Monroe Doctrine, and it was also a trial balloon, designed to see how far the West would allow Japan to go in determining China's future. Although it caused some consternation in Washington and London, there were no outright protests. In reply to a British enquiry Tokyo announced that she would not trespass on foreign rights in China, and would continue to observe the Nine Power Treaty and the principles of the Open Door. Here the matter was allowed to stand.[9]

Despite this attempt by Tokyo to stake an almost exclusive claim in China, the years from 1935 to 1937 marked a significant increase in Britain's interest in that country. The policy of concessions to Chinese nationalism had been checked by the Manchurian crisis, and for the next few years Britain was mainly concerned with her own economic problems. Efforts, such as they were, to stimulate recovery in the Orient were based largely upon plans for Anglo-Japanese cooperation in China, and this period was climaxed by the mission of the Federation of British Industries to Japan and Manchukuo in the autumn of 1934. Nothing came of the visit, and presently British policy began to change. Increasingly concerned at the troubled state of the Chinese economy, on 1 June 1935 London announced that Sir Frederick Leith-Ross, the Government's Chief Economic Adviser, would go to China, to investigate and report on conditions there. America, France, Italy, and Japan were invited to take similar action, but stood aside.

Leith-Ross left Britain in August, travelling through Canada and Japan before arriving in Shanghai; although the State Department wanted to send someone to talk to him as he passed through Toronto, the Treasury in Washington apparently managed to block the move, and Sir Frederick had no contact with the Americans. In Tokyo he probably tried to get Japan's agreement to an international loan, but generally the Japanese gave him a cold welcome.[10] His arrival in China coincided with a further deterioration of the economic situation, and presently, on 3 November 1935, the Minister of Finance announced a series of reforms which would take China off a silver standard, and put her on a managed paper currency. London and Washington immediately announced their cooperation, and British and American banks turned over their silver holdings to the Government, as required by the new law. The Japanese fell into line with more reluctance, evidently linking Leith-Ross's arrival to this manifestation of Chinese economic independence.[11]

Whatever part Sir Frederick played in the reforms, they had an initial apparent success, and China finally seemed to be pulling herself out of the depression. The mission also did something to stimulate the interest of the British investor in China, and when he left Shanghai, on 23 June 1936, Leith-Ross issued a statement saying that 'the fundamental economic conditions for a stable currency are fulfilled', and suggesting that after the settlement of certain loans then in default, further British credits for railway construction would be granted. He concluded with an optimistic picture of a peaceful, modernizing China,[12] and his optimism was repeated often in the next year by such British groups as the influential China Association, British chambers of commerce in the treaty ports, and others concerned with the China trade. On 19 October 1936 the Export Credit Guarantees Department announced the appointment of W. H. Kirkpatrick as its special representative to China, indicating Britain's interest in working alone there if necessary, and in ensuring that during the period of China's expansion, her orders for capital goods would be placed in British factories.

Nanking, of course, did all it could to reciprocate the new British interest. During 1936 and 1937 services on railway loans were resumed; some had been in default since 1924, and British holdings in them were high. There were reports of Sino-British agreements for the financing and development of Chinese mining and communications facilities; whether or not they were all true, they were nevertheless indicative of the renewed interest in China. Significantly, Nanking's mission to the Coronation in May 1937 was headed by Finance Minister H. H. Kung, and included Sir Frederick Maze, the Inspector-General of the Chinese Maritime Customs. These two men found time to discuss with British financiers both a £3,000,000 loan for a new rail line, and a general loan of £20,000,000.[13] Meanwhile China's improving economic situation was graphically shown by the increase of her primary source of income, the revenues of the Maritime Customs which, after falling to $385,519,712 in 1935, had climbed to $324,633,291 in 1936, and were well on their way to a record figure in 1937.[14]

By July 1937 Britain's relations with China both politically and economically were closer and more harmonious than would have seemed possible ten years earlier. Part of the reason for this no doubt lay in the improving economic prospects which a close relationship between the two countries seemed to promise. Yet perhaps even more important was the fact that these economic prospects themselves reflected a change in the Chinese political situation, a change which took the form of a significant lowering of the temperature of official Chinese nationalism in the decade between the triumph of the Northern Expedition and the outbreak at the Marco Polo Bridge. Threatened by the Communists and the Japanese, the Kuomintang had lost much of its early revolutionary fervor, and had managed to oust the Communists from their stronghold in the southeast, driving them up to the distant reaches of the northwest, where they were far removed from the western centres of power and influence in the treaty ports. Chiang's government, in short, had proved that it was safe, much as the Manchus had proved that they were safe when the Taiping rebels were advancing on Shanghai. And as the British had, after 1860, begun a period of cooperation with the Ch'ing government, so they were now hopeful of beginning a period of cooperation with the Nationalists. In 1932 many Westerners felt that Japan was fighting civilization's battle against Chinese nationalism and revolution during the Shanghai 'war' of that year. In 1937 there were still those who held to such a view, but they were far fewer in number, and less important in influence. Now it was to be the Japanese victors in Shanghai, not the Chinese vanquished, who were seen as the real threat.

British relations with Japan not surprisingly grew steadily worse as those with China grew better. The Japanese had resented the ending of the alliance with England in 1921, and never considered the Four Power Pact an adequate substitute. Many of the older generation looked back (as did many British) to the days of friendship between the two island empires who were thought to have so much in common. The motives behind Japan's imperialism in the 1930s need not be discussed here, but it is safe to say that many of the foreigners who had been willing to give Japan the benefit of the doubt in Manchuria and Shanghai began to realize within a few years that she was demanding nothing less than a hegemony over East Asia, and the exclusion of all those who would not cooperate. The depression had brought home to Japan the danger of her economic position and her need to establish safe roots on the mainland of Asia, to match the 'empires' of her rivals—America, Britain, and Russia. As she and Britain struggled towards economic recovery after 1931, disputes had flared, and the imposition of quotas and other restrictions on trade with the Commonwealth had naturally increased friction between the two countries, and had given point to the proponents in Japan of continental expansion, even at the risk of a showdown war with her rivals.

Nor was this all. Japan's changing ideological temper and her entry into the camp of the totalitarian powers was becoming clear enough. At home a spirit of radical nationalism was rising, the military men were increasing their control over the conduct of politics, and liberal thought and institutions were everywhere being stifled and terrorized. Abroad, Matsuoka Yosuke had led his delegation out of the League during the Manchurian crisis, and a few years later Admiral Nagano Osami led his delegation out of the London Naval Conference when his demands were not met. Japan's subsequent refusal to remain bound by the provisions of the 1922 and 1930 treaties was followed by an Anglo-American invocation of their 'escalation' clauses, and the spectre of a new naval race was raised in the Pacific. And finally on 25 November 1936 Japan concluded an Anti-Comintern Pact with Germany, establishing herself as the guardian against the spread of communism in Asia, the communism which, it was held, was coming not only from the Soviet Far East, but from China itself, from the party of Mao Tse-tung and his allies.

Nevertheless, early 1937 saw a significant attempt by Britain and Japan to improve their relations. Sato Naotake was named Foreign Minister in March 1937, in the cabinet of Hayashi Senjuro, and his conciliatory speeches to the Diet seemed to herald a milder approach towards the Chinese problem. That spring an economic mission under Kadono

Chokuro left for the United States and Britain. A Japanese delegation headed by Prince Chichibu (an eminent mountaineer, whose sporting instincts might appeal to the British) arrived for the coronation of George VI, and the cruiser *Ashigara* took part in the naval review at Portsmouth. Under the sponsorship of the newspaper *Asahi*, an aircraft named *Divine Wind* (*Kamikaze*) flew to Croydon as a gesture of goodwill.

More significant was the opening of talks in late 1936 between Ambassador Yoshida Shigeru and the Foreign Office. Very little is known of these, and not until May 1937 was their existence officially admitted.[15] Inevitably the suspicion arose that what was really being discussed was a plan to revive spheres of influence in China, but both sides denied this. What Yoshida apparently did suggest to Sir Alexander Cadogan (a former ambassador to Peking and now Deputy Under-Secretary of the Foreign Office) was a plan for the 'protection and rehabilitation of China', but Cadogan shied away, refusing to consider any special agreements without China and the United States. He assured the American ambassador that if Japan were in fact planning to try to negotiate a recognition of a special position in China, nothing would come of the talks.[16]

It is hard to believe that Britain would seriously have been prepared to make such an arrangement with Japan. The outcry over the Hoare-Laval plan had scarcely died down, and any similar agreement in the East would not only alienate the United States, but would also seriously undermine Britain's improving position in China. Anxious as she was to improve her relations with Japan, Britain must certainly have realized that the penalties attached to any bilateral arrangement of this sort would far outweigh the benefits. There were other ways to work for a *détente*. In February Secretary of the Treasury Henry Morgenthau had written to Neville Chamberlain, then Chancellor of the Exchequer, asking for his views on the reduction of world tension. Chamberlain answered in late March, proposing among other things that the time might be ripe for an Anglo-American-Japanese agreement which would prevent the simultaneous outbreak of war in Europe and the Far East. His letter was passed to the State Department, where in June a rather cold reply was drafted under Cordell Hull's supervision, pointing out that it was a traditional American policy 'not to enter into those agreements which constitute or suggest alliance', and concluding with a polite warning against any bilateral Anglo-Japanese arrangement which might deviate from the principles of existing treaties.[17] The State Department evidently did not feel that Japanese policy was changing for the better, and the implied disagreement with Britain foreshadowed many similar disagreements in the years to come.

At any rate, the outbreak of war prevented a development of Chamberlain's idea, although Prime Minister Lyons of Australia, addressing the Imperial Conference on 22 May, had proposed a regional pact for the Pacific, and the subject may well have been brought up in the Yoshida-Eden talks.[18]

At the time of the Lukouchiao incident in July, then, Britain was trying to improve her deteriorating relations with Japan without forfeiting her new friendship with China. In the spring of 1937, moreover, a new ambassador was posted to Tokyo—Sir Robert Craigie, then an Assistant Under-Secretary for Foreign Affairs—to replace Sir Robert Clive. Was this part of the effort towards better relations with Japan? Apparently there were those in the Government who considered Clive to be too intractable, and who thought that his successor might be more likely to serve the cause of Anglo-Japanese friendship.[19] It was a crucial choice; when Craigie arrived in Tokyo in September, war had already broken out, and the first of a number of serious incidents involving violations of British neutrality had taken place. Like his colleagues in Rome and Berlin, he found himself in the unenviable position of having to work for an understanding with a Government whose aims ran fundamentally counter to British interests. His chief assets were patience and considerable skill as a negotiator, as well as a genuine respect for certain of the Japanese statesmen with whom he worked, the 'moderates', such as General Ugaki Kazushige and Admiral Yonai Mitsumasa. Perhaps he was sometimes too patient, yet he was capable of advocating and defending on occasion a policy stiffer than London was willing to back. He was, in addition, able to remain on amicable terms with the American Embassy in the whole prewar period, a point of immense importance. He was not an expert on the Far East, although he had met the Japanese as negotiators during the London Naval Conference in 1936, nor had he much experience abroad, having spent most of his career in the Foreign Office.

Britain's interest in a rapprochement with Japan was more than simply economic; in 1937 the strategic advantages of such a solution were obvious, and Chamberlain's proposal for a Pacific understanding had been made largely to free his country to concentrate on the darkening situation in Europe. In 1902 Britain's growing preoccupation with Europe had been one of the chief factors in Lansdowne's conclusion of the Anglo-Japanese treaty; the problems of policing the western Pacific could be safely left to the new Japanese navy, while Britain could concentrate her sea power closer to home, and along the western approaches to India. That was all very well as long as Japan was friendly, and as long as her interests, concentrating on northeast Asia, did not clash directly with Britain's. Before 1914 the threat to imperial security—and in effect, this meant the threat to Indian security—had come from the West, but after the First World War, this was changed, and Britain gave notice that she recognized the change when she began to work on the Singapore naval base in 1921. For the first time it seemed necessary to protect India from the east, and there could be little doubt against whom the defences were being erected. Since 1902 there had been no significant British naval force in the Pacific, and in 1937 there was little chance that one might be sent there. Japan's gradual entry into the camp of the potential enemy, her refusal to sign the 1936 naval treaty, and Britain's own naval treaty with Germany in 1935 had entirely altered the strategic picture. Defence was very much on the minds of the Imperial Conference in 1937, as was the need to keep Japan from joining Hitler, should he attack in Europe. The base at Singapore was still unfinished, and although it would be opened in February 1938, few ships could be spared for Far Eastern operations. In 1937 Britain's forces in that theatre were slight. There were small ground and air units at Hongkong and in Malaya, and detachments of troops in Shanghai, Tientsin and Peiping. Her position, such as it was, was built on sea power, but the *Navy List* shows that at this point the China Squadron consisted only of some six cruisers, a light fleet carrier, ten destroyers, seventeen submarines, and various ancillary craft, including thirteen gunboats on the Yangtse and five on the West River.

In 1937 the Chiefs of Staff ranked Japan second only to Germany as a potential enemy. If an Anglo-French war came against Germany, Italy, and Japan, the security of the British Isles and of Singapore would be the two keystones for the survival of the Commonwealth, and no consideration for the Mediterranean position should be allowed to interfere with sending the fleet east. Yet it would take seventy days for the transit to Singapore, and ninety days would have to be allowed for the relief of Hongkong.[20] In this review, made for the Imperial Conference, lay the unspoken realization that British possessions in the East, as well as Australia and New Zealand, were becoming less likely to serve as outposts to protect British interests from attack, and more likely to become hostages to Japan for Britain's good behaviour.

A paper for the Sydney Conference on British Commonwealth Relations in 1938 defined British interests in the East as follows:

Great Britain is interested in the Far East territorially in respect of Hongkong, Malaya, Borneo and the South Sea Islands . . . and commercially and financially in respect of her trade with, and investments in, China, Japan and her Far Eastern dependencies. Great Britain is further interested ... in so far as developments in that area affect the defence of India, Australia, and New Zealand, and in so far as events in the Pacific area affect the general situation and have repercussions upon the balance of power in the world at large, and, indirectly, on the European continent.[21]

If the economic and the strategic represented two levels of interest the paper might well have added a third one: the general interest of Britain, as a nation bound by treaties in the East and by her undertakings as a member of the League, in the preservation of peace and the maintenance of such obligations. Nor was this a purely moral point. The British position in China was based on a series of treaties dating back to the end of the Opium War, and depended upon these and upon the maintenance of the Open Door. Despite the changes which had taken place since the rise of the Kuomintang, Britain and the other treaty powers enjoyed a number of privileges which signified that China was not yet a fully independent nation.

It is a difficult position to define. Most important was the privilege of extraterritoriality, the multitude of special arrangements, legal, financial, political, and administrative, which established the position of the Westerner in China. In the treaty ports along the coast and rivers, British citizens were covered by British law and tried by British courts. They, and the British companies which they served, were immune (in theory at least) from most Chinese taxes. Foreign warships as well as merchantmen were allowed to ply the coastal and inland waterways of China. Troops could be stationed in Tientsin and Peiping, and troops landed to protect foreign settlements and concessions in other treaty ports. So, for example, in 1927, British, American, Japanese, and Italian forces had landed in Shanghai to protect the International Settlement, and there they had remained, although in diminished number, together with the troops of the French Concession. Outside the treaty system Britain had a considerable interest in the Chinese Maritime Customs, built up in the nineteenth century by Sir Robert Hart, and in 1937 administered by his nephew, Sir Frederick Maze. An international service under the Ministry of Finance in Nanking, it remained preeminently British, staffed largely by British citizens, and run along British lines. It remained a vital British concern; as a Foreign Office memorandum some years earlier had put it,

... as regards its functions as mediator, between Chinese Government and foreign merchant, its importance is as great as ever, and every effort should be made to see that, however much the Chinese share in it may be increased, the old spirit of Sir R. Hart's creation should be, so far as possible, maintained.[22]

There are no satisfactory figures on British investment in China. An estimate of 1931 gave a figure of £197,961,800, of which some £130,000,000 were in Shanghai, £35,000,000 in Hongkong, and £30,000,000 in the rest of the country. Twenty-five per cent was in import and export trading, 14 per cent in transport, 18 per cent in manufacturing, 12 per cent in banking and finance, 12 per cent in real estate, 5 per cent in public utilities, 2 per cent in mining, and 3 per cent in other activities. An additional £46,400,000 was invested in Chinese Government obligations.[23] In 1937 direct investments in China were put at about £250,000,000, £200,000,000 in business investments, and £50,000,000 in Chinese Government obligations. About £180,000,000 of this was said to be invested in Shanghai.[24] This was calculated to amount to about 5.9 per cent of British overseas investments, and in a normal year contributed from £5 to £15,000,000 to the British national income.[25]

China supplied less than 1 per cent of British imports and took somewhat more than 1 per cent of British exports.[26] The figures, however, do not take into account invisible exports. Although Britain no longer maintained her nineteenth-century lead in China's trade, British shipping in Chinese waters remained predominant, a position especially marked in internal trade. In 1936 British tonnage accounted for 35.72 per cent of all the entrances and clearances in foreign trade in China (Japan, her closest rival, had 20.82 per cent), and 41.28 per cent of China's domestic trade (compared to 36.91 per cent for Chinese flag shipping).[27]

Territorially, besides her Crown Colony in Hongkong, Britain maintained concessions in Tientsin and Canton, and administrative privileges in her former concession at Hankow, in the Legation Quarter of Peiping, in the small International Settlement at Kulangsu in Amoy harbour, and, most important of all, in the great International Settlement in Shanghai, the heart of China's economic and commercial life.

This was the situation in July 1937. When fighting broke out at Lukouchiao, Britain was, despite the rapid growth of the Japanese position, still the predominant foreign power in a country which was not yet sovereign. As the fighting spread from north China to Shanghai, it was to be the British whose interests, both tangible and intangible, were chiefly affected, and for this reason they were to bear the brunt of negotiating with the Japanese to try to protect the treaty position which they, a century earlier, had done the most to develop. Undoubtedly Britain pursued a policy of self-interest; the paradox lies in the fact that as the war progressed, China began to discover what no patriot could admit, that her semi-colonial status actually helped her against Japan. The Japanese advance, rapid as it was at first, bogged down by 1939, and it was not only the Chinese armies and Chinese geography which slowed it; it was also the Western insistence on the maintenance of Western rights, and the ensuing mass of diplomatic protests, threats, and red tape which tangled the wheels of the Japanese war machine.

Chapter II

The Outbreak of War: Lukouchiao and Shanghai

Guernica, submarine piracy in the Mediterranean, the abortive Non-Intervention Agreement in Spain—Whitehall had more than enough European problems to keep itself occupied in the spring and early summer of 1937. In Africa Mussolini's ramshackle empire was being inaugurated, and from Radio Bari came torrents of anti-British propaganda, pouring into the Muslim world, and threatening to upset Britain's rather shaky position in the Middle East. Hence the rather slow reaction of London to the news trickling in from the plains of north China—another skirmish on the outskirts of Peiping hardly seemed at first to be of great importance. On 12 July Foreign Secretary Anthony Eden saw both the Chinese and Japanese ambassadors, and Quo Tai-chi, Nanking's representative, suggested to Sir Alexander Cadogan that his country might welcome Anglo-American mediation. Out of the question, he was told, unless there were some indication that Japan might agree,[1] but from Tokyo the British chargé, James Dodds, had warned that Japan would resent any direct representations of this sort, although an offer of British services might enable her to extricate herself gracefully from the prospect of general combat.[2] The next day a British proposal was made to Washington that expressions of concern in the two Asian capitals might have a salutary effect. France was ready; would America agree?

She would not; Secretary Hull had already been over this ground with the Chinese and Japanese ambassadors, but the British were welcome to parallel his action. This was simply a polite refusal, for the Department of State knew perfectly well that Eden had already paralleled Hull's action, and what London now wanted was a joint approach, to suggest greater Western firmness. The American viewpoint was carefully set forth to Ambassador Sir Ronald Lindsay: '. . . cooperation on parallel but independent lines would be more effective and less likely to have an effect the opposite of that desired than would joint or identical representations.'[3] Accordingly, Eden told the British embassies in Tokyo and Nanking to go ahead on the lines he had indicated, but independently of the French, presumably in order not to advertise America's absence.[4] Meanwhile Cordell Hull publicly set forth his views on the maintenance of treaty obligations and world peace in a declaration of 16 July, but magnificent as it might have been as a statement of principle, it had little effect on the situation.[5]

This exchange, seemingly of no great importance in itself, nevertheless marked the beginning of a serious divergence in policy between Britain and America. In a memorandum of 1 June answering Chamberlain's proposal for a Far Eastern agreement, the State Department had already said that it favoured a policy of 'consultation between and among the powers most interested [in the East], followed by procedure on parallel lines and concurrently',[6] and now as war threatened, this was repeated in the reply to Lindsay, a reply drafted by Hull and approved by the President. It was the line which Washington henceforth would follow, insisting always upon 'parallel' as opposed to 'joint' action, and it is one of the keys to Anglo-American difficulties in the ensuing years. From the outset, Washington was suspicious of British efforts to involve her in the East; and from the outset, London felt that America was refusing to pull her own weight, allowing Britain to do the dirty work as spokesman for Western interests against Japan. In retrospect, it might be added, each side had considerable justification for its estimate of the other.

The American ambassador in Tokyo, Joseph C. Grew, was by no means an isolationist, but he had his own ideas on how Japan should be handled, and they often ran counter to those of the British. In July 1937 he wanted to hold to a strictly neutral attitude, protesting only when it was necessary for the protection of American interests, or for humanitarian reasons. He opposed any offer of good offices, warning that Japan regarded the affair as a local one, and none of the West's business. His view was shared, in part at least, by chargé Dodds, who took it upon himself to tone down the statements which Eden ordered him to make to Foreign Minister Hirota Koki. Unlike the French or American ambassadors, however, Dodds did say that British assistance was there, should Japan seek it; Vice-Minister Horinouchi Kensuke, to whom he made the offer, thanked him, but added that so far it was not necessary.[7]

Dodds was hardly a man who lacked firmness, but probably he was convinced that too stiff a stand at this point would simply play into the hands of the Japanese military, at the expense of the civil government.

He was too late; despite Horinouchi's reassurances, the Foreign Ministry had bowed to army pressure, and agreed to the dispatch of reinforcements to China.[8] This was announced on the 15th; the next day Dodds again saw Horinouchi, and on his own initiative pulled from his pocket a wire from Nanking which told of Chiang's willingness to withdraw his troops to the positions held before 7 July, and to cease all troop movements if Japan would do the same. Horinouchi was silent, but on the 18th told Dodds that Japan could not accept this 'standstill' proposal, and again he insisted that she was doing her utmost for a peaceful local settlement, assuring the chargé that the military would be kept in hand.[9]

Already too much had happened to allow this. By 16 July the guns had already begun to fire again near Lukouchiao, and on the same day China made her first appeal for international support, circulating among the signatories of the Nine Power Treaty (less Japan), a memorandum which denounced Japan's moves as violations of Chinese sovereignty, contrary to the Nine Power Treaty, the Pact of Paris and the League Covenant.[10] On the 17th the Japanese embassy in Nanking called for China to agree to the ceasefire and withdrawal agreement which General Sung had signed on 11 July, rejecting the reply two days later which insisted that the Central Government must confirm any local settlement. The Chinese contention was reasonable enough, but Tokyo would have none of it, and from Nanking, Ambassador Sir Hughe Knatchbull-Hugessen glumly reported that now the military in the north were likely to force the situation to the point where China must either fight or surrender.[11] Surrender was out; Chiang Kai-shek made this clear in a speech of 19 July at the summer resort of Kuling, calling for a demonstration of militant national unity against the invader, lest north China become a second Manchukuo. Sir Hughe had tried to forestall this fiery pronouncement, but he realized that unless Chiang put himself at the head of the popular anti-Japanese movement, he would be committing political suicide.[12]

Chiang quite frankly admitted as much when he saw the ambassador on the 21st, and again he asked for an Anglo-American approach to Tokyo, but evidently Tokyo was still convinced that the Chinese were bluffing.[13] In the Japanese capital Dodds, again acting without formal instructions, tried to convince Horinouchi that this was a serious mis-reading of the situation, but got nowhere.[14] Meanwhile on 20 July Britain had again suggested to the State Department a joint approach to both sides asking them to suspend troop movements, while Britain and America put forward proposals for a solution. Again Washington demurred, and when Lindsay pressed for a clarification, he got a reply making quite clear the American desire not to get involved. 'We feel', the Department rather pompously declared,

that the courses of action thus far pursued by our Governments on parallel lines have been truly cooperative and that . . . both Governments should again, each in its own way, urge upon the Japanese and Chinese Governments the importance of maintaining peace.[15]

This was on 21 July, and in fact it looked at that point as if the storm clouds might be blowing away. Then, on the night of the 25th, a serious clash along the Tientsin-Peiping rail line led to the resumption of fighting and to a severe Chinese defeat. Within a few days, the Japanese were masters of the region around the two northern cities.

So far the West had stood by helplessly while war came on, and during this period only Britain was making constructive proposals. Rebuffed by America, she turned to Germany for support, but again got nowhere;[16] that country was clearly caught between sympathy for her ideological ally, and her very considerable business, commercial, and military interests in China. Eden made one more attempt to win American support for a joint *démarche* to end the fighting, but evoked no more interest than before; by now Hirota had privately admitted that the initiative had passed to the local military commander in north China, and with the army in control, neither Dodds nor Grew thought that offers of mediation in Tokyo were likely to accomplish much.[17] In a last try, however, on 10–11 August both men made private, separate calls on Hirota at his house to extend unofficial offers of help, but the Foreign Minister was by now more pessimistic and more conscious of the internal pressure driving Chiang to resist. He could only suggest that if the two countries really wanted to help, they would press China to return a favourable reply to the proposals for a settlement which Tokyo had just transmitted to Nanking.[18]

The proposals of which he spoke were, in fact, surprisingly lenient in the light of what was shortly to come.[19] They had no chance, however; before they could be considered, the tensions which had been building up in Shanghai for the past few weeks erupted into fighting, and as the war spread to central China, the talks were broken off. No longer could the fighting be considered as just another incident in the north; indeed it had been apparent for at least a fortnight before Shanghai that it was a good deal more serious than similar outbreaks in the past. Yet none of the powers took an effective lead to try to settle it. The American refusal to join Britain destroyed any semblance of unity which the West might otherwise have been able to uphold. France, despite an offer at mediation to the Japanese embassy in Paris, would take no further action without support from Britain and America.[20] No one knew what Russia's intentions were, and apparently no effort was made to find out. But probably she too would not have acted without support, and she may also have been discouraged by the weakness which the Red Army had shown, in its skirmishes with the Japanese along the Amur that summer.[21] Britain had been alone, offering mediation while others contented themselves with counsels of moderation, and she was now to find herself isolated in trying to end the fighting in Shanghai.

Even before the outbreak at Lukouchiao, Shanghai had begun to suffer from a severe case of war nerves. The truce agreement of 1932 had established a demilitarized zone around the city, policed by a special Peace Preservation Corps instead of by regular Chinese army units, and had set up a Joint Commission of Chinese, Japanese, and neutrals to oversee the armistice arrangements. On 23 June 1937 the Japanese called a meeting of this body—the first since 1932—to protest against alleged Chinese violations of the armistice, claiming that tanks and artillery were being moved into the demilitarized zone, and fortifications built there. Then, before the Commission had acted, came the news of fighting in the north, and the city's nervousness mounted; it remembered the brief, violent, outbreak at the time of the Manchurian episode, and wanted to avoid a repetition. By 3 August there were rumours of a plan to neutralize Shanghai, but it was already apparent that a crisis was in the making, and each side suspected the other of working to reinforce and consolidate its position before the first shots should actually be fired.[22]

On the 9th, Japanese citizens evacuating the hinterland began to arrive in the city, and that evening at the entrance of Hungjao airport, a Chinese sentry, and a Japanese naval officer and his driver, were shot and killed. Japanese reinforcements came in during the next two days; this was followed by the arrival of some 20 to 30,000 Chinese regulars in the area immediately north of the Settlement, next to the Japanese units. At a meeting of the Joint Commission, Mayor O. K. Yui admitted that he had no control over these troop movements.[23] Meanwhile in Nanking the ambassadors of the five Western countries most concerned—Britain, America, France, Italy, and Germany—acted together in seeking assurances that the peace of the city would be kept, but the answers they received showed only that the situation was developing too fast to be arrested simply by appeals of this sort. Each side protested its innocence, expressed the hope that the war would not spread to Shanghai, and blamed the aggressive moves of the other.[24] All during the 13th in Shanghai, the

French, British, and American consuls-general worked to secure agreement to a mutual withdrawal of reinforcements, but to no avail; fighting broke out late that afternoon in northeast Shanghai, and spread as darkness fell over the city.[25] The next day the horrors which war could bring a modern city were made evident when a flight of Chinese aircraft, attempting to raid the Japanese flagship *Izumo*, dropped five bombs into a crowded intersection in the heart of the city.

Again the British took the lead in trying to end the fighting, and again they found themselves alone. On the 16th the five ambassadors in Nanking had worked out a plan for pacifying the city, but it was never advanced by the Shanghai consuls, who felt it to be impractical.[26] On the 18th, however, Dodds presented a variant of their scheme to Horinouchi, stating that if both sides withdrew their forces, Britain would undertake the responsibility of protecting Japanese citizens in the Settlement, as long as the other neutrals would join her. France agreed, but Washington refused; Japan was apparently opposed, and America wanted no further military or police responsibilities in China.[27] Horinouchi gave Dodds an official refusal on the 19th, insisting that the Chinese must retreat to the boundaries of the 1932 truce. He did, however, say that his country might reconsider, and on the strength of this hope London once more sought Washington's cooperation. This time the State Department made no secret of its exasperation, replying acidly that it 'could not but view with the opposite of gratification the pressing upon us by the British Government of a project which we regard as already having been disposed of adversely by the Japanese Government.'[28] The British *démarche* accordingly failed (it was, incidentally, accepted by the Chinese on 25 August), and with it went the last chance of saving the peace in Shanghai. But at a higher level the front of official Anglo-American solidarity was maintained, and on 25 August, Chamberlain, Eden, and Halifax issued a statement observing with satisfaction the 'close collaboration' which had been maintained throughout the crisis with the French and the Americans. The same issue of *The Times* that reported this also carried an editorial criticizing the lack of cooperation—but this was just a case of 'irresponsible journalism', said the Foreign Office blandly, trying to soothe the ruffled feelings of a plaintive official from the American embassy.[29]

If the diplomats could not protect Shanghai, the foreign community would have to do what it could to protect itself. It took a while for them to realize that this was more than just another brief affair which would not interfere with the normal business of finance, commerce, and manufacturing, but presently it became evident that peacetime Shanghai was

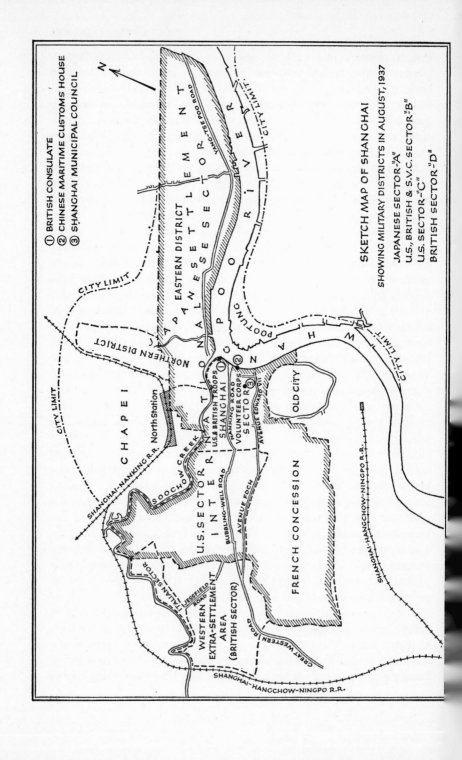

SKETCH MAP OF SHANGHAI
SHOWING MILITARY DISTRICTS IN AUGUST, 1937

JAPANESE SECTOR-"A"
U.S., BRITISH & S.V.C. SECTOR-"B"
U.S. SECTOR-"C"
BRITISH SECTOR-"D"

① BRITISH CONSULATE
② CHINESE MARITIME CUSTOMS HOUSE
③ SHANGHAI MUNICIPAL COUNCIL

gone forever, and that the city would remain in a state of siege, even when the front had moved hundreds of miles up the Yangtse into the interior. Because of the city's importance as the centre of Western interests in China, the events which took place there are not just local history; until 1940 at least they had a vital bearing on the relations of the West with Japan, and it was only the greater issues of Pacific strategy which, after the fall of France, thrust Shanghai's affairs into the background.

The Municipal Council, in accordance with a plan reached earlier, proclaimed no official state of emergency when the firing started; this would have activated the foreign military forces under the Settlement's Defence Plan, and placed them all under the senior foreign officer, who happened to be the Commandant of the Japanese Naval Landing Party.[30] Instead, the Council simply ordered the mobilization of the Volunteer Corps and Police Specials, under the direction of the British commander, Brigadier A. P. D. Telfer-Smollett. Early on the morning of 13 August, the forces were in position. Two sectors were held by the British: 'D' sector, in the so-called western extra-Settlement area, where the Municipal Council held jurisdiction over a number of roads where many foreigners lived, and 'B' sector, which embraced downtown Shanghai. Within a few days British, French, and American reinforcements had been sent, and plans for the evacuation of women and children were drawn up.

Meanwhile both Chinese and Japanese dug in for war. Any technical objections that might have been raised to the use by the Japanese of the Settlement as a base for their military were quickly brushed aside in view of the fact that the Japanese Defence Sector, comprising almost all of Hongkew, Yangtsepoo and the north Hongkew salient, was in the hands of the Naval Landing Party. Despite the neutrals' attempts to restrict the area of fighting it was inevitable that the other parts of the Settlement would sooner or later become involved. The Chinese had already killed over a thousand in their raid on the *Izumo*, and although the neutrals prevailed upon the Japanese to shift the flagship's berth, and upon the Chinese to restrict their own naval operations in the part of the river fronting the Settlement, the danger continued.

In both Shanghai and Tokyo unsuccessful protests were made against the flight of Japanese aircraft over the Settlement, and against the Japanese use of wharves in Hongkew for the unloading of troops and military supplies.[31] Such exchanges, however, served little purpose except to prove that the Japanese were determined to stay where they were. From a tactical point of view they had little choice, and in the early days of the battle for Shanghai they were literally fighting for survival against the superior numbers of Chiang's crack German-trained 87th and 88th divisions. Then the course of the fighting changed. On 23 August troops were disembarked at Woosung to relieve the Landing Party, and more reinforcements followed on 1 September. In late October the Chinese were driven out of Chapei, and on the last day of the month the Soochow Creek was crossed. Five days later a landing in force on the shores of Hangchow Bay outflanked the Chinese; these troops drove north and by 10 November had effected a juncture with the forces in Shanghai, encircling the defenders. On 11 November Nantao was evacuated and the battle for Shanghai was won.

During this period the main base of the Japanese military had been their sector in the Settlement, and it was apparent that the Western powers were unwilling to go beyond protests in opposing this, and were ready to write off the northern and eastern regions as a loss until the fighting had moved beyond the city. Until then they would concentrate on keeping the area below the Creek neutral by denying entry to the troops of either side. Yet the frequent exchanges between Japanese and Western officials did much to embitter relations, and when the Japanese charged that the Settlement was in fact being used by the Chinese military, they left unsaid the fact that they regarded Britain as mainly responsible, for after all, it was Britain who played the leading role in the Settlement's administration.[32]

There is little point in speculating whether the British proposals to end the fighting in north China and Shanghai would have worked if they had had American backing. Probably nothing short of the imposition of some form of sanctions would have influenced Japan, and neither Britain nor America was ready for such a move. In London on 20 July the American ambassador had suggested an embargo on Japanese trade, and although Eden apparently was willing, both men were ahead of their Governments. Chamberlain was horrified by the idea, and the United States, which was then baulking at the mere suggestion of a joint diplomatic approach to Japan, would hardly have gone along with anything so drastic.[33] Yet it was evident that Britain had done more than America to work for a settlement, and both Chinese and Japanese realized this. Chiang Kai-shek, in fact, in appealing for American support of the British efforts, had gone so far as to compare Hull's policy in 1937 with Simon's in 1932. Nor was he the only one to see the parallel; Ambassador Grew noted in his Diary:

Humorists might find humor in the complete turning of the tables between 1931 and 1937. Then it was we who stepped out in front and the British who would not follow. Now it is the British who are taking the lead while we are moving slowly and very, very carefully.[34]

Nothing could hide the fact that there was a rift in the fabric of Anglo-American cooperation. In Tokyo Grew criticized privately what he felt to be an inept and naive British policy, and tried to hold Washington's line to one of stricter neutrality than London's, protesting less often and less strongly to the Japanese.[35] Nor was the Foreign Office of one mind on the correct policy. Dodds had taken the liberty of modifying London's instructions, and the new ambassador, Sir Robert Craigie, who arrived in Tokyo early in September, seemed to be closer in his thinking to Grew than to Eden. That, at any rate, was the impression he had managed to give the American legation in Ottawa as he passed through Canada on his way to the Orient. Here he stressed the fact that although the military were in the ascendant in Tokyo, it would be important to do everything possible to strengthen the hands of the civilians and the moderates, and this meant avoiding any joint or concerted action against the civilian government. Washington and London must keep each other informed, but must act separately, and while Tokyo must never feel that they were divided, she must also never feel that they were acting in league against her. He continued that he did not agree with those in the Foreign Office who wanted joint action with America; the Japanese knew perfectly well that there was no group in either country willing to take a position sufficiently firm to stop Japan, and such a course would only weaken the moderates. With a laugh, he admitted that perhaps he had spoken too frankly, since some of his views ran counter to the official mind of the Foreign Office.[36] Craigie's opinions were duly reported to Washington; but was the ambassador as ingenuous as he seemed? While he was by no means an advocate of strong collective action against Japan in September 1937, his agreement with American policy at this point may have been more apparent than real, a way of winning the trust of those with whom he was going to have to work.

Among Craigie's views were a number which would be repeated over and over again in the next few years. The belief that the military were not in firm control in Tokyo, that public opinion would revolt against the high taxes and the austerity of war and would help drive out the generals, to allow a return of the 'liberal' party politicians, who would pursue a less aggressive China policy; the belief that firm Western action would only solidify public opinion behind the military; and the feeling that Western partisanship for China should not be overstated; these themes were echoed and re-echoed in the dispatches of both Craigie and Grew as long as there seemed to be even the slightest chance that Japan might be persuaded to soften her policy in China. And unquestionably such views

coming from the Tokyo embassies helped forestall any plans for concerted action on a large scale which a preoccupied and none too powerful
Britain or America might have taken before 1941.

If Britain could not work out a common policy with America, she was
not likely to be able to do so with any other country. France, while
proclaiming her willingness to follow in the Far East, was determined not
to lead, convinced that she was doing enough in permitting the shipment
of war material over the Indochina rail line into Yunnan.[37] There is of
course no clear evidence as to how firm a stand the Soviet Union would
have taken with the West. On 21 August Russia had signed a non-aggression pact with China, giving rise to a flood of rumours about intervention
in the East, and it appears that in London Ambassador Ivan Maisky did in
fact broach the subject, only to have Eden pour cold water on it. Britain
was probably no more anxious to work with the Russians in the Far East
than she was in Europe, and in any case, how effective an ally would
Moscow be? The apparent Japanese victory in the settlement of the Amur
incident that summer seemed to indicate that Stalin's bloodletting was
weakening the Red Army. Yet Russia may have had her own reasons to
welcome a war which would divert Japanese strength from the Siberian
frontier, and for that reason, among others, would supply aid to China
through central Asia, and work on the Chinese Communists to support
Chiang against Japan.[38]

Among the great powers this left only Germany, and it was obvious
that she was highly annoyed by what the Japanese were doing in China.
She had developed considerable interests in that country, maintained a
military mission in Nanking, and was quite realistic enough to see the
advantages to Moscow of a Sino-Japanese war; hence she refused Tokyo's
plea for support under the Anti-Comintern Pact.[39] Yet apart from an
approach on 24 July to Berlin, Britain made no attempt to exploit this
split, and it was unlikely that any attempt would have worked. Ribbentrop's influence on foreign policy was growing, and he would shortly
become Foreign Minister; he was pro-Japanese, and by autumn Berlin's
policy of neutrality was giving way to one of support for Tokyo. The
only cooperation between Britain and Germany, paradoxically, came in
the shipment of arms to China, as large quantities of German and Italian
military supplies made their way through Hongkong to the forces of the
Central Government.[40] But this was simply a matter of convenience (and
profit) to both sides, and hardly provided the grounds for any common
action.[41]

Chapter III

First Reactions at Home

In public the British Government was as cautious as the United States in private, in holding to a position of neutrality. Anthony Eden, addressing the House of Commons on 19 July, refused to blame either side for the outbreak of fighting,[1] but the Opposition had already made its judgement and was holding the Government responsible for the continuation of the war. From the Labour benches Hugh Dalton called for cooperation with America above all: '... we should go in step with the United States, not rushing ahead of anything they are prepared to do, but being prepared to go as far and as fast as they'.[2] The line which the Government's critics would henceforth take was implicit here. As Britain had failed to follow an American lead in 1932, so she was failing again in 1937. No publicity had been given, of course, to the unsuccessful approaches to Washington, and no one contradicted the easy assumption that Britain was once again holding back an America devoted to the principles of collective security.

On both official and unofficial levels relations between London and Tokyo cooled perceptibly. The fighting in north China had ended the hopes for a rapprochement, and Yoshida's discussions with the Foreign Office were quietly ended by the British.[3] The Federation of British Industries, not perhaps as sensitive to public opinion, did embark on a programme of talks with the Japanese trade mission, which arrived in London just before Lukouchiao. Yet here too, there was no result, and the mission left on 29 July, announcing that further discussion had been postponed until a more propitious time.[4] Never again were the relations of the two countries quite so promising as they had been just before the outbreak of fighting, and the Japanese visitors who were to come to Britain in the next few years would be primarily concerned with explaining and justifying their country's actions in China. A final ironic note came in the form of an announcement from Tokyo that among the 'patriotic contributions' made by Japanese citizens to the War Office for the prosecution of the 'China Incident' was the sum of ¥30,286, given by pilots Iinuma and Tokagoshi. It was the money they had received for their goodwill flight to London in the *Divine Wind*.[5]

Nothing showed more clearly the state of British sympathies than the fact that the Chinese bombing of the International Settlement on 14 August brought little editorial comment other than generalizations on the horrors of war. Most people were ready to accept the contention that this was an accident, and a similar disastrous mistake on 23 August did nothing to change their minds. Yet undoubtedly similar Japanese accidents would have brought a quite different response. Immediately after the second Chinese bombing came another serious incident, and this time it was Japan who was at fault. On 24 August Sir Hughe Knatchbull-Hugessen, driving from Nanking to Shanghai with two members of his staff, was wounded when his automobile was attacked by a flight of Japanese aircraft. In London, Yoshida immediately expressed his personal regrets, but he was ahead of his Government.[6] Tokyo proceeded to handle the case with a combination of arrogance and stubbornness which managed to alienate a good deal of whatever British sympathy remained for Japan. Not for a month was the case settled, and then the formal expression of regret dodged the issue of punishment for those responsible. Furthermore the Japanese also asked for British cooperation 'to give notice in advance in the future to the Japanese authorities before entering a danger zone', implying that the British ambassador had to report to the Japanese his movements within a country with which Japan was not even legally at war.[7] On 3 September Sir Robert Craigie had arrived in Tokyo; the settlement of the affair was his introduction to the problem of Anglo-Japanese relations.

On 12 October there was another attack on three British embassy cars near Shanghai, and there were a number of British military casualties caused by fighting in the city itself. More spectacular was the growing intensity of the Japanese air raids on the cities of south and central China. More than any other single factor it was these attacks which inflamed opinion, in Britain and elsewhere, against Japan, and which caused the growth of a serious anti-Japanese protest movement. The German blitz on Guernica had taken place that spring, and a nation shocked by the attacks on civilians in Spain now saw the Japanese air force using similar tactics against the crowded cities of China. There was a public outcry, and it was partly in response to this that the Foreign Office sought to pass through the League of Nations a resolution condemning the Japanese action. On 27 September Lord Cranborne addressed the League's Far East Advisory Committee, and there was nothing neutral about his words.

There is one step which I suggest the Committee could immediately and properly take. It could express its view with regard to the air bombing, and I hope it may be possible for it to do so in unmistakable terms. . . . Words cannot express the feeling of profound horror with which the news of these raids has been received by the whole civilized world. They are often directed against places far from the actual areas of hostilities. The military objective, where it exists, seems to take a completely second place. The main object seems to be to inspire terror by the indiscriminate slaughter of helpless civilians. . . . [Therefore] His Majesty's Government in the United Kingdom desire here, in Geneva, to place on record their profound horror at the bombing of open towns which is now taking place in China and to express the hope that this committee may condemn such practices in no uncertain terms. Their effect on world opinion is, I suggest, a factor which those responsible would do well to take into account.[8]

A resolution embodying Cranborne's proposal was passed by the Committee that day, and by the League Assembly on the 28th. The protest seems to have had some temporary effect; Canton suffered no serious bombing till mid-November, nor did Nanking until mid-December. Yet the fact that it was a British resolution on which the League acted did not go unnoticed by the Japanese.

The League's failure to take any action more concrete than this spurred the move in Britain for sanctions in the form of an embargo on Japanese trade. A year earlier Freda Utley, in those days still a popular voice on the Left, had published a widely read book, *Japan's Feet of Clay*, which pointed to the weaknesses of the Japanese economy and the strains which a Chinese war would impose upon it. Others stressed Japan's lack of raw materials, her failures to exploit Manchurian resources, and her dependence upon America and the East Indies for oil, upon Malaya for tin and rubber, and upon Indochina and Australia for iron ore. In a letter to the *New Statesman* explaining 'How Japan Could be Stopped', Miss Utley told her readers that the British Empire and the United States took half of all Japanese exports, and supplied 62 per cent of her imports; an embargo would thus be 'quite sufficient to stop Japan's aggression'.[9] *The Spectator* called for a severance of trade relations with Japan by Britain, Holland and the United States. Britain could not act alone—'that would be to invite failure'—but effective sanctions with American and the Netherlands would work if, unlike those which had been imposed upon Italy, they were complete. *Time and Tide* wanted the supply of arms and credits to Japan

31

to be cut off, and called for a popular boycott of Japanese goods in protest against the bombings.[10]

Nor were these ideas restricted to the press. On 24 August the National Council of Labour issued a strong denunciation of Japanese aggression and urged the Government, in concert with the United States and others, to take measures 'to secure respect by Japan for international law and treaty rights'.[11] Clement Attlee, in a speech of 3 October at Bournemouth before the opening of the Labour Party Conference, asked his country to take the lead in pressing for action by League members and America 'to bring such pressure to bear upon Japan as will stop this abomination. I believe this can be done; Japan's economic position is weak. A resolute boycott of Japanese goods and a refusal of all financial assistance will make her position difficult'.[12]

At the Conference he moved an emergency resolution condemning Japan, calling for the withholding of credits and war material, and for British cooperation with other powers to impose economic pressure on Tokyo. In keeping with the still undefined Labour Policy at this period, no suggestion was made that armed force might be necessary to enforce sanctions, once they were imposed.[13]

Attlee's statements at Bournemouth were echoed by a host of other men and women before organizations official and unofficial, large and small, peaceful and not so peaceful, that autumn in England. The League of Nations Union came out for international measures against Japan, and on 12 October its president, Lord Cecil, asked for economic sanctions, even if they meant war. A China Campaign Committee was formed to raise funds for relief, and to rally opinion against Japan. There were a variety of protest meetings, culminating in a massive demonstration at the Albert Hall on 5 November, organized by the London *News Chronicle*, and presided over by the Archbishop of Canterbury.[14]

With a large and vocal part of British opinion reacting in this way, it was not surprising that President Roosevelt's speech in Chicago on 5 October should have met almost as sensational a response in England as in America. The kernel of the speech lay in Roosevelt's deploring of 'international lawlessness', and his suggestion that nations responsible for 'international anarchy' be 'quarantined', like the carriers of an epidemic disease.[15] The point has been made that this was not so much a trial balloon to test American opinion as an effort to find some non-belligerent way of isolating an aggressor by a form of neutral cooperation, and that Roosevelt himself never quite faced up to its implications.[16] Nevertheless for those who wanted to read into it a strong American lead, it was easy enough to do so. So Lord Cecil gave his immediate backing to what appeared to be the President's recommendation, a quarantine which 'means a cutting off from all relations with other people. . . . I believe that the President is absolutely right in thinking that that is the line on which we should proceed'. To Sir Norman Angell this was the third time that the United States had offered to become an economic ally of the League. The Labour *Daily Herald* saw it as a chance to secure American cooperation, but doubted if Whitehall would take it, while *The Manchester Guardian*, assessing the situation from a less doctrinaire and more accurate point of view, wondered if Washington really knew itself what action it might take.[17]

Chamberlain, in public, hailed the speech as 'a clarion call', and pledged his Government's cooperation in 'a concerted effort in the cause for peace'.[18] But in private he was less confident.

I read Roosevelt's speech with mixed feelings . . . seeing that patients suffering from epidemic diseases do not usually go about fully armed . . . something lacking in his analogy . . . when I asked US to make a joint *démarche* at the very beginning, they refused.

And later, more disillusioned: 'It is always best and safest to count on nothing from the Americans but words.'[19] There were other dissenters. Sir Geoffrey Clarke, speaking to the Association of British Chambers of Commerce on 14 October, came out flatly against sanctions, which he called both futile and injurious to trade[20]—overlooking the fact that their intent was precisely to injure trade. Nor, as yet, were those two organs of staunch conservative opinion, *The Times* of London and the *North China Daily News* of Shanghai, ready to admit that the time for sanctions had come.[21]

As far as one can gather from the press of the day, this marked the high point of British concern for the Far East—at least prior to the Tientsin crisis of 1939. Perhaps China was too far away to engage the sustained attention of the British public, but more important was the fact of the Spanish civil war, which had now been going on for over a year, and which from an emotional point of view, remained the primary issue in British foreign policy. It was this conflict which took on the nature of a crusade, stirring up the partisans of both sides, crystallizing and catalyzing opinion as the Sino-Japanese war never did. There on the Iberian peninsula the great contest was taking place between good and evil, and it was easier to see the Spanish Republic as the guardian of democratic liberalism than to try to fit Chiang Kai-shek into this role. At the same time, however, China's cause would eventually have a broader appeal in Britain than that of the Spanish Loyalists; men who might be quite willing to accept Franco's argument that he was fighting a holy war against the forces of bolshevism were less apt to be convinced by the Japanese claim that they were doing the same thing. It was hard to see Chiang as a Communist, despite the Popular Front, and it was obvious that Japan was more intent on ousting British business and commercial interests from China than in acting as a bulwark against the Soviet Union. In 1937, however, it was still possible to believe in Japan's promises to respect the Open Door, and not until the following year would the threat to the British position in the East become clearer.

Yet what could be done by a powerless Britain to stop a war so many thousands of miles away? Some still believed in the efficacy of public opinion; if the world protested loudly enough, Japan would have to behave better. Even Sir Alexander Cadogan told the American chargé that he could not regret the demonstrations in London, because such outbursts of 'honest indignation' might impress Japan, and in Geneva a British delegate observed that something must be done to meet the popular demand, adding that in 1932 it was the Government which had tried to give a lead to public opinion, but now public opinion was running ahead of the Government.[22]

Despite Chamberlain's apparent dislike of the idea, his Government continued to consider the question of sanctions. Shortly after Lukouchiao the possibility of economic action against Japan had been examined,[23] and a report by the Industrial Intelligence Centre prepared, which had concluded that after the exhaustion of existing stocks, Japan 'could not continue without supplies *ex hypothesi* under our control', but that unless the United States and the whole of the British Empire cooperated, 'no measure of boycott would achieve its object'.[24] On 1 October London cautiously sounded the State Department, in a note drafted by Eden and toned down by Chamberlain, saying that while she was not convinced of the usefulness of sanctions, Britain would be willing to examine the question in concert with Washington. An equally guarded answer on 5 October—the day of the quarantine speech—replied that although America would not lead, she would be willing to examine any plan to 'cooperate by pacific methods . . . toward bringing to an end the present hostilities in the Far East'. It was hardly an answer distinguished by its clarity—were sanctions 'pacific methods'?—but as long as the League was in session, no one was going to take any action.[25]

Then came the quarantine speech, and Eden followed it up, his questions sounding half anxious, half fearful, that America was at last going to make her power felt in the Orient. What exactly did the President mean? he asked. Was America thinking of a boycott? Had she considered the possibility of Japanese retaliation? These were the same questions that were on the minds of all those who had heard or read Roosevelt's speech and already the State Department was trying to extricate American foreign policy from the rather awkward situation in which the President had put it. Sumner Welles sent the Foreign Secretary an answer: no boycott was immediately in the offing, and all that Roosevelt had meant was that the United States should try to find a solution of the Chinese question which would satisfy everybody.[26]

Welles's reply can hardly have left Eden much wiser than he was before, but the American Government was in a difficult position. Roosevelt's Chicago speech had touched off a violent reaction by pacifist and isolationist groups, and their outcry did much to convince the Administration that America should steer clear of any sort of international punitive action in the East.[27] America's sympathy was with China, but above all America wanted to stay out of trouble in Asia. Lindsay had earlier told the State Department that his country did not want to embarrass America in its proposals for common action, and he explained that while Chamberlain was being urged to 'do something', Roosevelt was being told to stay out.[28] Nowhere else does the difference in public opinion between the two countries emerge more clearly than here. In America, efforts were being made to have Washington invoke the Neutrality Act, and even to withdraw all American civilians and troops from China, rather than risk war.[29] In Britain, on the other hand, Whitehall was being urged to take stronger action, not only by Labour and the Left, but increasingly also by the Right, by the business circles which were beginning to realize that Japan posed an immediate and very real threat to their interests. America would not act; without America, Britain could not act; yet there remained, in Geneva, some hope that the war might be ended by international negotiation.

Chapter IV

Conciliation Fails: Geneva and the Brussels Conference

On 30 August 1937 the Chinese delegation at Geneva forwarded to the Secretary-General of the League of Nations a 'Statement on Japanese Aggression in China since the Lukouchiao Incident', and two weeks later followed it with a supplement describing the situation as it then stood from the point of view of Nanking.[1] With none of the neutrals (save perhaps Russia) apparently willing to give much help more concrete than diplomatic protests, China had decided to take her case to Geneva. Yet while the League's moral support would be helpful, the crucial question, of course, was that of America's attitude at Geneva, and America (as the British embassy in Washington was told) was not yet ready to commit herself, and would prefer to wait upon the course of events.[2]

China planned to appeal under Article XVII of the League Covenant. By its terms Japan would be invited to accept the obligations of League membership for the purposes of arbitrating the dispute, and if she refused, the provisions of Article XVI—sanctions—would apply. Through Ambassador Quo Tai-chi, Sir Alexander Cadogan tried to talk China out of the move; nevertheless on 13 September Wellington Koo officially asked the League to take cognizance of the fact that Japan had invaded China, and invoked Articles X, XI, and XVII of the Covenant.[3] Thereupon Eden, with French Foreign Minister Delbos and Secretary-General Avenol, took Koo aside, and pointed out the dangers implicit in his move; it might lead, among other things, to a Japanese declaration of war, the enforcement of the American Neutrality Acts, and the consequent cessation of arms shipments from the United States to China. Koo accordingly modified his requests when he addressed the Assembly on 15 September, suggesting now that the matter might be referred to the Far East Advisory Committee.[4]

This was the body which had been formed in 1933 during the Manchurian crisis, and the transfer thence of the Chinese appeal had several advantages. Above all, the Committee might include an American representative (as it had earlier), and even if he were again only a non-voting observer, his presence could be useful. Furthermore, it was a far more flexible body than either the Council or the Assembly, and its participants were less likely to become bogged down in the embarrassing technicalities of Article XVII. The Council accordingly accepted the Chinese request, and the Committee held its first meeting on 21 September, under the chairmanship of Latvian Foreign Minister Munters. American participation was as it had been in the past; Leland Harrison, the minister to Bern, sat as an observer, and maintained a polite silence throughout the proceedings. Invitations were issued to China, Australia, Japan, and Germany, none of whom were represented, and to no one's surprise, only the first two accepted. Then on 27 September the Committee passed the Cranborne resolution condemning Japanese bombing, and thereby killed any chance that Japan might be induced to cooperate with the League.

On 21 September S. M. Bruce of Australia broached to the League Assembly the idea of a conference of powers with interests in the Pacific, in order to allow the League 'to transcend the limitations of its present membership', as he tactfully put it, and Cranborne promised British support if the other powers agreed.[5] Privately, however, it was felt that this might embarrass the United States, and Cranborne subsequently told Harrison that Britain would not press for the conference at that time.[6] By early October, however, Koo was growing impatient for action on a resolution condemning Japan and declaring her an aggressor under Article X, and it was to forestall this that on the 4th Cranborne proposed a variant of Bruce's plan, calling for a conference of the signatories of the Nine Power Treaty, together with other nations with interests in the Far East (this to bring in Russia and Germany). That, at any rate, was how he privately explained his action to Harrison later, expressing his regrets that there had been no time to consult Washington before he announced his plan.[7] It may well be that Koo's impatience was genuinely the cause of Cranborne's sudden proposal; but it is also true that only in such a conference would the United States be actively, rather than passively, involved.

On 5 October a subcommittee drew up two reports which were, essentially, a watered down version of Koo's original declaration. The first concluded that Japan had violated her treaty obligations; the second contradicted the Japanese assertion that the fighting could be settled only

37

by the two countries involved, without third power intervention, and recommended a conference in line with Cranborne's proposals. In the meantime, the League would 'express its moral support for China', advise its members to take no action which might weaken China, and to consider 'how far they can individually extend aid to China'.[8] The two reports were adopted by the Assembly the next day, and a statement from Washington gave America's blessing to the League's position.[9]

This indecisive action came as no surprise to a world which had already seen the failure of Geneva's peacekeeping machinery in Abyssinia and the Spanish civil war. Although the word 'aggression' had been avoided, Japan stood condemned of violating her treaty obligations, and the League's moral support was clearly on the side of China. However, as a compromise on what Koo had wanted, it was a move dangerous in its weakness; there was no firm pledge of any kind for aid to China, yet the condemnation of Japan *in absentia* gave that country a ready excuse to have nothing to do in the future with international arbitration. Nevertheless the League had succeeded in shifting its burden to the signatories of the Nine Power Treaty, and managed to bring in the United States. This could have been a move of capital importance; Eden has written that while he had no great hopes for the conference, he felt that at least it might demonstrate Anglo-American solidarity.[10] This was something Geneva could not do, and perhaps he hoped that despite Hull's insistence on parallel rather than joint action, the State Department might find it easier to take what would amount to joint action in concert with the other treaty powers, rather than simply with Britain and France alone.

Everyone favoured the idea of the conference, but no one wanted to be held responsible for it. London at first suggested that it take place at The Hague, but the Dutch were fearful for the safety of the East Indies. The Belgians, who were next on the list, were hardly more enthusiastic, but finally agreed to the use of Brussels as long as the wording of the invitations made it clear that they were not responsible for the idea. So the invitations would be issued 'at the request of the American and British Governments'; but now it was Washington's turn to object, and ultimately they were sent out 'at the request of the British Government and with the approval of the American Government'.[11]

With the unexpectedly troublesome question of paternity thus settled, it remained to be seen what a conference could do. Many saw the imposition of sanctions as the next step, and this was the line taken by Clement Attlee, when the House of Commons debated foreign affairs on 21 October. He warned of the possibility of an Oriental Hoare–Laval pact, and asked for an undertaking that, if China accepted and Japan refused an armistice, Britain would propose an 'international embargo' against Japan. He scoffed at the possibility of war; Japan was too weak. 'I do not believe for a moment that Japan would challenge the world. The world has given its verdict at Geneva. A verdict like that, followed by no action, is perfectly useless.'[12] More cautiously, the Liberal Sir Archibald Sinclair asked first for an attempt at mediation, and only if that failed, for the imposition of sanctions. Sanctions were dangerous, he admitted, and should be undertaken only as a last resort, but Roosevelt's Chicago speech showed that America was willing to take the lead.[13]

The Government spokesmen were more guarded in their views. Eden called it 'unwise' to discuss what Brussels might or might not do. The conference offered the best chance there was of ending the fighting; if it failed, 'then we enter a new situation which we shall have to face', but he did not suggest how.[14] The Prime Minister deplored all talk of sanctions before the conference: 'We are here to make peace, not to extend the conflict.'[15] In the House of Lords, the Earl of Plymouth followed a similar line, over the objections of Labour's Lord Snell, who wanted immediate sanctions, and of Lord Lothian, who argued that too great an emphasis on peace would only mean the betrayal of China.[16] The Government was being cautious; the League had already condemned Japan, and Japan's methods of waging war, and further threats were pointless now that Japan's presence at the conference table was sought.

Once again what the British were saying in public the Americans were saying in private. On 19 October a British note to the State Department had suggested that the two countries should go to Brussels at least prepared to deal with the likelihood that Japan would not change her position, and that some further action would have to be taken.[17] This time Washington made it clear that sanctions could not be considered, even in private; the question simply 'did not arise in a conference which had for its objective the finding of a solution of the conflict in the Far East by agreement'. America wanted an armistice, followed by negotiations, and for the moment would not look beyond this. A few days later the American ambassador drove home the point to Eden: no one nation, he said, should take the lead at Brussels. Britain should neither lead, nor force the United States to lead. Furthermore, the British attempts to pin America down as to just how far she would go, and just what the Chicago speech meant, were 'objectionable and damaging'. Eden agreed that no one should lead, and denied that he had ever tried to put America on the spot—what had been said on this subject was 'irresponsible newspaper stuff'.[18]

D

Obviously, few plans could be made in this sort of atmosphere. Washington was afraid of its isolationists, and afraid also that it might appear to be leading an anti-Japanese coalition. It was doing its best to temper the popular interpretation of the quarantine speech as the harbinger of a hard new American line, and London and the rest of the world were simply going to have to wait and see how America would react if the conference failed. All this, of course, gave point to the public British line that Japan should not be unnecessarily antagonized, and that every way must be tried to bring her to Brussels. In Tokyo, both Grew and Craigie urged Hirota to accept the forthcoming invitation, but Vice-Minister Horinouchi had already frankly told Craigie that Brussels would have not the slightest effect on the terms which eventually would be given to China. Craigie got nowhere when he argued to Hirota that while Japan had lost her case at Geneva by default, she would now be offered another chance to present it.[19] On the evening of 27 October Japan officially refused the invitation, and issued a declaration setting forth her position. She was fighting in self-defence; what was really needed was a change in China's attitude and policy; the League had already adopted an unfriendly resolution; no 'fair and just results' could possibly be expected from the nations seated at Brussels; and only direct Sino-Japanese negotiations could solve the problem.[20]

In other words, there could be no public third power intervention. In private, however, Yoshida talked to Eden and the American ambassador, urging that no resolution condemning Japan be adopted, and he suggested that, with the conference as a screen, Britain and America might be able to negotiate secretly with Japan. Eden agreed that this would be the only practical way of bringing Japan in, but he also realized that a man like Yoshida—a liberal, oriented towards the West—was hardly representative of the real rulers of Japan, and that for all his good intentions, his ideas might represent more hope than reality.[21] Nor did the Western ambassadors appear much more optimistic; Craigie, Grew, and Arsène-Henry (the French ambassador) all wired home warnings against any step which might look like diplomatic pressure, and against any declaration blaming Japan for the war.[22] Craigie went even further, and just after the conference opened, suggested to London that Hongkong be closed to arms shipments from China. This might well have brought Japan to Brussels, but it could only have convinced her further of Western pliability. Eden, in any case, was unwilling to take such a step until American intentions were clearer; Japan, he noted, might be 'going to her "1812" in China . . . [and] we should do what we can cautiously to make it possible'.[23]

Before leaving for Brussels Eden again promised Parliament that he would do his best to gain the 'full cooperation on an equal basis with the United States',[24] and this was the point which he emphasized to the cautious Norman Davis, who led the American delegation, when they met at Brussels. Davis backed away; no form of pressure could be considered until every possible means of bringing peace by agreement had been explored. And, he continued, American public opinion was suspicious of British attempts to involve the United States in the saving of British interests. Eden replied that he knew and deplored this feeling, and he summed up the British position: London would go as far in positive action as America, but would neither lead nor force the United States to lead. If peace by agreement could not be achieved, she would join fully in pressure against Japan, but would not embarrass the United States by advocating such a course if it were unwelcome. Eden would second any American initiative, and throughout the crisis, would base his policy on that of America.[25] In other words, if he were not actually trying to push the United States out in front, it sounded very much as if he would prefer an American lead, and while promising support, would wait for America to move first. Since Washington had already made it clear beyond a doubt that there would be no American lead, and no American support for anyone else's lead, the conference was apparently doomed before it met.

It opened on 3 November. Of the major non-treaty powers, only Italy and Russia were represented; Germany, like Japan, had refused her invitation. Paul-Henri Spaak, the Belgian Foreign Minister, opened with a speech reviewing the conditions which led to the calling of the conference, and urged that the meeting should not consider itself a tribunal summoning Japan to defend herself, but should work instead for 'conciliation and peace without prejudice or passion'. Eden, Davis, and Delbos followed on the same note. Only three men upset the pacific unanimity of the proceedings: Koo, whose long speech was an indictment of Japan, Maxim Litvinov, who warned against appeasement, and Aldrovandi-Marescotti of Italy, who, as attorney for the defence, stressed the futility of the conference.[26]

Now the work began, and immediately a number of tacit but serious differences of opinion began to make themselves felt. No one, except perhaps the British, really believed that Japan might be willing to talk. The United States simply saw the conference as a forum to educate public opinion; Italy, of course, opposed any move even remotely unfavourable to Japan and underlined the point by adhering to the anti-Comintern Pact on 6 November; the Soviet Union called for strong action; and France seemed to be mainly interested in extracting from Britain and America a guarantee of Indochina, and in encouraging Roosevelt to assume the leadership of a democratic bloc.[27]

The immediate issue, of course, was what would happen if Japan, by rejecting a second invitation which had been sent to her on 7 November, refused to have anything to do with the conference. The question of coercion was the crucial one, and although Davis himself seems to have favoured a strong move, the United States remained resolutely opposed to any discussion of it. On 10 November Eden and Delbos met with Davis, and gave the American an opening by promising their support for any action Washington might decide on, although, Eden admitted, embargoes and boycotts were 'none too popular' in Britain since Abyssinia. Davis refused to take the hint, and all the meeting did was to postpone the day of decision. It was agreed that if Japan refused the second invitation the delegates would meet again, send a stiffer message to Tokyo, and after a week's recess, draft a final resolution.[28]

On 12 November Tokyo sent the expected refusal to Brussels, and the next day the delegates assembled to hear a round of speeches upholding the principles of international law. Koo took a different line.

Now that the door to conciliation and mediation has been slammed in your face . . . will you not decide to withhold supplies of war material and credit to Japan, and extend aid to China? It would be, in our opinion, a most modest way in which you can fulfill your obligations of helping to check Japanese aggression and uphold the treaty.[29]

Two days later a resolution was adopted rebutting the Japanese statement that peace could best be reached by direct negotiations between the two sides, and concluding that the nations assembled at Brussels would have to consider what was to be their common attitude towards Japan.[30]

It was a very vague threat. But what more could have been said in the circumstances? Everyone of any importance at Brussels had promised to back the United States, but each had made it clear that an American lead was expected. Nothing, of course, was less likely to appeal to the State Department, and Welles told Sir Ronald Lindsay on 13 November, that while Davis might have talked of sanctions, he was in no position to commit his country.[31] Yet if no one would lead, what more could the conference do? How could it possibly avoid the appearance of failure? Here too, London and Washington differed. Both Eden and Hull were concerned with the state of public opinion, but in different ways. To Eden, if the conference recessed as planned, and then simply issued another declaration, the effect would be disastrous. Hull, on the other hand, was worried about the growing tendency of China's partisans to blame Washington for the failure at Brussels, and about the growing feeling (hardly an accurate one) in Tokyo that America was replacing Britain as the nucleus of an anti-Japanese coalition. Contradictory as these opinions might be, they both denied the genuineness of America's neutrality, and caught between them Hull could only repeat his belief in the possibility of educating public opinion. Yet to offset a feeling of anti-climax, he could suggest nothing better than a 'strong reaffirmation of the principles which should underlie international relationships'.[32]

This would simply mean a moral pressure, and no imposition of the comparatively mild sanctions which London wanted: a declaration of a policy of non-recognition and the witholding of loans and credits to Japan. Nor was Davis responsive to Cadogan's suggestion of a further attempt at mediation outside the conference. He refused even to consider writing into the final declaration the statement that Britain and America were prepared to tender their good offices, on the grounds that this would be the assumption by two nations alone of a responsibility which properly belonged to all the powers.[33]

The British recommendations, mild as they were, accordingly were not put into effect. On 21 November the British and American delegations drafted a Report which, they agreed, would look better than a Declaration of Principles, although in fact it amounted to much the same thing. Adopted on the 24th, with Italy abstaining, it set forth once more the beliefs that a solution of the problems of the Far East could not be achieved by force, that it could not be achieved through Sino-Japanese negotiations alone, and it concluded with the statement that the conference would suspend its sittings in order to allow further time for study. Cranborne, Davis, and de Tassan of France all tried in their final speeches to find positive achievements in the meetings of the last three weeks, but their eloquence was unconvincing. Wellington Koo and Jordan of New Zealand both said outright that the conference had failed, and in general public opinion agreed with them.[34] The delegates thereupon adjourned, subject to a recall which never came, and left the world with the impression that the powers were unwilling to take any serious risks to stop Japan.

Brussels must thus go down in history as another episode in the list of dreary failures of the diplomacy of the 1930s to keep the peace of the world. Here, if anywhere, it had seemed possible that something might be done, for here the United States was represented, and represented fully, not simply through an observer as at Geneva. 'The contrast with Nyon (the meeting on non-intervention in Spain) could scarcely have been more marked,' Eden has written, 'for preponderant power was at the disposal of the conference.'[35] It is difficult and perhaps futile to try to apportion the blame in such a case, but the history of the conference appears to prove, if proof be needed, that at this late date it would take more than American participation to spell the difference between success and failure. The new world had been called in to redress the balance of the old; but the new world was, if anything, rather less willing than the old to act. No single nation dared take the lead against Japan. By pledging support to Washington, Britain, France, and Russia had implied that they sought an American initiative, although Washington's refusal to make any such move was quite clear and had been clear before the conference met. On the other hand, by not promising her own support to a British lead and, in fact, by discouraging it, Washington assured its failure, for neither Britain nor France would dare in the autumn of 1937 to stand up to the Japanese, unless sure of the military, naval, and economic backing of America. A month later Chamberlain told the House of Commons: 'There was only one way in which the conflict could have been brought to an end, as it proved, and that was not by peace but by force . . . [but] coercion would not have obtained the support of any member of the Brussels Conference.'[36]

This was close to the truth. A Foreign Office study, undertaken in November, had warned that sanctions would prove no quick and easy solution to the problem of stopping Japan.[37] Uncertain in effect even with American support, such measures would have been useless, and perhaps worse than useless, without it.

The Nine Power Conference was—with the exception of the special case of Munich—the last attempt of the prewar world to end a conflict through collective international action. It was also the last great test of the Pacific treaties of 1921 and 1922, and it was a test which the treaty powers failed. Henceforth all efforts to reach a settlement would utilize the older channels of secret diplomacy, either through the form of clandestine Sino-Japanese negotiations, or through half-hearted attempts by Western nations to mediate, either singly or in groups. Never again was a serious effort made to achieve peace in the same glare of publicity which had attended the meetings in Geneva and Brussels.

The conference had done little to clear the air. To Craigie, who had been against it in the first place, it 'left the situation more rigid and lessened the prospects of friendly mediation'.[38] What prospects in fact existed? Although he never told the Americans, Craigie was involved in a sort of mediation himself during October and November, acting as middleman in the transmission of new peace terms from Tokyo to Nanking. His efforts to moderate them were consistently blocked by the military, however, and as they emerged, they had little to recommend them to Chiang.[39] Nevertheless, as late as 5 November, Hirota told Craigie that England was 'still the most suitable country' to mediate; Germany, he added, would not do at all.[40]

This simply was not true. In early November, terms similar to those transmitted by Craigie, were given to the Chinese through the German ambassadors, Herbert von Dirksen in Tokyo and Oskar Trautmann in China, but were again rejected. Just what sort of a game Japan was playing is unclear; Dorothy Borg has interpreted the Japanese refusal on 27 October to go to Brussels as a veiled invitation to outside nations to proffer their services as intermediaries, an invitation which Germany accepted, but whose point was lost on both Craigie and Grew. In mid-November, after the fall of Shanghai, Tokyo tried harder to make peace, partly to forestall the passage of an anti-Japanese resolution at Brussels, and partly to prevent the fall of Chiang's government and the consequent extinction of all law and order in China.[41]

Nevertheless Craigie, probably unaware of the entry of Germany on the scene, continued to press for some sort of Anglo-American mediation, while in London Ambassador Yoshida remained hopeful that his country might accept such a move. Despite the American refusal to consider mediation outside the Brussels Conference, Craigie was encouraged by Horinouchi's repeated denials of any German role, and suggested to Grew that Britain and America might simply transmit messages from one side to the other, assuming no responsibility for the terms involved, and bringing no pressure on China to accept. He did not tell Grew that he had already been involved in such dealings himself; perhaps he hoped that with American support he might have more success in softening the Japanese terms. Grew, however, took a considerably less optimistic view, and Washington was unhappy at the possibility of being in any way associated with terms incompatible with the Nine Power Treaty, as the Japanese proposals almost certainly would be. Meanwhile Horinouchi told Craigie that the only form of good offices acceptable would be to persuade China to enter into peace talks. The British ambassador remained hopeful, however, feeling that if the process could once be started, it might proceed more satisfactorily, and Britain and America could act simply as a 'post office', giving advice only when asked for it.[42]

London, however, was becoming cooler to this course by now, and

Washington stood firmly by its refusal to take part.[43] On 13 December Lindsay again discussed the subject with Hull, but met with no encouragement, and after this the British efforts were apparently dropped. The situation, it appeared, had passed the point where such a course could have succeeded; the Japanese penetration of China, after the occupation of Shanghai, was resulting in more and more damage and threats of damage to British interests. On 3 December the foreign missions, who by now had abandoned Nanking for the greater safety of Hankow, were officially informed of the German mediation efforts,[44] and finally, on 13 December the Japanese naval air and ground forces had precipitated the most serious crisis yet, by attacking British and American shipping on the Yangtse and sinking an American gunboat, the uss *Panay*.

Chapter V

The West Under Attack, I:
December 1937 – January 1938

The sinking of the USS *Panay* and the shelling of HMS *Ladybird* and *Bee* on the Yangtse in December, brought a sudden and shocking end to the unrealistic atmosphere of optimism which the public pieties of the Brussels Conference had sought to produce. The severity of the December crisis was something new, but the situation which had led to it was not. Ever since August Japan had sought to restrict navigation by Western warships and merchantmen along the coasts and inland waterways of China. In August and September the commander of the Japanese Third Fleet, Admiral Hasegawa, had announced the closure of all coastal ports save Tsingtao to Chinese shipping, and while he promised that this would not affect the 'peaceful commerce' of third powers, in fact his order meant that neutral ships could in the future be held up by Japanese men-of-war.[1] The Chinese themselves closed the Yangtse below Chinkiang on 13 August, and after the fall of Shanghai, both sides placed restrictions on navigation of the river as the war moved upstream. Hasegawa demanded that no foreign ships were to move without Japanese permission, and trade on the river was brought to a virtual standstill, save on the upper reaches beyond the war zone.[2] Nor was it ever resumed, and the restrictions on navigation of the Yangtse were among the major irritants to Anglo-Japanese relations in the next few years.

For the time being, however, these were petty annoyances compared to the attacks of December. On the 5th, during a Japanese raid on Wuhu, two British ships and a British hulk, all of which had refugees aboard, were hit and damaged, and the nearby gunboat, HMS *Ladybird*, was hit by splinters. Craigie protested, but worse was to come. On 12 December at Wuhu, a British tug was fired on by a Japanese machine gun position ashore. *Ladybird* steamed to her aid, and herself came under fire from a

Japanese field gun. Four shells hit the warship, killing one man, and wounding several others, including Captain Crabbe, the flag captain to the Rear Admiral, Yangtse. Crabbe landed, accompanied by two members of the embassy and protested to the local Japanese commander, Colonel Hashimoto Kingoro. Hashimoto admitted that he had been mistaken in attacking British ships, but said that he was under orders to fire on every ship moving on the river. Shortly thereafter HMS *Bee* arrived, drawing fire herself, and another protest was made to Hashimoto.[3] The climax came that afternoon, when a flight of naval aircraft bombed and sank the USS *Panay* and two Standard Oil ships in her company. The survivors struggled ashore to the village of Hohsien, from which they were able to get word to Nanking. *Bee* and *Ladybird*, with the USS *Oahu*, went to their aid, while the British obtained assurances from Hashimoto that Hohsien would not be attacked until the evacuation of the survivors was complete.[4]

To this day it is not certain how far these attacks were an error by the Japanese, and how far they were calculated. There is little doubt that the shelling of *Ladybird*, if not on orders from Tokyo, was intentional on the part of the military. Hashimoto was no ordinary Japanese artillery officer, but a notorious nationalist, deeply involved with the political action wing of the army; according to Craigie, after he was recalled he boasted that he knew perfectly well that *Ladybird* was British when he attacked her, and a recent historian has seen the affair as an attempt by the army to force a war with Britain and the United States.[5]

Craigie immediately protested to the Foreign Office, and Hirota, seriously worried, called to express his regrets. The next day a preliminary note promised measures to prevent a recurrence, said that those responsible would be punished, and that compensation would be paid; but the full British protest which followed on the 15th pointed out that the Japanese assurances only covered attacks on warships, and not on merchantmen.[6]

Now more clearly than ever before, Britain and America were presented with a chance to take forceful action together. Trying to make the most of it, Eden and Cadogan told the American embassy on the 13th that the attacks might well have been intentional, and urged that before Washington did anything, it might consider acting, if not jointly with Britain, at least with a closer degree of parallelism than before. But once again Hull refused to be drawn into any *démarche* which would imply premeditated action with the British. Despite Cadogan's strongly expressed feeling, that in these circumstances the American attitude towards joint action should be reconsidered, Grew was told to present his protest to the Gaimusho without waiting for Craigie.[7] On the 14th Sir Ronald Lindsay, more outspoken than usual, called on the Secretary of State to tell him how disappointed London had been when the United States acted alone, and added that no single country was likely to make a showing sufficient to force the Japanese to stop and think. In the utmost secrecy an appointment with Roosevelt was arranged for the night of the 16th, but there seemed little likelihood that American policy would change; the next day Welles gave the ambassador a further justification of the American preference for 'parallel' as opposed to 'joint' action, and added firmly that he was stating the President's wishes in this respect.[8]

For a while, though, it looked as if something stronger might follow. After the failure at Brussels, London had revived its earlier suggestions for a show of strength in the East, and on 27 November Lindsay showed Welles a telegram asking whether, in view of the events in China, America would support Britain in future representations with 'an over-whelming display of naval force'. Furthermore, should Washington be willing, the two countries might initiate staff talks. Welles promised to refer the matter to Hull and Roosevelt, but reminded Lindsay that some ten days earlier the ambassador had said that because of Britain's European commitments she would be unable to divert many ships to the East, and therefore the overwhelming display would be, it appeared, over-whelmingly American.[9] Lindsay seems not to have mentioned any specific figures in his talks with Welles, but a few days later—after the attack of 5 December—Eden sent him another telegram, this time stating that Britain was thinking in terms of preparing for the East a force of some eight or nine capital ships, together with supporting craft, on the condition that the United States would match them. When he saw the President on 16 December, Lindsay told him this, but Roosevelt felt that the ships would do more good remaining in Europe. He was, however, very interested in the question of staff talks, and suggested also the possibility of a blockade to cut off Japan's supply of raw materials.[10]

There followed a rather curious episode, which unfortunately can be reconstructed only from the American side; there is not a hint of it in any British source. As the evidence of Japanese guilt in the *Panay* sinking grew more and more apparent, Roosevelt began to consider economic retaliation against Japan, and instructed Henry Morgenthau, the Secretary of the Treasury, to sound London. Morgenthau accordingly telephoned the Chancellor of the Exchequer, Sir John Simon, on the 17th, outlining Roosevelt's plan, and suggesting that Britain cooperate. Simon, according to Morgenthau, was rather taken aback, and indicated that he preferred not to do business over the telephone, that he considered this to be more in the province of the State Department and the Foreign Office, but—with memories of 1932 in his head—he had no desire once more to turn down an American offer of cooperation, and would talk to Chamberlain. On the 18th Morgenthau telephoned again, to say that the economic considerations were a corollary to the naval conversations which were to take place, and with this in mind Captain Royall Ingersoll of the Navy Department, who would shortly be sent to London, would be instructed to see Simon. A few days later Simon called back to say that he would be glad to meet Ingersoll, but pointed out that if Britain were to join in the sort of sanctions Morgenthau had proposed, special legislation would be required. Nor, he continued, was the Cabinet by any means convinced that economic pressure would help.[11]

It is hard to tell how interested the Cabinet was in the American proposals. However, Roosevelt himself soon lost interest in the idea, and with the settlement of the *Panay* incident at Christmas, nothing more was said of the possibility of sanctions. Captain Ingersoll's instructions apparently did not deal with the question of economic retaliation against Japan; he was sent for technical discussions about the British building programme, and was to investigate what might be done if war came with Japan, but any meeting with Simon was to be left to the Chancellor's initiative. On Ingersoll's arrival in London on 1 January, he had one meeting with Eden, telling him that the Navy Department did not favour any drastic move as yet, and after that he saw only his opposite number in the Plans Division of the Admiralty, Captain Sir Tom Phillips. He never saw Simon, who presumably either expected Ingersoll to approach him, or else simply preferred to wash his hands of the whole question, and let the Foreign Office consider it. The talks with Phillips resulted in an informal agreement whereby, in the event of war with Japan, Britain and the United States would use each other's waters. Yet there was a wider significance to the Ingersoll mission, for although at the time of Pearl Harbor four years later, not much more had been decided specifically on Pacific strategy, this marked the beginning of Anglo-American naval cooperation in the Second World War.[12]

London still was not ready to give up the idea of a show of force in the Orient. Early in January Craigie discussed this with Grew: a substantial number of British ships might move to Singapore, while the American fleet would go to Hawaii, and London and Washington would then warn Japan that they were prepared to take steps to protect their interests. Should the warning be disregarded, the next move would be to establish a blockade against Japan at Singapore and the Panama Canal, ruining

Japan's export trade, and cutting off most of her supplies. It must have sounded rather far-fetched to Grew, although Craigie insisted that the Royal Navy had the capability to carry it out, as long as the French could be left to guard the Mediterranean. The American ambassador, at any rate, was convinced that such a plan would lead to war, and after some thought told Craigie that he could not recommend it to his Government; in effect it would mean that America should fight for her interests in China, and she was not prepared to go that far. Craigie protested that he had no such drastic step in mind, but felt rather that the two countries should simply consult on plans for common action, and then show Hirota in private what they would do to protect their interests. To Craigie, a private threat of this sort would encourage the civil government to extend its control over the actions of the military; to Grew, on the other hand, such a step would only encourage the military to increase their independence.[13] A week later, however, the British ambassador told Grew that he was waiting to see how his talks on the Chinese Customs would come out before moving further, and after that the idea of a naval show of force was apparently dropped. Perhaps, as Grew suggested, he had himself discouraged Craigie, or perhaps London had realized that the United States was not likely to go along with such a course; more probably the ideas were simply Craigie's own, and were too strong for his Government.[14]

The crisis thus blew over, and with it, one more opportunity was lost. As Dorothy Borg has pointed out, Roosevelt's refusal to consult with the British, and his deliberately proceeding without them, showed the Japanese that they had nothing to fear in the way of a united front.[15] Certainly the lack of unanimity encouraged Tokyo, and the wave of humiliation that had swept over Japan after the *Panay* sinking quickly subsided. Furthermore, the Japanese replies to the protests of the two countries were very different in tone, that to America being considerably softer. To Craigie it was obvious that Tokyo was thus trying to drive a wedge between Britain and America, and he was all the more concerned because Grew did not agree with him.[16] Nevertheless the crisis did provide one demonstration of Anglo-American solidarity, for when the great new naval base opened at Singapore on 14 February, the only foreign ships present were three American cruisers. The Japanese, complaining that they should have been invited as well, were only partly mollified by Craigie's assurances that the American visit had been arranged informally, and the press commented icily that America and Britain should cultivate greater discretion in the future.[17]

The attacks on *Ladybird* and *Panay* were simply the most spectacular of a number of incidents which were beginning to occur with increasing frequency as more and more of China passed under Japanese control, incidents which were symptomatic of the problems facing any neutrals who insisted upon their treaty rights in occupied China. After Shanghai's fall, the victorious armies of General Matsui began a drive up the Yangtse into the interior. On 13 December, Japanese troops entered Nanking, breaking loose to sack the city and to provide the world with a foretaste of the atrocities that were to come; but the military effect of the capital's fall was slight. The Central Government simply withdrew further up-stream, establishing a new capital at Chungking, safely above the Ichang gorges, and leaving the Foreign Ministry at Hankow. Most of the dip-lomatic corps followed, but not the British. Their interests lay in the treaty ports, and while they kept a diplomatic mission with the Central Govern-ment, the embassy itself returned to Shanghai. In the meantime, Sir Archibald Clark Kerr had arrived in China, to replace the injured Knatchbull-Hugessen as ambassador.

On 16 January 1938, as the German mediation effort stalled and failed, the Japanese announced a formal break in relations with the Central Government, pending the establishment of a new Chinese régime with which they could cooperate.[18] Hirota set forth his country's aims more fully in a speech to the Diet on 22 January. It is worth quoting at some length, as the first official statement of the conditions which Westerners in China were going to have to face.

Japan has no territorial ambitions in China, nor has she any intention of separating North China from the rest of the country. All she wants is that China, taking a broad view of the situation, will collaborate with Japan towards the fulfillment of the ideal of Sino-Japanese cooperation for the common prosperity and well-being of the two countries. . . .

In Europe and America there are some who are apt to entertain misgivings regarding Japan's intentions, as though she were trying to close the Chinese door and expel the interests of the Powers. . . . Not only will Japan respect to the fullest extent the rights and interests of the Powers in the occupied areas, but she is prepared, for the purpose of promoting the welfare of the Chinese people, to leave the door wide open to all Powers and to welcome their economic and cultural cooperation there. It is earnestly to be hoped that the Powers by recognizing the new conditions prevailing in China . . . will cooperate for the establishment of a new order in the Far East.

Finally (and this must have worried Craigie) he praised America for her 'fair and just attitude', while warning England 'to comprehend correctly Japan's position in East Asia'.[19]

In Hirota's speech there appeared for the first time the phrase, 'new order'. Vague and undefined for the present, and appearing in the midst of promises to maintain the Open Door and to respect the territorial integrity of China, it nevertheless had a menacing ring to it. Already its political ramifications were beginning to become evident. As the Japanese armies advanced, they set up puppet governments in their wake, made up largely of old politicians who had seen active service in the warlord period before the Northern Expedition, and who had retired with the coming of the Kuomintang. In Chahar and Suiyuan, the Kwantung Army established an Autonomous Government of Inner Mongolia, and on 14 December the North China Army unveiled a Provisional Government of the Chinese Republic, under Wang Keh-min, in the city now renamed Peking (northern capital) rather than Peiping (northern peace) for the benefit of local pride. Both Prince Konoye and the army spokesmen announced that the Wang government would be a nucleus around which other régimes could gather, but for the time being Tokyo was cautious, and showed no intention of recognizing her new child. She showed a similar reserve when a new puppet government of Central China was formed at Nanking in March 1938.

Hirota's statement, and Japan's subsequent actions, left little doubt of Tokyo's intentions to prosecute the still undeclared war to a finish. No longer could the 'China Incident' (as the Gaimusho insisted on calling it) be regarded merely as the struggle for the five northern provinces, or for the protection of Japanese interests in Shanghai. It now meant an extension of Japanese power, not only in the north, but in central China as well, a power which would be political and economic as well as military. Matsui was already driving up the Yangtse valley, the gateway to the heart of China and to the vast interior markets which had been the dream of China traders for a century. South China too, and with it the great entrepôt of Hongkong, would be in danger. Even western China might fall, where a British road was being built from Burma over into Yunnan. The Japanese advance would not only mean a terrible destruction of life and property in China, but would also bring Japan's armies to the very gates of the Western empire in Southeast Asia.

For the moment (as far as the neutrals were concerned) the chief question was that of Japan's treatment of foreign interests in China, and if what had happened in Manchukuo was any indication, the prospect was far from promising. Or, should China win (bringing Japan to her '1812', as Eden hoped) her victory might mean a return of the aggressive nationalism and anti-foreignism of the days of 1927. In either case the foreign position would be changed, and the British—and others—were now faced with a number of questions which they could no longer afford to ignore.

First of all, there was the question of economic interests. How far would they be affected by the war, how far hurt by the political changes stemming from Japanese occupation? How far would a China, dominated by Japan, maintain the traditions of the Open Door? Second, there was the question of what policy to follow. Should Britain try to back the winning horse, and hope to make the best of the situation? or should she simply insist on her neutral rights and (as the Shanghai magazine *Finance and Commerce* had suggested) try to carry on business as usual, ignoring the actual war as far as possible?[20] Or should she take seriously her commitments as a signatory of the Nine Power Pact and a member of the League of Nations, and extend aid—military as well as diplomatic—to China? For the moment this last alternative had faded into the background; for the moment many still believed that business could be carried on as usual despite the war and despite Japanese occupation. American isolationists might be frightened, might be pleading for a total withdrawal from the Far East, but why should Britain abandon the position which she had built up over the last century? Certainly Japan's advance would mean some changes—the experience in Manchukuo had already shown that— but Japan could not hope to dominate all China, and it seemed inconceivable that she should want to oust every foreign firm, shipping line, bank, and business house. Viscount Ishii told the Japan Society in London, on 17 February 1938, that Tokyo would need English cooperation in developing China; this would provide Japan with a natural market, and do much to eliminate trade rivalries.[21] These were reassuring sentiments, and they were echoed by men like Yoshida Shigeru and Matsuidaira Tsuneo, men who spoke the language of a more liberal era, and looked back longingly to the days of Japanese friendship with Britain. But it was not men like Yoshida and Matsuidaira who controlled Japan, and to the more far-seeing it was becoming evident that an attack on foreign interests was in the making, that cooperation with Japan in the new China would be a one-sided compromise, and—the logical corollary to this—that the problem of the survival of British economic interests was thus inextricably linked with the problem of the survival of China herself. The alternatives were not to be business as usual or aid to China, but aid to China in order to have any business at all.

In late 1937 and early 1938, however, this was not yet as obvious as it would shortly become, and for the time being the chief problems plaguing Britain's relations with Japan were ones which dealt with the protection of

British enterprises in those parts of China which were either occupied or, in the war zone, were presently to become occupied. Most of the incidents which arose here were less spectacular than the December attacks on the Yangtse, but they stemmed from the same causes, and in the long run, were equally important.

Chapter VI

The West under Attack, II: 1938

The British interests in China which came under attack from the Japanese in late 1937 and in 1938 may be conveniently broken down into five separate headings. In the first place there was the question of the Maritime Customs, which was to be of special importance for the first five months of 1938. Second, there was the question of those Chinese railroads in which British capital was still invested, and on whose revenues loans were secured. Third, there was the problem of restrictions on the navigation of British shipping, and the general reaction of British shipping to the war. Fourth there were, particularly in north China, new trade and exchange regulations imposed, which were designed as a first step in bringing that area into an economic bloc with Manchukuo and Japan, and which operated to the detriment of foreign firms. And last, there was a continuous attempt by the Japanese to increase their control of foreign settlements within the Treaty Ports. The first four will be examined in this chapter, and the next chapter will concentrate on Japan's campaign against the two major foreign areas with which Britain was concerned: the International Settlement in Shanghai and the British Concession in Tientsin.

The Customs

The future of the Customs was first called into question after the fall of Tientsin in the summer of 1937, when the Japanese consul-general opened talks with the British Commissioner of Customs in that city.[1] The problems involved were by no means of importance only to China and Japan. Officially the Customs Administration was an organ of the Central Government, and the Inspector-General, Sir Frederick Maze, was a servant of Nanking, responsible to H. H. Kung at the Ministry of Finance in the Chinese capital. In fact, however, the Maritime Customs was a body which was international both in its outlook and in its duties. It was staffed by an international force, and Maze regarded himself as serving not only the Central Government, but also the interests of the traders dealing with China, and his viewpoint, which was shared by many of the senior Customs officials, was that whatever helped China's trade would help China herself. In a country where localism had always been strong, the Customs, since its founding had had to fight to hold together in one piece, divorced as much as possible from Chinese politics, and Maze continued this tradition. Above all, he sought to maintain the integrity of the Service, even if it meant some compromise with the Japanese and their puppets, and he lived with the constant fear that his organization might split into two parts, one for occupied, the other for free, China. Yet if the Customs was both Chinese and international it also had a strong British complexion. Britain's stake in the Customs was not what it had once been, but it was still high. Of the forty-two Commissioners (the chief officers in the treaty ports) in 1937, twenty-one were British, and no other nationality had more than five representatives.[2] A number of Chinese foreign loans, in which there were considerable British holdings, were secured as a first charge on the Customs revenues; on 1 January 1938 these amounted to a total outstanding of £25,877,475 and US $28,800,150.[3] A default on loan services would hurt Chinese credit abroad, and to prevent this it was necessary (or so it seemed at the time) to maintain the operation of the Administration unimpaired.

There were considerable difficulties standing in the way, however. By January 1938 every significant port north of Hangchow Bay was in Japanese hands, and the invasion of Fukien and Kwangtung was rumoured to be imminent. Second, the Japanese blockade affected the ports still under Chinese control, although some, such as Canton and those of the Kowloon Customs District, profited from the diversion of trade from the north. And last, the Japanese were of course interested in securing control of the revenues, or at least in making sure that they did not find their way to the Central Government.

From the viewpoint of the Western bondholder, for whom Britain was emerging as spokesman, it seemed that despite the problems the fact remained that trade still continued with both occupied and unoccupied China. In 1937, even with five months of war, the Customs returns had showed an increase of revenue over 1936.[4] Funds for loan services were therefore available in theory, and it remained only for a compromise to be worked out which would satisfy all sides. These were the points around which the negotiations turned as an effort was made from September 1937 to May 1938 to find a settlement which would protect the bondholder, and to which Chinese and Japanese would agree. The foreign position was weakened early by the action of W. R. Myers, the Tientsin Commissioner, who after two months of talks with the Japanese agreed to deposit the revenues from that city's Customs in the Yokohama Specie Bank, maintaining only a theoretical control over them. He also agreed that while the fighting lasted he would make no remittances to the Inspector-General in Shanghai for Tientsin's quotas of the loan services. 'Unsatisfactory, unilateral, and entirely in favour of Japan', Maze called it privately when he first heard of it, and it created a precedent which dogged all the later negotiations.[5] This became apparent after the fall of Shanghai when the Japanese tried to force on the local Commissioner an arrangement similar to that in Tientsin. Maze's appeal to the West for support had some effect, and the British, French, and Americans let Tokyo know that they expected to be consulted on the situation.[6] As time went on, however, it was the British who took the lead in the negotiations; by mid-December the United States had refused support to any specific plan which might then have to be forced on the Chinese, and Washington preferred to talk simply in terms of the larger principles of Customs integrity.[7]

A further complication came when on 21 January 1938 the new Peking Provisional Government announced a series of tariff reductions for north China; to no one's surprise Japan was the chief beneficiary. Western protests had no effect, and Maze was unsuccessful in his attempt to neutralize the action by recommending to Kung that China cut her own rates from the comparatively high 1934 level to the lower tariff of 1931, in order to prevent a diversion of trade to the north.[8] Nor was this all that Maze had to worry about, and on 8 January he wrote the French, American, and British representatives in Shanghai of his fears that Peking would appoint him its own Inspector-General, and when he refused, would take control of the Customs in the north. The French gave a general promise of help, the Americans left the letter unanswered, and the British refused to comment on a 'hypothetical' situation, although the embassy promised him its support, 'provided you keep us informed and are guided by our advice'.[9] For Maze the question was more than hypothetical; it embodied the whole question of his proper relationship to the puppets and to the Japanese, and the possibility of a separate Customs establishment for occupied China continued to haunt him until Pearl Harbor.

For the moment, however, the threat remained purely a latent one. Maze went to Hongkong in early February to see Kung, and while the Minister tacitly agreed to his retaining a working contact with the

Japanese, he otherwise took an unyielding stand, refusing to alter the tariff or to deposit the revenues of the occupied ports in the Yokohama Specie Bank.[10] In February the talks moved from Shanghai to Tokyo, and there, for all practical purposes, they evolved into bilateral negotiations between Craigie and the Gaimusho. By late February the British had indicated their willingness to consider the deposit of revenues in the Japanese bank (they had earlier held out for the Hongkong and Shanghai Bank) and by late March an arrangement providing for the full service of foreign loans had been reached. Craigie had originally envisaged an agreement between Maze and the Japanese in Shanghai, but the Inspector-General refused this,[11] and what emerged eventually was a draft agreement in Tokyo, accompanied by an exchange of letters between the ambassador and Vice-Minister Horinouchi. On 3 May a communiqué was issued in London and Tokyo announcing the agreement. Under its terms the revenues collected in occupied China would be deposited in the Yokohama Specie Bank, which would then remit to the Inspector-General funds for the service of foreign loans, the amounts to be proportional to the trade of the occupied ports. China would also pay Japan the arrears owed on the Boxer Indemnity, which Kung had held up the previous autumn. And, in addition, the revenues in the occupied ports which had been placed in the Hongkong and Shanghai Bank would be turned over to the Yokohama Specie Bank.[12]

Before the news was released, Craigie had shown the French and American ambassadors the preliminary drafts of the agreement, and while the French were ready to accept it, Washington refused comment. Craigie then told Grew that unless both France and America expressed 'no objection', the whole arrangement would collapse and the Customs would be seized. Still the United States refused, but before the final decision was made, the communiqué of 3 May was issued, and it implied that neither Paris nor Washington would object. Craigie apologized to Grew, but the damage was done, in spite of Hull's statement later that day trying to correct the impression thus given to the world.[13]

As it was, the agreement foundered on the attempt to gain Chinese assent. Kung was shown the text on 3 May and urged not to oppose it.[14] Yet nothing could disguise the fact, as the Chinese pointed out, that this was the first time since the Washington Conference that two countries had reached an important decision on China without consulting her. After some uncertainty Hankow issued a statement rejecting the arrangement, and Ambassador Quo told the Foreign Office that China considered herself in no way bound, and would reserve her full rights and freedom of action on Customs matters.[15] The agreement thus remained a dead letter, and only once, in June 1938, was a payment made under its terms. China kept up the full service of foreign loans, by authorizing the Inspector-General to overdraw on his account in the Central Bank of China, until 15 January 1939, when Chungking announced that payments could no longer be continued.

The importance of the Customs issue lay not so much in the agreement itself as in the attitude shown towards it by the British and Americans. The affair was one of the most obvious examples yet of a lack of cooperation. The British view, as Craigie expressed it, was that his country had done the dirty work, partly for the benefit of the Americans, who now threatened to sabotage the agreement by refusing to express 'no objection'. 'The whole wretched business has been far from enjoyable'. Grew wrote in his Diary, after talking to the British ambassador.[16] Britain had compromised with Japan and won a doubtful bargain; the United States had stayed clear, standing high on her principles. Here, it seemed to the world at large, was British appeasement at work. A few weeks earlier she had recognized the Italian conquest of Ethiopia, in return for some dubious promises for the withdrawal of foreign troops from Spain, and now in the East it seemed that she had come to an arrangement with Japan for the benefit of her own financial interests, at the expense of China. It was a pattern which was to be repeated again in the ensuing years, notably in the Anglo-Japanese agreements on the Tientsin Concession in July 1939, and on the Burma Road in July 1940, where Britain, forced into negotiations, would seek American support, fail to secure it, and would end up seriously compromising those principles which, Hull was fond of declaring, should influence nations in their dealings with one another.

Officially, Britain remained in favour of the agreement and during the next year there were efforts made both by the ambassador and the Inspector-General to have the Chinese implement it. With or without the agreement, however, both the British and international aspects of the Customs were seriously challenged and it began to seem as if the Administration, too, would be swept up in the *Gleichschaltung* of the New Order. Nevertheless it is hard in retrospect to consider the agreement a serious mistake, as many did at the time. Even though it was never put into effect, and although the question of the disposal of revenues went unsolved, the agreement helped the Customs to continue to function as a unit. In Shanghai Maze authorized his Commissioner to deposit current revenues in the Yokohama Specie Bank, but refused to transfer the balances from the Hongkong and Shanghai Bank unless the Chinese agreed. This proved to be the basis for handling the Customs's finances in occupied China in the future, and despite efforts on both sides to make changes, little more was done before Pearl Harbor. Maze thus still exercised a certain degree of control over his Service even in the occupied areas, and the prospect of an outright seizure of the Customs and their revenues by the Japanese was thereby averted.[17]

Economic Changes in North China

In June 1938 a speaker at Chatham House examined the situation of Western interests in occupied China, and concluded that a bleak future was emerging.

The application of the Open Door in Manchukuo provides a partial answer as to what is in store for North and Central China. For foreign interests in Manchukuo, the Open Door has been for one-way traffic—outward. . . . The foreigner has been ousted by two methods: the first consisted in a state-socialistic, monopolistic domination of all key industries . . . the second method was police or political pressure on the buyer, or non-interference with law-breaking activities of Japanese subjects.[18]

What these measures would mean to China proper became evident in 1938. The reduction of the Customs tariff in the north was followed by the establishment, on 11 February, of a Federal Reserve Bank (F.R.B.) in Peking, which was to issue yuan at parity with yen, eventually superseding in the north the Chinese national currency, or *fapi*. The bank opened on 11 March, but at first made only slow progress, hampered by the hostility of foreign bankers, the distrust of the north Chinese for the new currency, and the active opposition of the guerrilla 'Border Governments', who worked against the dissemination of its money.[19] Nor did the F.R.B. currency have sufficient backing in either foreign exchange or specie, since the Chinese banks in the north refused to hand over their silver stocks, safely stored in the foreign areas of Tientsin and Peking.[20]

These were the first in a number of moves designed to integrate north China into a yen bloc with Japan and Manchukuo. They were an effective bar to non-Japanese imports; they meant also that foreign manufacturing interests in Shanghai would be threatened, and that trade would flow from central China to the low tariff area of the north. 'Looked at from the standpoint of British trade', said a spokesman for the China Association in London, 'the outlook is decidedly menacing. . . . Non-Japanese exporters to north China now have no assurance that they will receive payment in a currency convertible to sterling, or other foreign exchange, while investments and profits in north China are immobilized for the same reason'.[21] In late March Craigie warned of the possibility of 'exchange control *à la Japonaise*', which would seriously harm foreign business operations, and he suggested that Britain might exert discreet pressure by discouraging loans and credits to Japan.[22] His warning was premature, and exchange controls for north China were still a year away. Efforts to drive out the *fapi* continued in 1938, and in March 1939 it was outlawed, but where the two currencies competed on equal terms, in the free markets of the Peking Legation Quarter and the British and French Concessions in Tientsin, the F.R.B. notes remained at a discount to *fapi*, and gained little ground before the end of 1938.[23]

Although there were no general controls imposed on the north yet, there was one major northern port which had no foreign settlements, and where the local government could therefore legislate as it saw fit. Tsingtao became a sort of testing ground for Japanese economic policies, and thus provided the foreign trader with an example of what a system of controls might mean. All exports were forbidden save those covered by a Japanese naval permit. Until April 1938 these were easy enough to obtain, but after the institution of the F.R.B. permits were refused for cargoes financed through foreign banks which did not handle the new currency. The local Chamber of Commerce ordered its members to close their accounts with foreign banks, and to do their business only with the Yokohama Specie Bank. For a while the Deutsche-Asiatische Bank accepted the F.R.B. notes, and acted as a channel for the granting of export permits, but after 24 July the permits stopped completely. Meanwhile Japanese exporters continued to trade to Europe at current market prices, not working on the artificial exchange rates set up by their own authorities, but using the Shanghai open market rates for *fapi*. In the autumn of 1938 a concession was made which allowed foreign merchants to negotiate their exports through the current Shanghai rates, provided that the remittances from Shanghai to Tsingtao were made through the Yokohama Specie Bank, which then would take a high commission. The fact that in a port like Tientsin, where such controls were lacking, the export business went to the foreign banks, which could offer *fapi*, diverting business from the Japanese banks, must have caused foreign businessmen to wonder how long Tokyo would allow this state of affairs to last.[24]

Railroads

China's railways, particularly those in which Britain held interests, had suffered considerably from the war. On 30 June 1937 there were still some £13,898,950 in loans outstanding, and in addition to the purely financial considerations, Britain had had such rights as the employment of British engineers-in-chief and chief accountants, the supervision of the expenditure of railway funds, and similar privileges, on those lines in which British capital was invested. The Japanese occupation meant the expulsion of many British employees, the expropriation of railway revenues, and the refusal of requests for the inspection of rail lines.[25] The war had also prevented the issuance of the loans which had been agreed upon in the summer of 1937 for the Canton–Meihsien, Shanghai–Nanking, and Pukow–Siangyang lines. The North Station, Shanghai terminus of the line from Nanking, had been severely damaged by fighting and in 1938 was occupied by the Japanese. The Shanghai–Nanking line itself was occupied and by the end of 1938 had lost an estimated Ch $5,000,000 in revenue, while the Shanghai–Hangchow–Ningpo line had lost some $1,500,000. The Canton–Kowloon railway had been bombed, and in the north the Peking–Mukden line, while operating normally, remained under Japanese control. Nor had the situation improved much by the end of the year, and though the Shanghai–Nanking and Shanghai–Hangchow lines were again running as usual, their foreign bondholders could neither inspect them, nor had they any voice in their management. The Peking–Mukden line, too, continued to function under the Japanese, and its revenues were paid into a Japanese bank.[26] The *North China Herald* charged that the lines from Shanghai were carrying commercial as well as military traffic, but the Japanese repeatedly claimed that the railways were theirs by right of conquest, and that they were bound by no agreements with foreign companies.[27]

Navigation

Nineteen-thirty-eight saw a steady worsening in the conditions under which foreign shippers operated. Although there were isolated cases of foreign coastal ships being held up by the Japanese, the chief trouble spot remained the Yangtse. By early summer the drive on Hankow was in progress, yet though the fighting moved further and further upstream, there was no change in the situation on the lower reaches of the river. The Japanese denied that the Yangtse was actually closed to foreign shipping, but continued to insist that the river could not yet be opened to free navigation without prejudicing military operations.[28] There was undoubtedly some truth in the claim that the river was unsafe for general navigation, but the purity of Japanese intentions was open to question. Disquieting reports of trade discrimination begin to filter down from the hinterland. An American firm reported that while no foreign ships were allowed above Kiangyin, Japanese merchantmen would carry only Japanese cargo, or cargo in which there was a considerable Japanese interest. Agents of Butterfield's and Jardine's, reporting on conditions at Nanking and Wuhu, charged that commercial shipments were travelling in Japanese bottoms between those cities and Shanghai; above that point priority was given to military cargoes but downstream practically all loadings were commercial.[29] *The Times* on 28 July reported a regular Shanghai–Nanking service, with semi-regular runs to Wuhu, and accused a local Japanese sponsored company of dictating excessive freight rates by virtue of its monopoly of inland waters.

The Western shipper thus found himself hedged in by an increasing number of restrictions, conditions, and outright prohibitions of his business. On 20 March it became necessary for all ships plying the inland waters of central China to carry a military permit or risk seizure; Britain refused to recognize the order,[30] and apparently British shippers managed to carry on some trade without the passes. On top of this came the formation of a Kiangchek Steamship Company, which promised to secure passes for all ships cooperating with it, granting them the right to fly the Japanese flag, and carry Japanese guards. In return for this the shippers would pay half their net revenue to Kiangchek. And, said the *North China Herald*, the foreign shipper then discovered that the pass only permitted navigation, and another permit—generally granted only to Japanese shippers—was needed to offload or land cargo.[31] Finally there came the announcement of a new Sino-Japanese Shanghai Inland Navigation Company, which was to enjoy 'monopolistic privileges in the transport of passengers and goods, the operation of wharves and godowns, and the chartering of vessels'. No outside competition would be allowed, and foreign shippers could either take up shares in the new company, or go out of business, selling their ships at the Japanese company's evaluation.[32]

At Tsingtao, too, there were similar disabilities on foreign navigation. By May 1938 the Japanese had cleared the harbour entrance sufficiently to allow the passage of ocean-going ships, but only Japanese merchantmen (and, it was claimed, some German as well) were permitted to use the wharves. Foreign ships, forced to anchor in the outer harbour, had to pay the high transport rates charged by the Japanese sponsored lighterage organization, rates which, according to the local British Chamber of Commerce, were some 300 to 450 per cent higher than those which the shippers could have obtained privately. Protests to Tokyo brought only promises of better treatment in the future and the usual explanation that the difficulties were due to military needs.[33]

Miscellaneous Problems

Other lesser annoyances arose through 1938 to plague the foreign trader. On 28 June an embargo on the export of skins and hides was imposed in north China, and was extended on 18 October to cover wool and hemp. Although the prohibitions were later somewhat modified, the four products made up over one-third of the total volume of north China exports. With this came the formation on 25 July of the Mengchiang (Mongolian) Bank, and a form of exchange control in that territory. However an apparent effort to establish an oil monopoly similar to that in Manchukuo failed, partly due to the strength of British, American, and Dutch protests in Tokyo.[34] A more serious indication of what was to come was the adoption in 1938 of a Four Year Plan, which defined various fields for development, and called for state controlled monopolies in all key industries. In November came the formation of two huge semi-official concerns, the North China and Central China Development Companies, half of whose funds were put up by Tokyo, which in turn held supervisory powers. Under them came a number of subsidiary enterprises, such as shipping, railroad, power, and mining companies, while at their head was the newly formed China Affairs Board in Tokyo, the final authority in Sino-Japanese economic relations.[35]

Nevertheless, while the future was uncertain, and while many British businesses had already been severely hurt by the war, it would be a mistake to assume that the immediate prospect in all fields was entirely black. A few sets of figures will give some idea of the pattern of British trade in China after Lukouchiao.

BRITISH TRADE WITH CHINA
(in pounds sterling)[36]

	1936	1937	1938	1939
Imports	7,642,655	8,248,983	6,448,133	5,147,000
Exports	5,784,027	5,911,789	4,093,115	3,557,900

TRADE WITH HONGKONG

Imports	757,981	935,361	982,339	944,000
Exports	2,109,127	3,391,716	3,937,515	2,751,000

In other fields, British interests showed a mixed reaction to the war. Shipping advanced markedly at first, as Chinese tonnage was driven from the coastal waters and Japanese ships requisitioned for war purposes,[37] but as the following figures show, the relative increases were offset by an absolute decrease in the volume of trade.

BRITISH SHIPPING IN CHINA: TONNAGES AND PERCENTAGES, ENTERING AND CLEARING CHINESE PORTS[38]

	1936	1937	1938	1939
Foreign Trade	16,158,051 (35.72%)	12,940,748 (36.51%)	12,350,327 (41.97%)	8,297,449 (27.82%)
Domestic Trade	41,187,464 (41.28%)	23,165,047 (42.43%)	16,209,988 (54.65%)	10,936,086 (49.48%)

Mining companies had mixed experiences; the Peking Syndicate suffered badly from Japan's overruning of its mines in Hopei, Shantung and Shansi, and from the disruption of water and rail transport, but the Kailan Mining Administration was considerably more successful, and its production figures rose steadily until 1941.[39]

Craigie, late in 1938, pointed ironically to the fact that many of the British firms in Shanghai who were complaining loudest against Japanese restrictions were in fact doing a thriving business during the war.[40] The Chairman of the Chinese Engineering and Mining Company (which owned half of the Kailan Mining Administration) must have been speaking for many of his colleagues in China when he told the annual meeting of his company in 1938:

Neither the Kailan Mining Administration nor this company has any political ends to serve; we are concerned only with the prosecution by the Administration of our legitimate business interests. In doing so we are rendering an essential service to the business community of the Far East. . . .[41]

His company that year raised its dividend from 5 to 7½ per cent. Others prospered from the war too; the financial pages of the *North China Herald* are filled with reports of business successes that year. So, for example, the Shanghai Tug and Lighter Company saw 1938 as 'the best [year] in our history'; the revenue of the Shanghai Waterworks Company was up, and J. W. Keswick reported of Ewo Cotton Mills (a subsidiary of Jardine's) that 'despite the unhappy state of affairs which existed throughout 1938 our profits are the highest in the company's history and they might well have been larger but for the restrictions imposed north of the Soochow Creek'.[42]

The immediate business outlook therefore was not one of unrelieved gloom. Nevertheless many companies had been badly hurt by the war, and the general rising trend of Chinese trade since the Leith-Ross mission had been quite definitely reversed. The big question, of course, was that of the future; what did the Japanese mean when they said they wanted the 'cooperation' of foreign business? Finance Minister Ikeda and Kodama Kenji, the head of the newly formed Central China Development Company, both told Craigie that they were determined to prevent the formation of any monopolistic system, realizing the need for foreign economic cooperation in China's reconstruction. The Open Door would stay open, and Kodama admitted that it should not have been closed in Manchukuo. The main purpose of the new organizations, Craigie was told, was to keep control of Chinese economic affairs out of the hands of the military. Kodama repeated much the same thing to the press that autumn, and both he and the head of the North China Company promised that foreign businesses would be able to resume normal operations as soon as conditions permitted, and they invited foreign investment in their companies.[43] A year earlier some might have responded to these pleas for cooperation, but now they were greeted with scepticism. Of course Japan wanted foreign capital, said the *North China Herald*, 'but that is all they want—foreign financial assistance for a trade to be made as exclusively Japanese as possible'. Westerners were to give up trading, and become money lenders, 'wiping out the very substantial interests which have been created in the past century, and providing financial assistance for the policy of the Closed Door'.[44] As one writer pointed out, Japan had failed to win a quick victory in China, and now found herself in an economic pinch. She had to work for the development of north China and to stimulate exports from occupied China, in order to replace foreign imports and to revive a deteriorating balance of payments. A system of exchange controls and monopolies would eliminate foreign competition, and to pay for these she would have to increase her export of consumer goods to China, and stimulate this through a favourable tariff rate.[45] This was becoming more and more clear to British concerns in China, and although some of them might be enjoying a temporary wartime boom, they had the uneasy feeling that if Japan conquered China, she would use them only as long as she needed them, and that ultimately they had no future in a country which had become Japan's client. Thus their confidence in a policy of business as usual, and the earlier hopes which some had had of cooperating with Japan, or at least of not opposing her, gave way to the advocacy of stronger courses by the Government at home, involving both a programme of aid to China and economic sanctions against Japan.

Chapter VII

Shanghai and Tientsin: 1937–1938

To most Westerners, life in China meant life in the treaty ports, and the centre of treaty port life was Shanghai. Here, what was once a small walled town in the Yangtse delta, had by the twentieth century become the leading city of China, in terms of population, wealth, and influence. Modern Shanghai, in both its good and its bad aspects, was a creation of the West, and particularly of the British, who had opened it up as one of the five original treaty ports at the end of the Opium War. The British had discovered its potential as a port serving the vast hinterland of the Yangtse valley, and the British had taken the lead in building it as a modern city. Nowhere else in Asia perhaps was the meeting of East and West so obvious or so jarring; Shanghai was the centre of Western business activity in China, and the centre of the peculiar treaty port culture— an artificial Western style of life imported into Asia—which flourished in the century between the treaty of Nanking and the Communist triumph. Shanghai had long held a deserved reputation as one of the world's wickedest cities, a place where respectable British bankers and American-educated Chinese industrialists rubbed shoulders with impoverished refugees, and the derelicts of all countries who drifted ashore from the ships crowding the harbour. Shanghai was a centre of British parks, clubs, schools, hotels, and banks but beneath the opulence of the International Settlement could be seen the appalling poverty of Asia, and the elements which batten on poverty: the underworld of East and West, living from the proceeds of gambling, dope, prostitution, kidnapping, and murder.[1]

The city was divided into three administrative areas, each with separate and independent authorities, laws, and regulations. There was the International Settlement, the French Concession, and the Chinese municipality, which together comprised some 3,746,768 people in 1935, of whom

57,607 were foreigners.[2] Technically international, the Settlement in fact reflected a heavy British predominance; it was administered by a Municipal Council made up of fourteen members, of whom five were Chinese, five British, two Japanese, and one or two Americans. This predominance was based not on law, but on the British leadership in landholding and the payment of taxes, for the franchise was based on a property qualification. The Japanese made up the largest foreign colony in terms of size, but there were more British voters: 1284 in 1935, to 893 Japanese, and some 400 Americans.[3] Most of the officers of the Shanghai Municipal Police were British, as were those of the Shanghai Volunteer Corps, a local foreign militia unit. The Land Regulations of 1869, on which Settlement administration was based, had been largely drawn up by the British, and remained British in character. The British-owned *North China Daily News* (with its weekly edition, the *North China Herald*), was the city's most important newspaper, and the closest to being the organ of British treaty port opinion, while the weekly *Finance and Commerce* reflected the outlook of much of the British business community. Two British shipping firms, Jardine, Matheson and Company, and Butterfield and Swire, dominated the rich waterborne trade of the Yangtse Valley, while on land much was carried by the Shanghai–Nanking railway, in which there were substantial British holdings. There was heavy British investment in, or outright ownership of, the city's public utilities. Britain had built Shanghai in the nineteenth century, and in the twentieth she was working hard to retain her control, against both Chinese nationalism and Japanese imperialism.

On 11 November the Chinese evacuated Nantao, south of the Old City, and the main lines of battle moved back from Shanghai, leaving the city quiet and in a position to assess the harm that had been done. The most serious casualty among British concerns was the Marconi Maritime Wireless Telegraph Company, whose factory had been destroyed by fire, while elsewhere a number of cotton mills, lumber yards, dockyards, and wharves were hurt. The chairman of the British Chamber of Commerce estimated the material damage to British property at £500,000, adding that consequential losses were probably fifteen to twenty times as great. There was a serious loss in trade, as many Shanghai-bound cargoes were diverted to other ports, and in September Britain's share of the vastly reduced import trade was down 77.3 per cent from July, and her export trade down 56.5 per cent.[4]

In addition, Hongkew and Yangtsepoo—the northern and eastern sections of the Settlement, beyond the Soochow Creek—had been in the Japanese defence sector, and now remained in Japanese hands, for all practical purposes outside the control of the Municipal Council. This region, comprising over half the area of the Settlement, was particularly vital to foreign interests: according to one estimate, of the approximately £180,000 of British capital in Shanghai, £100,000 was invested here. Sixty per cent of the city's large scale industries and 70 per cent of the smaller lay here. Here were the bulk of the shipping properties, and most of the public utilities, including those that were British-owned: the Shanghai Electric Construction Company, which operated the tramcars, the Shanghai Waterworks, the Shanghai Gas Company, and the Anglo-American Shanghai Power Company. Here was 90 per cent of the Settlement's developed water frontage; outside it were no wharves capable of accommodating large ships, and here also were the godowns of the shipping companies.[5] Part of the Settlement was thus directly occupied by the Japanese, and the rest was (as the China Association reported) surrounded by Japanese forces who could, if they were willing to disregard the international repercussions, do just about whatever they wanted to bring it under their control.[6]

Nor was there much hope that the situation would change for the better. In Shanghai, as elsewhere in occupied China, the Japanese insisted that military necessity prevented the restoration of normal conditions, and even after the Chinese evacuation, they refused to lift the restrictions on entry into Hongkew and Yangtsepoo. However, when General Matsui Iwane, the local commander, reportedly threatened on 11 November to occupy the whole Settlement, Tokyo was quick to issue a disavowal.[7] Matsui may well have been misquoted; in fact what Japan sought in the period before Pearl Harbor was not an outright occupation of the Settlement, but an increasing share in its administration, coupled with severe restrictions on its use as a haven by pro-Central Government Chinese. This was essentially what Consul-General Okamoto asked for, when he presented the Council and the French authorities with a series of demands on 21 November, calling for the suppression of the Kuomintang and anti-Japanese organizations, literature, and propaganda, the eviction of Central Government organizations and representatives, and censorship of Chinese radio communications. His demands were accompanied by a threat from the military that if the Council did nothing, Matsui would be forced to act himself.[8]

Few in the Settlement were inclined to take a firm stand on these issues. The two most influential British papers called for acceptance of the terms as the only realistic policy. 'For the present Shanghai has to regard itself as an internee', wrote the North China Herald, adding that 'activities and expressions of view which might have been proper before . . . can no longer be indulged in without breaking the peace'. *Finance and Commerce* granted the Japanese the right to demand measures for their own security, and in a more optimistic vein continued that 'there is no reason why the Chinese and the Japanese and the other foreign communities should not live here in peace, and carry on trade, while the war . . . is waged else-where'.[9] It is only fair to add that this same paper would presently take a more realistic view.

In general the Council agreed to go along as far as possible with Okamoto's demands, and in fact had already begun to move against anti-Japanese organizations.[10] A number of Chinese post and telegraph officials withdrew of their own accord, enabling the Japanese to take over the Chinese Telegraph Office on 28 November, and the Wireless Administration on 5 January 1938. Yet inevitably there were troubles. The Japanese announced that there would be a victory march through the city on 3 December, and despite British and American efforts (and apparently those of the civil government in Tokyo) to dissuade them, the military went ahead with their plans. Inside the Settlement, a grenade was thrown, and four people wounded.[11] The parade continued, but the Japanese cordoned off about twenty-five blocks near Nanking Road, and that evening as they prepared to withdraw, Major Gerrard, the S.M.P. Commissioner, was handed a memorandum from Matsui's headquarters and asked to sign it. It represented an agreement which would allow Japanese troops to pass freely through the Settlement without notification, whenever they thought it necessary, and which would allow them to act independently within the Settlement whenever they found the Council's behaviour unsatisfactory.

In other words, the Council was being asked to abdicate its power over an already truncated Settlement, and hand it over to the Japanese, and this is precisely what the Japanese were going to press for during the next four years. Gerrard naturally refused to sign, and merely promised to bring the memorandum to the Council's attention.[12] The Japanese were evidently embarrassed by the affair, and tried unsuccessfully to retrieve the document before the Council could see it and issue a statement presenting its own side of the case. At a meeting of the consular body on 6 December Okamoto said that the Japanese would treat the memorandum as if it had never been presented, but he was unable to give any assurance that the military had agreed to its recall.[13]

Here the matter was dropped for the time being, but the peace which followed was uneasy, and it later became evident that this episode had simply been the first thrust in a Japanese campaign to gain control of the

F

policing of the entire Settlement. The Japanese had a number of reasons, both political and economic, for wanting this control (and not only in Shanghai, but in the foreign areas of the other treaty ports as well), but it was the security of their forces which gave them a ready and very real issue. A Kuomintang underground had stayed behind in the cities after the retreat of the regulars, taking asylum in the Western settlements, and their activities remained a continual source of friction between the Japanese and the foreign communities.

A bad outbreak of crime at the end of 1937 led to the issuance of a proclamation on 1 January 1938, by which the Shanghai Municipal Council assumed a number of emergency powers designed to crack down on anti-Japanese terrorism. It said nothing, however, about S.M.P. cooperation with the Japanese gendarmerie.[14] Then on 4 January Consul-General Okamoto presented the Council chairman with a new set of demands for changes in the administration of the Settlement. He wanted the Japanese position strengthened, and asked that a Japanese Secretary be appointed to the Council to rank with the British Secretary. Again, however, the most important points were those which dealt with the police. Among other things, Japanese policemen were to be detailed to conduct investigations bearing on Japanese interests; Japanese strength in all ranks of the S.M.P. was to be increased; the Japanese Deputy Commissioner was to be put in charge of the northern areas, while Japanese officers would command units there; and a special Japanese police officer was to be appointed to rank next to the Commissioner, Major Gerrard.[15]

The British embassy opposed making any concession, even under threat of force, and recommended that the Council reject the demands, pointing out that in any case the treaty powers would have to agree to any changes made in the Council's constitution. Both the French and the Americans refused even to comment, and lacking any firm backing, the Council fell back on procrastination as a weapon, not calling a meeting to consider the demands for over a month. By that time its British and American members were moving towards a compromise, agreeing to meet some of the Japanese demands, if the Japanese would improve their relations with the Settlement authorities, and would restore the northern and eastern areas to the Council's control. Sir Herbert Phillips, the British consul-general, backed this position, and a cautious statement in Parliament on 15 February seemed to give it London's blessing.[16] Finally, after two months of deliberation, in early April the Council agreed to appoint a Japanese Special Deputy Commissioner of Police, as a proof of their good intentions, and then to wait for a similar move from the Japanese side before proceeding further.[17] Here the matter rested, however. The northern districts remained under Japanese control, and although some of the restrictions were eased, the military refused to set a date for their abolition, and the compromise remained unimplemented.

The struggle for control of the Council and its police force was the overriding issue in Shanghai, but here as elsewhere, there were a number of lesser points of friction. Two other international bodies—the Whangpoo Conservancy Board, which kept the shipping channel dredged and clear for navigation, and the Shanghai Customs House—became objects of the Japanese struggle for power.[18] In Shanghai, too, came the first serious evidence of discrimination against foreign traders, as the Japanese refused to allow Customs control over the merchantmen docking at their wharves and were thus able to carry on what amounted to a duty-free import and export trade with the city.[19] Meanwhile a new Shanghai City Government—the Ta Tao Government—was formed under Japanese auspices, to administer the Chinese municipality, and to pose a new problem for the S.M.C., which now was forced to deal with a puppet authority which it could not officially recognize.

Elsewhere, a British civilian was stabbed and detained by the Japanese; two British merchantmen were boarded by Japanese soldiers, one being released only when a gunboat was sent to the scene; and the British instituted military patrols in the central district of the city, ostensibly to 'protect' a Japanese force which had taken up positions along the Nanking Road after a bomb went off.[20] More serious perhaps was the dispute arising over the western extra-Settlement roads. Here, where many foreigners lived, the S.M.C. had no firm legal right to police the roads, to maintain public works, or to tax or issue licences of any sort, but before the Japanese occupation they had performed these duties under the terms of a gentleman's agreement with the Chinese authorities. Now there arose the question as to whether the new city government would recognize the agreement. Furthermore, the fighting in the northern Settlement had caused swarms of refugees to move into the extra-Settlement roads, where they had put up makeshift tenements, factories, and workshops. This posed considerable problems of sanitation and policing, but worse yet were the gambling and opium dens, and the brothels which began to spring up in the city government enclaves between the roads themselves. In March 1938 a Residents' Association was founded to work for better conditions, but found itself powerless.[21] Another problem was presented by the Settlement's two Chinese courts, the First Special District Court and the Second Branch, Kiangsu High Court. Since 1933 these had been part of the Chinese judicial system, although a measure of foreign control remained, and in 1938 they were still staffed by officials of the Central Government. In May 1938 the new Nanking 'Reformed Government' appointed its own president of the District Court, and made a polite but ultimately unsuccessful effort to take control. Here too, the situation hung fire for the present.[22]

It was terrorism which remained the chief problem however, and which gave Japan an ever-present excuse for intervening in the Settlement's affairs. On 19 July 1938 the S.M.C. reissued its emergency proclamation of January in an even stronger form, threatening to expel anyone found to be connected with terrorist activities. At the Council's request British and American approches were made to the Central Government, urging it to put a damper on the operations of the Shanghai underground, and on 10 July Chiang Kai-shek, while disclaiming all responsibility, promised to use his influence to prevent the recurrence of crime.[23] Nor were the Chinese alone at fault. On 13 August the Settlement was put under virtual martial law, to prevent any trouble during the first anniversary of the outbreak of fighting in the city. Despite these precautions, there were disturbances, but they were caused principally by members of the Special Service Section of the Japanese army, who entered the British and American sectors (sometimes in cars carrying Shanghai Defence Force licence plates) and forced the removal of Kuomintang flags. Meanwhile a Japanese aircraft rained leaflets on the city, attacking both Chiang and the West. Furthermore, according to the S.M.P., a number of the terrorist outrages in the Settlements had actually been caused by a Chinese secret society which, it appeared, was operating under the aegis of the Nanking puppet government.[24]

In Tientsin, as well as in Shanghai, the proximity of Westerners to Japanese led to trouble. Here, there was no international settlement, but four concessions—British, French, Italian, and Japanese—existing side by side with the Chinese city. Here, however, terrorism was (during 1938 at least) a secondary issue; the primary one was economic, and this needs some explanation.

In November 1935, at the time of Leith-Ross's mission to China, Nanking had nationalized all silver stocks, requiring every bank under its jurisdiction to pay over its silver to the Currency Reserve Board in Shanghai; in lieu of silver currency, the three chief government banks would issue paper. Some provinces, however, particularly those under Japanese influence in the north, did not actually send their silver to Shanghai, but were allowed to keep it themselves, although it was nominally under the local branches of the Board. How much of this there was, and where it was kept, is uncertain. At the time it was estimated that some Ch $14,000,000 was held by the Bank of China in the British Concession in Tientsin, and some $20 to $40,000,000 by the same bank in the French Concession. About $6,400,000 was believed to be in a vault owned by an Indian in the Legation Quarter of Peking, and several millions more in French banks in the Legation Quarter. The issue of ownership was complex: did the silver belong to the Central Government, to the northern branches of the Chinese banks, or (as the Japanese later maintained) to the 'people of North China'?

In 1938 the new Federal Reserve Bank, struggling to establish itself in the face of both Chinese and Western hostility, desperately needed the silver to back its own currency. Accordingly on 30 July 1938 Peking declared the local branch of the Currency Reserve Board dissolved, to be replaced by a Peking-Tientsin Silver Committee. The Japanese, in notifying the British embassy in Peking of this, stressed the importance of transferring the silver to the puppet government for the welfare of the local populace.[25]

Then, in the late summer of 1938, came a mounting pressure against the British and French Concessions in Tientsin. Japanese complaints of counterfeiting in the French Concession led to a number of arrests, and Consul-General Shigenori Tashiro complained that the foreign areas were centres of 'anti-Japanese communist' activity in north China.[26] This was followed by a communication, which at the time seemed to order all Japanese residents in the British and French Concessions to leave, because of the 'absence of cooperation' shown by the officials of those two countries. In fact, as the Westerners were quick to point out, Japanese business concerns had actually been moving into the two Concessions since the war because of their very peacefulness. In the face of Western protests the Japanese backed down, denying that the order had ever been given, and saying that they were only preparing for a possible evacuation.[27] The first Japanese thrust had been rebuffed, but it brought only temporary relief. The refusal of the Concession authorities to outlaw the use of the *fapi* in their areas added to Japanese grievances, providing one more issue to the many which were plaguing Anglo-Japanese relations in the summer and fall of 1938, and which would nearly explode into war in 1939.

Chapter VIII

The Search for Policy: 1938

Nineteen thirty-eight was the year which saw British diplomacy in Europe at its lowest ebb. Appeasement was the policy of the day in dealing with the problems of Germany, Italy, and Spain, and it is against the background of this familiar story that Britain's oriental troubles must be considered. In November 1937 Lord Halifax had gone to Germany to talk to Hitler and Goering as the Brussels Conference was stumbling to a close. In January 1938 Roosevelt made his first hesitant step towards greater solidarity with the European democracies, only to have his proposal turned down by Chamberlain, who feared its effect on his dealings with Italy. Anthony Eden resigned and was replaced by Halifax. In March Austria disappeared; in April Chamberlain recognized the conquest of Abyssinia, in return for the hollow promise of an Italian troop withdrawal from Spain. Finally in September came the greatest of the pre-war crises, culminating in Hitler's stunning diplomatic victory at Munich.

All this had one obvious and immediate effect on the search for an Eastern policy: it was now imperative for Britain to avoid serious trouble there. The Singapore naval base had been opened on 14 February, but it was empty, waiting for a fleet which was desperately needed on the other side of the world. Obviously, if she were to take any forceful steps Britain would have to realize what had been from the outset one of the cardinal aims of her Eastern policy: to bring into being an alliance with the United States, an alliance which, although unwritten, would be clear enough for Tokyo to recognize as a threat. Was this ever a realistic hope? For a while it seemed as if it might be, when Roosevelt made his proposal in January 1938 for American cooperation to relieve world tensions; but when Britain hesitated he drew back. Eden, whose resignation stemmed partly from the plan's rejection, and Sumner Welles, who originated it, both have stressed the importance of Chamberlain's failure to act, seeing it as one of the great missed opportunities of prewar diplomacy. Others, including Cordell Hull, have been less sure.[1] Acceptance of the American initiative certainly could not have made the outcome worse, but given the state of American opinion, and given Hull's views on foreign policy, there is considerable doubt as to whether Roosevelt's move would have led to anything significant. Since Lukouchiao London had already presented Washington with a number of opportunities for common action, and neither Hull nor Welles nor Roosevelt had ever allowed themselves to hint that America might join Eden's united front. A month before Roosevelt took his step he had turned down the British plea for common action on the Yangtse bombing; was it realistic to believe that he would or could now lead his country in a great international effort to deal with the world's problems? or might not the result simply have been a re-echoing of the principles of international behaviour which the Secretary of State had enunciated on 16 July 1937?

In any case, American policy and American attitudes remained much as they had in the past. What did this leave for Britain? She could try again to end the war by mediation, or through the League of Nations; she could work for an understanding with Japan; or she might work against Japan, by imposing sanctions, by expanding aid to China, or by a combination of the two. These last possibilities, of course, were the most difficult and the most dangerous. Officially Britain remained neutral, and if there were those who wanted to see Japan defeated, there seemed to be few ways of hastening the process, apart from keeping the supply routes to China open, and refusing to send war materials to Japan.

Furthermore, London would have to decide what was to be the aim of British policy in the East. Was it to defeat Japan and maintain the independence of China? If so, what sort of independence, in how much of China? Or was it simply to protect British interests in China, while ignoring the changing political situation as far as possible? As the year progressed, it began to grow clearer that the problems of Chinese independence and of the state of British interests were linked. This was true not only because of Japan's discriminatory policies in occupied China, but also because it was increasingly obvious that the Western (and particularly the British) insistence on treaty rights was handicapping the Japanese advance. Early in the year, however, this was not as clear as it later became, and for the time being both Britain and America generally restricted themselves to attempts to safeguard their positions in China, without directly trying to influence the outcome of the war.

Neither inside nor outside the League did the prospect of mediation seem to offer much hope. In February 1938 Yoshida once again told Eden his country might be ready for a peace offer, and once again he seemed to be only the victim of wishful thinking; a few months later, in June, when R. A. Butler publicly announced Britain's readiness to help, a Japanese spokesman in Shanghai rebuffed the offer.[2] Meanwhile the Chinese persisted in hoping for some strong action from Geneva, but when they let it be known in January 1938 that they might invoke Article XVII of the Covenant (making Japan liable to sanctions if she refused League arbitration), the British managed to persuade them to back down. The Chinese delegation then agreed to settle for a resolution similar to that of the previous October, and which also called on League members to collaborate on action to refrain from weakening China's powers of resistance. Even this proved too strong, and what finally emerged on 28 January was a resolution which simply urged the consideration of 'further steps' for a settlement. Only a desperate Chinese stand blocked a French move to tone this down still further, and it was made public on 2 February.[3] Wellington Koo then wanted British help to have the Nine Power Conference recalled, but London managed to kill this proposal simply by passing it on to Washington.[4] There the matter rested, unchanged by a further League resolution of 14 May which asked the powers to give 'serious and sympathetic consideration' to Chinese requests for aid.[5] The peace-keeping machinery of both the League and the Nine Power Treaty had broken down under the strain, and no one in the West was doing much to help it recover.

Another alternative would be for Britain to patch up some sort of an understanding with Japan. This would (if it worked) have the advantage of protecting British interests in China, and of fitting in with Chamberlain's efforts to prevent the formation of a German-centred coalition against Britain. Japan and Italy were indeed already bound to Berlin by the Anti-Comintern Pact, but this was not yet a military alliance and might be kept from becoming one. A judicious policy of appeasement—concessions to Mussolini and a *détente* with Japan—might perhaps have the effect of restraining Hitler by depriving him of foreign support. Or so it seemed in 1938. It is hard to dignify this by calling it a policy, for at best it was a rearguard action, cautious and unimaginative. Yet there were signs that it might work, that Tokyo was trying to cultivate London's good will. Thus General Matsui was replaced as commander in central China by General Hata—'a good soldier, [and] less interested in politics', Horinouchi told Craigie.[6] Tokyo welcomed Eden's resignation in February as indicating a 'reorientation' of Britain's foreign policy, and this view was privately, and unhappily, echoed by the Chinese. In March Tani Masayuki, just appointed minister-at-large in China, told the Shanghai press that Japan must be careful not to infringe British rights, especially since the replacement of Eden diplomacy by Chamberlain diplomacy meant the replacement of idealism by realism.[7]

Earlier in the year the Foreign Office had drawn up an essay embodying British ideas on a Sino-Japanese settlement, and on 14 February they sent it off to Washington for comment. Based on the assumption that the League and the Nine Power Treaty had failed, it suggested that Britain could help restore peace only 'by action taken in defence of purely British interests'. The three prime British interests in the East were defined as (1) peace and stability, (2) equality of opportunity and the Open Door, and (3) the security of Hongkong. The crux of the matter was seen as the administration of Shanghai; any return to the conditions of July 1937 would be open to objections both on the grounds that it did not take into consideration the growth of Japanese interests in the city, and might be seen as contrary to the spirit of the Nine Power Treaty. The suggestion was made that the Settlement might be returned to China, and that the S.M.C. be absorbed into a new body which, although Chinese, would fully represent foreign interests. There would also be a demilitarized zone around the city. All this would open the way for a general peace on the basis of the Open Door and 'in the spirit of the Nine Power Treaty', probably involving the evacuation of all foreign troops. In return China would redress Japan's legitimate grievances by suppressing anti-Japanese propaganda and by granting tariff reductions for Japanese goods. Furthermore (and here the writers were on more delicate ground), China might recognize Manchukuo, and concede Japan special facilities for economic cooperation and capital investment in north China.[8] In short, this would amount to a recognition of a special position for Japan in the north, in an economic, if not in a political or military, sense.

The plan was unofficial, and ultimately came to nothing; its interest lies chiefly in the fact that it was indicative of at least one strand of official thinking about the pacification of the Far East. There is no way of telling how far it represented the ideas of 'Eden diplomacy' as opposed to 'Chamberlain diplomacy', though it inevitably invites comparison with the Anglo-Italian agreement which was then in the making, and which in a few days would lead to Eden's ouster. There were parallels between this plan and the agreement with Mussolini, but the determining factor in Eden's resignation was the unwillingness of the Prime Minister to insist on compromises by the Italian dictator to meet those which Britain was preparing to make. In the Far East, on the other hand, all three parties—China, Japan, and the West—were to make definite compromises to ensure the peace, and the plan was in no sense a wholesale sellout to an aggressor. What really prevented its serious consideration was the fact, as its authors readily admitted, that the terms were made 'on the assumption that H. M. Government are in a position to enforce respect for vital British interests, and thus dictate terms of peace', which would mean the 'backing of naval forces adequate to defend any vital British interests that might be threatened'. These, of course, simply did not exist. In the light of later events, what was perhaps the most significant part of the plan was that which defined Britain's role almost solely as defender of her own interests. This was the line which she pursued through most of 1938, and in a limited sense it did help China. Yet at the same time it was obvious that a policy made on such a basis might also very easily countenance an Anglo-Japanese agreement made at China's expense.

Lacking the naval and military strength needed to force a settlement in China, Britain could rely only on the less direct pressures of sanctions against Japan or of a programme of aid to China. In the spring and summer of 1938 both of these courses were considered and rejected.

The deteriorating position of Western interests in occupied China had led to agitation, both in and out of Parliament, for efforts to secure a stronger stand for British rights. Both Houses of Parliament discussed sanctions, and the issue was pressed not only by the forces of the Left who had led the agitation of the previous autumn, but also now by the business interests, whose position in China was now more clearly endangered by Japan. Sir John Wardlaw-Milne and Adrian Mòreing, two of the most vociferous champions of Britain's China interests in the Commons, hammered away at the Government for action, and when on 23 February a Liberal introduced a Bill to ensure that imports from Japan be so marked (to make it easier to boycott them) it was a Conservative who suggested clearing the way by denouncing the 1911 Treaty of Commerce with Japan. On 15 February Lord Elibank initiated a long debate in the Lords on the subject, and called for a combination of powers against Japan.[9] The British businessmen who were concerned with China certainly did not speak for British businessmen as a whole, and certainly not for the Conservative party; nevertheless there were few issues in foreign affairs in the thirties where even this limited harmony between the two sides of the House could be matched.

Behind the scenes Whitehall was still considering sanctions. In February

1938 a plan, ordered by the Committee of Imperial Defence, was produced and again it stressed the importance of Anglo-American cooperation. This was about as far as the project went however, and when Washington inquired about sanctions in April, London answered that nothing definite was yet planned, but that sanctions were being considered—not so much to end the war, as to force some respect for British interests.[10] On 25 July in a statement to the House of Commons, Butler implied that the 1911 trade treaty might be abrogated, unless Japan eased her discriminatory policies,[11] and that was as close as Britain came to making an overt threat.

Technically, this treaty did not allow the prohibition of any single category of exports (such as arms) to Japan. Nevertheless, no licences for arms exports in fact seem to have been issued after February 1938, and before that the amounts licensed were insignificant. If Japan ever did try to buy British arms, Britain's own needs for rearmament gave the Board of Trade a ready excuse to refuse their sale, and in some cases pressure was applied to prevent British firms from accepting Japanese arms orders.[12] Nothing ever appeared, however, to indicate that there was an explicit government policy in this regard.

Another alternative for Britain would have been an increased programme of aid to China. That country had already made during the Brussels Conference a rather grandiose request, asking for the delivery of a long list of war materials, with credits totalling £100,000,000 from Britain, America, and France. Needless to say, it was refused.[13] Expanded arms sales to China were considered impractical; they would slow down Britain's own rearmament, they would anger Japan, and they could not have been made in sufficient quantity to do China much good. Where help was desperately needed, however, and where something might be done by a neutral power, was in the sphere of China's civilian economy. The outbreak of fighting had brought a run on foreign exchange holdings in Chinese banks, and despite efforts to tighten the currency, from 13 August 1937 to 3 March 1938 the Government had had to sell an estimated US $50,000,000 in foreign exchange.[14] Nor was this the only danger. Having forced the F.R.B. currency into the north, the Japanese now were calling in the *fapi*, or national currency, to sell it in Shanghai for the foreign exchange that they so badly needed. According to the *North China Herald*, demand for foreign exchange from the Central Bank rose from a normal £50,000 a day to some £500,000,[15] and accordingly on 14 March 1938 the Central Government instituted exchange rationing, thereby managing briefly to stabilize the Chinese dollar. Then in April it began to fall again, going from a normal level of 1s 2d to a little over 8d in September, where it levelled off before a further decline in 1939.[16]

In March 1938 Quo Tai-chi asked the Foreign Office for a loan of £20,000,000 to keep the currency from collapse, but Leith-Ross, to whom he spoke, held out little hope of this, though he did suggest that commercial credits might be arranged.[17] British business circles in China also were beginning a campaign for the support of the Chinese dollar,[18] but while the Treasury and Foreign Office apparently favoured a loan, the Cabinet was undecided. On 11 July Halifax told the American ambassador that Britain was considering a stabilization loan of up to $100,000,000, but Washington was unreceptive to his suggestion that the United States might join in the project.[19] Perhaps it was this lack of American interest which now led the Cabinet to decide against the loan—this, and the feeling that it was going to take more than £20,000,000 in any case to make a difference. On 14 July Simon told the House that while the Government would probably approve of a loan by a British bank to China, they had no power themselves to grant or to guarantee a loan without the special legislation needed, 'which, in present circumstances, they have not seen their way to introduce'.[20]

The Japanese were delighted, of course, and hailed Simon's refusal as an indication of a new look in British policy. In Hankow Chiang warned that China might soon have to reappraise her own policy, and Clark Kerr wired home that unless Britain did something, the Chinese would turn towards Russia—reluctantly perhaps, but they would turn.[21] The currency loan was shelved for the time being, however, over protests from such diverse quarters as the *New Statesman* and *Finance and Commerce*, the latter organ suggesting that Simon needed to be educated about Japan's plans for China.[22] Meanwhile in London, a Chinese Vice-Minister of Finance was looking for a grant of £10,000,000 from the Export Credit Guarantees Department, while another concern wanted £2,500,000 to build a rail line from Chengtu to the Burma border. Yet here too, no decisions were taken, and the opponents of the currency loan within the Government appeared to be set against British intervention in any other form.[23]

Perhaps the chief reason leading to the decision against the Chinese loan was the fact that in Tokyo Ambassador Craigie was about to embark upon a series of talks with the new Japanese Foreign Minister. In May Hirota had resigned from the Cabinet following a clash over the proposed establishment of a new governmental agency, the China Affairs Board, which would have undercut the authority of the Foreign Office. His successor,

General Ugaki Kazushige, proved to be no more pliable than Hirota, and the disfavour in which the army held him further weakened his position. He managed nevertheless to hold office until September, and it was during this period that he and Craigie made a concerted effort to clear up some of the outstanding differences between their two countries. Craigie liked the new minister, and was impressed by his evidently sincere desire to improve relations; furthermore, Ugaki was considered to be a moderate, and when he joined the Cabinet he had made it clear that he planned to work for a *détente* with Britain.[24]

On 26 July Craigie called on Ugaki, and gave him a list of five British desiderata, which Clark Kerr had drawn up, and which might serve as a basis for a settlement. Three of them dealt with Shanghai, calling for the resumption of normal conditions in the northern district of the Settlement, the removal of restrictions on certain British-owned and controlled concerns in the city, and the removal of restrictions on the work of the Whangpoo Conservancy Board. The other two asked for the reopening to inspection of railways lying outside the immediate war zone, and for the reopening of the Yangtse to navigation. Ugaki read them, apologized for the delays, and said that a satisfactory settlement might be worked out although, he added, the Yangtse question was difficult, since the river remained unsafe for foreign merchantmen.[25]

With this the talks began. Despite the efforts of both men, the atmosphere in which they worked became more and more strained, and their job was made increasingly difficult by the attitude of press and publicists on both sides. The Japanese papers continued to insist that Britain must show a 'correct understanding' of Tokyo's position before her claims could be considered. The British lack of understanding (in the Japanese sense) was made evident in the debates of 26 and 27 July in Parliament, which saw a number of speakers calling on the Government to initiate economic measures against Japan.[26] Chamberlain took a more neutral stand, and once again he offered to mediate, promising that in the meantime the Government would do its utmost 'to see that British interests shall not suffer in a conflict for which we have no responsibility and in which we have no concern'.[27]

The mention of mediation aroused a flicker of interest in the East, and led to some discussion in diplomatic circles in both Hankow and Tokyo, but the general feeling was that such an offer would be premature.[28] Thus when Craigie next met Ugaki on 17 August, he made no mention of the plan. Furthermore, it was obvious that relations had become considerably cooler since their last talk, and when he left the Foreign Office, deeply discouraged, Craigie wired home that Ugaki was now under strong pressure to drop the talks altogether, and that the statements in Parliament had given him an excuse. Perhaps, Craigie suggested, the negotiations were just leading up a blind alley, and pressure would have to be tried, and to the American ambassador he said that the first step might be a denunciation of the 1911 trade treaty, adding that a similar American move would help.[29]

Prince Konoye did in fact send Craigie a personal message saying that Tokyo was anxious to find a basis for cooperation, but when the ambassador next called on Ugaki on 20 August, he found the Foreign Minister's position growing even more difficult. 'He is now being accused in circles extending beyond normal reactionary ones of preparing to yield to British pressure', wrote Craigie, and he urged that the British press, particularly *The Times*, show 'special discretion' in its comments on Far Eastern affairs. Ugaki read him a statement attacking the British authorities in China as being the most unfriendly of the neutrals, although, he added, there still might be some room for Anglo-Japanese cooperation in that country. Anxious to save both Ugaki's position and with it the talks, Craigie seized on this, and wired home to Halifax a recommendation that he be allowed to promise that Britain would cooperate in the sense in which she understood the word, and providing that such cooperation worked to China's benefit rather than detriment.[30] Halifax, backed by arguments from Clark Kerr, vetoed this, and unquestionably he was right in doing so.[31] A year later, during the Tientsin crisis, Britain was forced into a position where she had to give what amounted to a formal assurance of cooperation, and it aroused a cry of opposition from the entire democratic world. 'Cooperation', in the Japanese sense, was a dangerous word, and whatever Craigie's qualifications might mean (when he said it would be only for the benefit of China) the Foreign Secretary was rightly wary of any British commitment on this score.

Craigie and Ugaki met three more times, on 8, 14, and 22 September, but it was obvious by now that the summer's hopes for a settlement had vanished, and for their two governments, the Tokyo negotiations had become simply a sideshow. London, of course, was chiefly concerned with the mounting crisis in Czechoslovakia, while Tokyo was waiting to see if a general European war would break out. Furthermore, within his own Government, Ugaki was continuing his fight to safeguard the authority of the Gaimusho by trying to prevent the establishment of the China Affairs Board, and was not going to weaken his position by appearing as an appeaser of the West. Neither side was much inclined to give way, therefore, and Ugaki continued to insist that Britain must understand Japan's position, and must take a more friendly attitude—which would include the cessation of aid to Chiang Kai-shek. The closest he came to any real proposal for a settlement was in the bargain which he suggested for Shanghai: Japan would restore the Council's authority in Hongkew and Yangtsepoo, if she were given 'full cooperation' in the maintenance of order—in other words if she gained control of the Chinese courts, and if her demands on the Municipal Police were met.[32]

Neither man realized it at the time, but the meeting on the 22nd was their last, and a week later Ugaki had resigned. His advocacy of dealing with Chiang, his talks with Craigie, and his opposition to the China Affairs Board had all hurt him, while his Prime Minister, Prince Konoye, had given him little support. When Ugaki left, Konoye temporarily took over the Gaimusho himself, but he was not made of the same stuff as his predecessor, and was unwilling to endanger his position by appearing conciliatory towards Britain. On 3 October he announced that while the talks would continue if Britain wanted them, they would now largely be in the hands of the Vice-Minister.[33]

This marked the end of the last broad effort to reach a general Anglo-Japanese agreement. With the tide running strongly in favour of the Axis, there was little reason why Tokyo should give in on any substantial points—even if it meant a greater freedom of action, in return for a pledge of non-interference in British interests. The China which Japan was trying to overcome was, after all, a China in which Western interests had a substantial place, and they, as well as Chiang and the Nationalists, were the target of Japan's war effort. So too for much the same reasons it seems unlikely that Britain could have made any arrangement with Japan, even if she had been willing to do it at China's expense. The prevailing attitude of London—that intervention in the conflict could only take the form of direct efforts by Britain to protect her own interests—was a two-edged weapon, which could serve either Chinese or Japanese aims, but under the conditions of the present war, was more likely to serve the former. As long as Britain sought to maintain her position in China she would find cooperation with Japan difficult if not impossible, as she would also have found cooperation difficult with an untrammelled Chinese nationalism. The danger would come only if London were persuaded by Craigie's rather facile argument that cooperation with Japan would serve the best interests not only of Britain but also of China. How far Craigie would have been willing to go in this direction it is difficult to say. General Ugaki at least received the impression—perhaps from Cragie, perhaps from others—that Britain was contemplating an eventual withdrawal from East Asia, and that in five to eight years her economic position in China might almost have disappeared. But she could in no case withdraw under the threat of force, and events must be allowed to take their natural course.[34] This, needless to say, was not a viewpoint which would have been shared by the China Association, or the British communities in the treaty ports and Hongkong.

In any case, whatever chances there might have been of a successful settlement had vanished by the end of September. Despite the general sense of relief which swept over the world after the Munich agreement, the repercussions of the Sudetenland crisis had added to Craigie's difficulties. On 14 September the Gaimusho had expressed its 'admiration and sympathy' for Hitler's stand, and shortly thereafter Konoye let it be known that Japan was considering the question of strengthening the anti-Comintern axis. This was the first public announcement of a move which had been underway for the last two months, and which looked to the possible conversion of the 1936 pact into an outright military alliance between Germany, Japan, and Italy.[35]

Not only had Hitler won a major victory in Europe in October, but by autumn the war in China also seemed to be going more and more in Japan's favour. The summer skirmishing between Russian and Japanese troops, at Changkufeng on the Manchurian border, had ended in August, and with the danger of a Russian war once again temporarily removed the military were left free to concentrate on the drive to Hankow, and to work out their future policy in China. On 22 September the puppet governments of north and central China had been brought closer with the inauguration of a United Council of the Republic of China, consisting of representatives from both Nanking and Peking. Furthermore, the ascendancy of the military in Tokyo seemed to be confirmed by Konoye's agreement to the formation of the China Affairs Board, which was to be the highest organ of China policy. This was the move which both Hirota and Ugaki had tried to resist, and even Konoye did not surrender unconditionally, for relations with third powers in China remained under the cognizance of the Foreign Ministry.[36] Then, on 12 October, thirty thousand Japanese troops swept ashore at Bias Bay, north of Hongkong, opening a new campaign in south China. By the 21st, the supposedly strong Kwangtung garrison had fled, the Japanese were in Canton, the rail line to Kowloon was cut, and Hongkong virtually isolated from the mainland. Four days later General Hata's troops climaxed the Yangtse campaign by storming into Hankow.

The Kwangtung campaign helped bring an end to any chances which Craigie might have had to continue his talks with the Foreign Office. So did the action which the League of Nations took in September. In the face of efforts by both London and Paris to dissuade them, on 11 September the Chinese appealed to the League Council to give immediate effect to Article XVII of the Covenant. On 19 September, in private session, the Council agreed, and sent an invitation to Japan to accept the League's mediation.[37] When the expected refusal came, three days later, the League, after some hesitation, adopted a report on 30 September, which declared the provisions of Article XVI (sanctions) now applicable, and said that member states could individually take the measure called for. But, the report admitted, 'as regards coordinated action in carrying out such measures, it is evident from experience of the past, that all elements of cooperation which are necessary are not yet assured'.[38]

In other words, although a state might apply sanctions on its own, the report admitted that none in fact would. The League was hardly issuing a challenge to Japan; instead, it was now Japan who challenged the League. After the report, Tokyo proceeded to accuse Geneva of having recognized the existence of a state of war in East Asia, a viewpoint 'at variance with the attitude of member states which, in regard to the question of respect for their interests in China proves that no war exists'. Actually the report had been careful not to admit the existence of a state of war. But sanctions could not be imposed without war, and Tokyo was now warning that if the Western powers treated the China Incident as a war, Japan would invoke belligerent rights, and ride roughshod over their interests and properties in China.[39] Needless to say, the report ultimately made not the slightest difference in the situation.

Nor was Japan's threat the only one facing the West. On 6 November, Clark Kerr met Chiang Kai-shek in Changsha, and the Generalissimo warned that Britain and China might now have reached a parting of the ways. Then, in the closest he had yet come to making a threat, he stated that if China were willing to join her in a policy of excluding Britain from the Far East, Japan might well agree, yielding everything she had taken thus far.[40] In Hongkong, the ambassador saw T. V. Soong, who also spoke of Japanese initiatives for a policy of 'Asia for the Asiatics', and this, coupled with a statement on 1 December by Konoye which hinted at the same thing, seemed to indicate that the possibility of Sino-Japanese cooperation was not so far fetched as might first be thought.[41]

In such circumstances, it was going to take more than bilateral negotiations to solve the problems between Britain and Japan. Already the tactics of the West were changing from conciliation to something stronger. Not aid to China, yet; Clark Kerr had appealed for this, and indeed went on appealing, but he got nowhere.[42] On 6 October, Ambassador Grew had presented a formal note to Tokyo which was the strongest indictment yet of the Japanese programme in China. It protested against the violations of the Open Door in Manchuria and occupied China; it criticized the formation of Japanese monopolies; it complained of interference with American rights of residence, freedom of trade and of the mails; and it demanded a stop to discrimination in the form of trade and exchange controls. In keeping with Washington's diplomatic practice at the time, no prior notification was given to Britain, and Craigie did not learn of the note until 3 October, the date on which an advance copy was handed to Konoye.[43] Nevertheless, for a while after that it looked as if Washington and London were about to close ranks, and that the united front which Eden had wanted, and which Tokyo feared, was going to come into being.

Chapter IX

The New Order Proclaimed:
November 1938 - January 1939

In November 1938, a month after the settlement of the Munich crisis, there came the first real evidence of a concerted policy between the three major Western powers in China. The issue was the closure of the Yangtse River, and although it was Britain whose interests were primarily concerned, the initiative for a protest came from the United States. By now the entire coast and most of the Yangtse Valley were in Japanese hands, and after the fall of Hankow on 25 October, there seemed to be a chance that trade restrictions might be eased. Both Ugaki and Horinouchi had suggested as much to Craigie, and the ambassador now took it up with the Gaimusho, pointing out that there were bound to be awkward questions about British interests in China asked in the forthcoming session of Parliament. At the same time he warned his own Government to avoid any harsh statements, which could only play into the hands of the extremists.[1]

Ministers accordingly took a mildly non-committal stand on the question when the House debated foreign affairs on 1 November. Chamberlain, in fact, far from criticizing Japan, tried to look for the bright side of the picture, and wound up angering both sides of the House. Rising to reply to Clement Attlee (who had taken Japan to task for closing one of the largest potential markets in the world), the Prime Minister chided the Labour leader for his pessimism. 'Potential' was the key, he said; a good deal of capital was going to have to be poured into China before she could take her place as one of the world's great markets. Where would it come from? Certainly Japan could not supply it, and therefore to talk in terms of a future in which she monopolized the trade of China was 'flying in the face of facts. It is quite certain', he continued, 'that when the war is over and the reconstruction of China begins, she cannot be reconstructed without some help from this country. (*Interruption*)'.[2]

Interruption there was indeed. Howls of fury arose. To the Left, here was another proof of the heartlessness of the capitalists who ran the country. To the capitalists themselves (at least those for whom *Finance and Commerce* spoke) it was another proof of the 'bland (or blind) optimism' of the Prime Minister who, having sold out Czechoslovakia, was now ready to surrender China for the sake of cooperation with Japan. Other British trade groups in China protested, and Chungking voiced its dismay, while Quo Tai-chi politely asked for an explanation.[3]

The Government tried to explain away the Prime Minister's statement, but the harm was done. Unfortunately for Chamberlain, a few days later Konoye issued a new pronouncement on foreign policy, and in pledging his country to the building of a 'New Order' in East Asia, presented the most concrete challenge yet to the Western position in that part of the world.[4] Slowly, however, the West was changing its stance, and the American note of 6 October ushered in a new series of stronger protests. No longer was there even a pretence of belief in Japan's good faith, and now, slowly and hesitantly at first, the West began to show its partisanship for China. A few days after Konoye's New Order speech there came the closest approach yet to joint action by the Western democracies.

Despite both repeated Western protests and the presentation of evidence of Japanese trade in the Yangtse Valley, Tokyo had continued to insist that military conditions prevented any easing of the restrictions on the river's navigation. Furthermore, the south China campaign had led to the closing of the Pearl River on 13 October, and it was apparent that the situation on the Yangtse might serve as a model for the southern river as well.[5] Accordingly, the West protested, and Washington this time not only took the initiative, but also invited London and Paris to make parallel representations.[6] On 7 November the ambassadors of the three countries delivered similar communications to the Gaimusho, thus facing Tokyo for the first time with some tangible evidence that they were beginning to concert their efforts.

Craigie's note protested against the Japanese transport of merchandise on the river, criticized the pleas of 'military necessity' for the continued restrictions, and asked for free navigation as soon as possible, at least below Hankow.[7] The American and French notes were substantially similar. The Japanese replies, predictably, repeated that the river must remain closed, denied that there was any substantial civilian trade, and expressed the hope that the regulations might soon be relaxed. Both Craigie and Grew wanted to press the matter further, but Washington demurred, and

the United States, after its one brief fling at initiating a combined diplomatic action, withdrew again into isolation.[8]

For all its importance, however, the Yangtse was fundamentally a local
issue, and the real question remained the larger one of Western interests
in a China dominated by Japan. After the victories at Canton and Hankow,
when China at last seemed to be crumbling before an invincible Japanese
military machine, Tokyo issued its clearest statement yet of Japan's plans
for the future of East Asia. On 2 November the Gaimusho released the text
of a statement for publication the following day (the birthday of the Meiji
Emperor) announcing that now

. . . all the vital areas of China have thus fallen into our hands. The Kuomintang
Government exists no longer except as a mere local régime. However, so long as it
persists in its anti-Japanese and pro-Communist policy our country will not lay
down its arms—never until that regime is crushed.

What Japan seeks is the establishment of a new order which will ensure the
permanent stability of East Asia. In this lies the ultimate purpose of our present
military campaign. This new order has for its foundation a tripartite relationship
of mutual aid and coordination between Japan, Manchukuo and China in political,
economic, cultural, and other fields. Its object is to secure international justice, to
perfect the joint defense against Communism, and to create a new culture and
realize a close economic cohesion throughout East Asia. . . .

What Japan desires of China is that the country will share in the task of bringing
this new order in East Asia. . . .[9]

Konoye elaborated on this in a speech of the 3rd.

History shows that Japan, Manchukuo, and China are so related to each other that
they must bind themselves closely together in a common mission for the establishment of peace and order in the Far East by displaying their own individuality.

China had been misled by the reactionary policies of the Central Government, which had failed to prevent the 'steady bolshevization and coloniza-
tion' of the country, unlike the policies of great patriots of former times,
who had fought for a new China[10]—the reference was presumably to Sun
Yat-sen's readiness to cooperate with Japan. Meanwhile, as a counterpoint
to Konoye's speech, the Japanese press began to talk of the 'obsolescence'
of the Nine Power Treaty.[11]

Here was an outright challenge to the whole Western position in the
Far East. The Foreign Office statement and Konoye's speech clarified and
gave official sanction to what had hitherto been a misty concept of a
tripartite bloc in East Asia. Not only that, but they also appealed to China
to join Japan in making common cause against the West—a fact of some
significance in light of the vague threats and warnings which had been

given to Ambassador Clark Kerr on his recent trip into the hinterland. Arita, who had recently become Foreign Minister, sounded less uncompromising in private than his government in public, but clearly the issue was, from Japan's standpoint, one between the haves and the have-nots. Powerful economic groups, he told the ambassador, like Russia, America, or the British Empire, might be able to dismiss such moves as the imposition of sanctions, but Japan's position was different, and the only way to secure a measure of economic appeasement was to group the smaller powers into blocs, such as the one which Tokyo was now trying to form in East Asia. Other countries must realize that the situation had changed, and while Japan had no intention of driving foreign trade from China, still—as he warned the American counsellor a few days later —previous assurances about foreign interests might no longer be valid.[12]

What all this meant, judging from Japanese press articles, and a memorandum which Arita gave Craigie on 8 December, was that within the new bloc of Japan, Manchukuo, and China, foreign interests were likely to be ousted from certain fields which were considered to be essential for defensive, economic, or strategic purposes. Here, 'as a matter of protection', monopolies might be formed, and while foreign capital, techniques, and materials would be welcomed, there could be no competitive business. Otherwise, however, third power economic activities would 'not all be restricted, but rather welcome';[13] and this situation, as the *Asahi* reminded its readers, was no more than that under which foreigners had to work in most sovereign states.[14]

The New Order statement of November was followed on 22 December by Konoye's announcement of the peace terms which Japan was now prepared to offer, terms which would establish the political basis of the New Order. China was to recognize Manchukuo, join the Anti-Comintern Pact, allow the stationing of Japanese troops at certain points to combat communism, agree to the designation of Inner Mongolia as a 'special anti-Communist area', and concede Japanese citizens trade and residence rights in her interior, with facilities for participation in the development of natural resources.[15] Chiang rejected the offer four days later. He could hardly have temporized without touching off a crisis, as both the Communists and the Left wing of the Kuomintang would have fought any settlement on these lines. Not all the party hierarchy felt as he did, however, and Wang Ching-wei, who had already been in touch with Tokyo, fled from Chungking to Hanoi, and thence to Japan, to throw in his lot with the New Order. Japan had thus outlined her plan for East

Asia, and had induced one of the most influential members of the Kuomintang to join her, for Wang was a man who could, with some justice, claim to be as much entitled to the mantle of Sun Yat-sen as was Chiang himself. Yet Wang alone was of no great importance; the danger was that his example might inspire a mass defection from Chungking. Nor was the only danger the one presented by the deteriorating situation in China; there were now more and more indications that Japan might be drawing closer to Germany and Italy, preparing to sign a military alliance. London's information on this point was not perfect—Halifax was under the impression that Tokyo was anxious to conclude the agreement, when actually the Government was bitterly divided—but his main facts were correct: negotiations for an alliance were under way, and if it came, it would be directed against the West as well as against the Soviet Union.[16]

In the summer of 1938 there had been hope that Britain and Japan might work out some sort of a *modus vivendi*. By the onset of winter that hope was gone, blasted by the fall of Ugaki, the capture of Hankow, the south China *Blitzkrieg*, and the enunciation of the New Order. Once more the familiar alternatives of policy were rehearsed—sanctions, aid to China, and diplomatic protests, and this time, although inhibited by doubts and uncertainties, the policy makers in London and Washington began to act.

The heavy bombing of Canton and south China during the summer had given new impetus to the popular campaign for sanctions, and although on 1 November R. A. Butler told the House that no thought was being given to such measures,[17] this was somewhat less than the whole truth. In late August the Foreign Office had suggested a programme of progressive action, starting with the 'institution in British-controlled territories of various petty administrative vexations on [the] Japanese model', and leading up to a denunciation of the 1911 trade treaty.[18] At first Craigie objected, arguing that denunciation might mean war, and pointing out that even after denunciation, the treaty would still have to run for a year, so that no practical results would be achieved until early 1940—by which time the belligerents would be exhausted and ready for peace. In a later dispatch on 4 November, however, he seemed more receptive to the idea, and underlined the choice which British policy makers had heretofore avoided making. Would sanctions be applied to weaken Japan? he asked, or simply to ensure respect for British interests? If for the latter, steps such as increasing duties on Japanese imports into the colonies, or imposing further import quotas against Japan, would simply irritate Tokyo, and Britain would lose more than she gained. But if London decided that the object of sanctions was to hurt Japan, then, he said,

... there is no doubt that it is in our power to take action to decrease Japan's export trade which would be very effective, in view of her diminishing stock of gold. Such actions would be indistinguishable from sanctions, and, I should say, would definitely rule out our prospects, such as they are, of improving Anglo-Japanese relations, weakening the 'axis', and exercising a salutary influence on the initial peace settlement.[19]

As long as Ugaki had remained in office, and as long as there had been a chance of the talks continuing, Craigie had been willing to make a considerable effort to stay in Tokyo's good graces. Since Munich, however, little had happened to justify this course, and now, in the late autumn of 1938, the ambassador began to urge on his Government a harder line in its dealing with Tokyo. Because of this, and because he was encouraged by the apparent firmness of recent American policy, Craigie took the matter up with Grew, and suggested that they both recommend a programme calling for a currency loan to China, the denunciation of the commercial treaties, and the raising of the French embargo on the passage of arms over the Yunnan-Indochina rail line. Grew remained absolutely opposed to sanctions, however; since one of Japan's purposes was to achieve immunity from such action, it was doubtful if she would abandon the New Order in response to pressure.[20] Craigie did not give up and at the end of the year he forwarded to Grew the opinion of the British embassy's economic advisers that an embargo would have a drastic effect on Japan's economy, in view of her steadily dwindling gold reserves.[21] And, at the same time, to Halifax he argued that the time was now more favourable than ever for a joint Anglo-American effort in support of China, particularly because Washington had asked for Britain's views, and even though Grew remained unwilling to recommend such a course.[22]

Yet Craigie was not only ahead of the Americans, but this time ahead of his own Government as well. Indeed, at the time of the Yangtse notes, Washington had cautiously asked London what might be done in case of an unfavourable reply, and Ambassador Lindsay had returned an equally cautious and noncommittal answer.[23] Late in November, Sumner Welles had asked what measures London had already taken against Japan, and on 30 December Lindsay returned a preliminary answer, referring to the limitation on arms shipments and the restriction of credit facilities.[24] On 25 January 1939, he gave the State Department a full answer which quoted, among other points, Craigie's opinion that an embargo would have an 'immediate and disastrous effect' on Japan, and his arguments that such action should be taken now. Yet London's reply fell short of recommending sanctions, and merely stated that while Britain had opposed such a step in the past, she was willing to change her mind.[25] In other words, London was still looking for an American lead. And rightly or wrongly, when Ambassador Kennedy was shown the reply by the Foreign Office, he came away with the impression that Britain was unwilling to take measures strong enough to 'break' Japan, since this might lead to a situation even more disastrous than the present one.[26] Here in Kennedy's report is one of the very few explicit acknowledgements of the problem which had been implicit in Britain's dealings with Japan since Manchuria: how to maintain Japan as the bulwark against Asian communism which she claimed to be, and at the same time keep her from ousting Britain from China, from driving Chiang closer to the Communists—both Chinese and Russian—or from reducing China to the state of disruption and collapse that would encourage the spread of communism?

In any case, Craigie strongly objected to the timidity of the British reply to Washington. London was still tied to the idea that the protection of trade interests was Britain's paramount concern, whereas the scope of sanctions should be wider. What was really at stake, he argued, was not simply British investments in China, but the whole future of 'countries with interests in the Pacific to say nothing of the urgency of ensuring the observance of treaty obligations as a matter of principle', and this justified the taking of greater risks.[27] His views represented a considerable advance over the Foreign Office's essay of the previous spring, but London was not yet ready for them, and both the British and American Governments agreed that sanctions were not advisable at present, and that aid to China would be preferable to measures against Japan.[28]

This was as close as the two countries had yet come to retaliation, but they had failed to take the decisive step. They did, however, make some progress in the sphere of aid to China, as the year drew to a close. In November 1938 the project of a loan to stabilize China's currency was brought up again, and Craigie backed the move, commenting that 'the knowledge that we are prepared to proceed from words to deeds might be wholesome rather than the reverse', and adding the hope that America would join.[29] In fact, the United States ultimately refused,[30] but this time the project was not dropped as it had been the previous summer, and in the meantime China began to benefit from the increased concern in the capitals of the West. In November came the announcement of an agreement in principle between British and Chinese interests on a £10,000,000 loan to finance the construction of a railway from Yunnan to the Burma frontier.[31] Then came the introduction of legislation into Parliament, empowering the Board of Trade to guarantee £10,000,000 worth of exports of which, Chiang was privately told, about £500,000 would be allotted to China to buy trucks for the Burma Road. And finally, on 15 December the United States announced a grant of $25,000,000 in credits to finance the export of American products to China.[32] None of this was as much as Chungking would have liked—Quo Tai-chi suggested his country would be much happier with an outright grant of £4 to £5 millions, to use as she saw fit,[33] but at least the West was beginning to act, and to act in a manner which suggested that the powers were capable of moving together.

Yet the major diplomatic weapon, if it can be called that, remained the protest. Craigie had been impressed by the strong American note of 6 October and this, coupled with Konoye's announcement of the impending New Order in East Asia, gave point to his arguments that Britain should strike while the iron was hot, in order to take advantage of America's new firmness. On 30 December Grew sent another protest to the Gaimusho,[34] and this time, although Craigie had no prior notification, the American action coincided with similar steps on the part of both Britain and France. Craigie and the Foreign Office had earlier been hammering out the text of a protest against the implications both of the New Order statement, and of Konoye's peace terms of 22 December. What Konoye really wanted, ran the British argument, was the surrender by the Chinese 'of their political, economic and cultural life to Japanese control, the indefinite maintenance in China of considerable Japanese garrisons and the virtual detachment from China of the territory of Inner Mongolia'. Britain, it continued, while not contending that treaties were eternal and unchangeable, meant to abide by the Nine Power Treaty and could not allow any unilateral modification of its terms. If Japan had any constructive suggestions to make, let her make them, but in the meantime His Majesty's Government would reserve its rights as they stood under the existing agreements.[35]

Grew and Arsène-Henry saw the note, approved it, and Craigie gave it to Arita on 14 January. Five days later, Arsène-Henry handed the Foreign Minister a similar communication,[36] and thus, although the three notes had been neither simultaneous nor identical, their presentation suggested a certain unity. The unity was more apparent than real, the timing of the notes more a matter of fortunate coincidence than of premeditation; nevertheless Japan might be given pause by the action, all the more so since force was lent to it by the British and American grants of credits to China in December. All three notes attacked the concept of the New Order as it was emerging from official Japanese pronouncements. All three denied

Japan's right unilaterally to change the existing treaty structure, but expressed a willingness to consider multilateral revision. And all three attacked not only Japan's actions, but the premises on which those actions were based. Furthermore, their attack was directed not simply against Japanese mistreatment of Western interests, but against the Japanese treatment of China herself, insofar as that meant China under the treaty system.

The presentation of the three notes coincided with a new cabinet crisis in Tokyo, and Konoye's government, which had been weakening for some time, resigned on 4 January. The new Prime Minister was the former President of the Privy Council, Baron Hiranuma Kiichiro, a man whose ultra-nationalist background and reputation was to be somewhat belied by the comparative moderation of his leadership. The Foreign Ministry remained in the hands of Arita. Yet neither the notes nor the change in government brought any significant modification in outlook or relationship towards the West. The Gaimusho complained that Craigie's note lacked 'realization of the present trend in Far Eastern affairs', and the press echoed this, saying that as long as the West was concerned only with trade and investments, an accommodation was possible, but if the powers should insist on the validity of the old treaties, Japan could not agree. Meanwhile, sanctions would only mean retaliation, a point repeated by Hiranuma, as he simultaneously invited the West to participate in the building of the New Order.[37]

What effect these first suggestions of a stronger combined policy had on the inner councils of the Japanese Government, it is hard to say. Certainly they frightened Japan neither into mitigating her demands on China, nor into improving her treatment of Western interests in that country. On the contrary, the new year brought an attack, stronger than ever before, against the Western position, an attack directed in particular against the international settlements and foreign concessions, the last strongholds of Western influence in occupied China.

Chapter X

The Coming of War in Europe: January – September 1939

When the notes challenging the New Order were presented to Tokyo in January 1939, Europe had not quite eight months of peace left. Hitler, unsatisfied with his gains at Munich, continued his advance, taking Prague and the Czechoslovakian rump in mid-March, while Mussolini's armies seized Albania on Good Friday, establishing the Axis in the eastern Mediterranean. On 30 March Chamberlain announced a British guarantee of Poland, and two weeks later London and Paris pledged their support to Greece and Rumania. This further drain on resources which were already inadequate made it less likely than ever that the West would take any forceful action in the Orient, and Japan seized the opportunity which was thus presented. After the dramatic victories of the autumn of 1938, her military advance had stalled, and in the ensuing year she fought her most important campaigns not on the battlefields of the interior, but on the diplomatic and economic fronts. To conquer China she had first to deal with the Westerners in China, and from now until Pearl Harbor, they were her primary targets. It was the West, and primarily the British, whose influence over Chinese economic life had to be broken, if China were to take her place in the New Order, and it was the West whose political hold in the foreign settlements of the treaty ports had to be broken, to keep those settlements from becoming centres of subversion against the Japanese overlord. Japan, on paper at least, was now master of the wealthiest and most modern part of China, but as long as the Western powers remained there—neutral, technically friendly, but jealous of their treaty rights— Japanese control could not be complete.

Thus in 1939, Japan's plan of action consisted of a series of moves directed largely against the remaining economic and political positions of the West in the treaty ports, while unofficially a Japanese-sponsored campaign of exceptional bitterness broke out, calling for the expulsion of the Westerner and all his goods. In Shanghai, Amoy, and Tientsin, pressure on the foreign settlements was particularly severe, and it was the fight for control of the British Concession in the latter city which precipitated the worst crisis in the entire history of Britain's relations with Japan.

Yet if the campaign against the foreign settlements was the most important issue of 1939, it cannot be understood without examining the background against which it was fought out. By late 1938 Britain (like America) seemed to be embarking on a new and stronger course against Japan, but in fact she still had not decided between the two fundamental alternatives facing her in the Far East. Should she end all pretence of neutrality, and declare herself definitely on China's side? or should she keep trying to work for a settlement in the war, maintaining as good relations as possible with both sides, in the hope of making her influence felt at the peace tables? The first course would mean treating Japan as a full-fledged member of the Axis, and might well drive her into alliance with Germany and Italy; the second would mean treating her as an erring, but not as a lost soul, who could still be turned away from the momentarily seductive attractions of the European dictatorships.

In any case a decision had to be made, and it was this that Craigie emphasized in a long telegram to London on 2 December 1938, arguing that the lack of a definite policy was simply earning Britain the enmity of both sides. The only way in which she was likely to be given satisfactory treatment, he said, was to take a strong line in concert with America, not baulking at reprisals 'and other forcible actions' if necessary. However, since it was clear that Washington was unprepared to go beyond protests, and would rather withdraw from the East than risk war, Craigie argued that the possibility of 'cooperation' should be reviewed. This would not mean abandoning China, but it would mean ceasing all aid to Chiang, recognizing Japan's military and economic predominance on the mainland, assuring her access to raw materials and markets, and trying to win back 'ultimate Chinese independence through cooperation. . . . Not an attractive policy at first sight', Sir Robert admitted, but it should be considered, if it were necessary to separate Japan from her German and Italian friends. In any case, if Britain continued along her present path of 'alienating one party to this conflict without assisting the other', nothing would be accomplished, and she might then have to face the very real possibility of a China so completely dominated by Japan as to become 'the willing instrument of her imperialistic designs'.[1]

In short, Britain should make up her mind and take a strong line, either

99

of positive cooperation with Japan or of increased aid to China. The first course was open to the obvious objections (as both Clark Kerr and Halifax pointed out) that it would mean placing a blind trust in Japan's leaders, would alienate the other democracies, and would raise the cry of appeasement, a word just then beginning to take on the meaning of weakness and failure which it has since acquired.[2] The second alternative—of stepped up help to China—was under consideration, but action came slowly, delayed by the knowledge that Japan was herself considering a military alliance with Rome and Berlin.

In early February 1939, Arita had admitted to Craigie that talks for a strengthening of Japan's ties to Germany were under way, but he insisted that they were directed only against the Comintern. Although he opposed the alliance himself, he realized its value as a threat against the democracies and, as Grew observed, worked hard to make the most of this aspect of it.[3] Craigie, on the other hand, was aware of the opposition to the alliance which was particularly strong in court, naval, and business circles, and he too could use a threat, in making sure that Arita remained aware of the possibility of an *entente* between London, Paris, and Moscow.[4] Halifax had already stated publicly that the talks with the Soviet Union, which had begun after the fall of Prague, might extend to the Far East, and Craigie and Arita were thus driven to a sort of unofficial *quid pro quo*: Britain would steer clear of alliances in the Far East if Japan would stay away from those in Europe.[5] No one spelled this out, but both men were aware of the situation, and the alliance's opponents carried the day in Tokyo. The Pact of Steel, which was concluded in Berlin on 21 May, embraced only Italy and Germany, and Britain, it appears, never brought up the subject of the Far East in her conversations with Moscow. Nevertheless, the chance remained that Japan might change her mind (Prime Minister Hiranuma was in favour of the alliance), and the threat never quite vanished during the next several months.

If, as the new year opened, there were signs that the Western powers were becoming more partisan in their attitudes, it was evident more in the projects of aid to China than in reprisals against Japan. For the latter, unity was needed, and it simply did not exist. The French complained that they had cut off iron ore exports to Japan, to the economic detriment of Indochina, while Tokyo could buy all the ore it wanted from Malaya. Suggestions that Malayan exports be reduced brought the reply that Japan would then turn to America. The French wanted to take the case to Washington, but the State Department pointed out that such a move would put a crimp in its own plans to embargo certain types of iron and

steel scrap.[6] So too, when China wanted to set up a 'coordinating committee' of League powers with the United States to work for trade measures against Japan, the State Department would have nothing to do with
it, and asked London to keep Chungking from 'making a fool of itself'.[7]
As usual, the fear of acting alone, without American backing, was
probably the deciding factor in discouraging a British imposition of sanctions, but there may have been other causes involved. 'The real trouble is',
wrote Stanley F. Wright a few months later, 'not that we could not stop
Japan by economic pressure, but that the mind of the London Chamber
of Commerce is divided. One section of that Chamber trades with Japan,
and another with China, and both are equally importunate at the Foreign
Office with their rival points of view. It seems to be a case of Pull devil;
pull baker; with the odds slightly in favour of the baker'.[8]

On a more positive note, France, apparently stimulated by the Japanese
occupation of Hainan in February, eased her controls on shipments over
the Indochina railway, which since the fall of Canton had become the
most important trade route into unoccupied China. She also undertook to
delay shipments of war materials (mostly iron ore, copper, and coal) from
Indochina to Japan, and, as Wellington Koo remarked jokingly, French
red tape could easily become the practical equivalent of an outright
embargo.[9] The British had opened the new Burma Road to traffic in
December 1938, and war materials for China had already begun to arrive
in Rangoon in November. By May 1939 some 900 to 1200 tons of supplies
monthly were arriving in Yunnanfu, their transport eased by the reduction
of customs duties on trans-Burma shipments from 3 to 1 per cent.[10] Yet
this was only about a fifth of the capacity of the Indochina railway, and
furthermore the Road had to be shut down during the rainy season, lasting
from May or June until November.

Most important, however, was the decision, taken after almost a year's
deliberation, to go ahead with a loan for the stabilization of China's
currency. After the project had collapsed in the summer of 1938, the
Chinese dollar had remained in serious trouble, and by the end of the
year had fallen from a normal value of 1s 2d to about 9d. The Federal
Reserve Bank, after a slow start, was beginning to meet with some success
in imposing its own currency, and by early 1939 the *fapi* had been driven
from circulation in the occupied parts of north China, although it continued to be used freely in the Western settlements, and in those parts of
the countryside where the guerrillas were in control.[11] Early in 1939 the
Japanese announced their intention to open a new bank in Shanghai, in
what looked like an attempt to capture the exchange market of that city.

And on 11 March 1939, the day after the old Central Government notes had ceased to be legal tender in the north, Peking extended a system of trade and exchange controls to the whole of north China.

All these moves helped inspire a reconsideration of a loan to shore up the Chinese dollar, but once again London was reluctant to move without American support. Washington seemed willing at first, but then drew back, afraid of the appearance of Anglo-American collusion[12]; the possibility that such 'collusion' might have a salutary effect on Tokyo was not mentioned. To complicate the situation further, on 15 January China announced that she could no longer continue to service the foreign loans secured on the Maritime Customs.[13] Clark Kerr seized the opportunity to try to persuade Chungking to implement the Customs agreement of May 1938, but his efforts here only led to a sharp exchange with Finance Minister H. H. Kung, who denounced British policy at length, and renewed the threat that China might join Japan to oust the West from Asia.[14] London was not going to press the point, however, in view of the City's growing concern over the flight from the Chinese dollar, which had been touched off by the announcement of the new exchange control measures in the north. On 24 February the Foreign Office wired its mission in Chungking the authorization to tell Chiang in strict secrecy of the Cabinet's decision to grant the loan.[15]

The agreement, as it was worked out during the next few days, was to be in three sections. First, an undertaking between two British banks— the Hongkong and Shanghai Bank, and the Chartered Bank of India, Australia, and China—and two Chinese banks—the Bank of China and the Bank of Communications—providing that each pair would subscribe £5,000,000 for a Stabilization Fund to be used to prevent undue fluctuations in the sterling value of the Chinese currency. A joint Sino-British Committee in Hongkong would handle the operations, and the agreement would remain in force for a year, renewable for a further six month period. Secondly, there would be an agreement by the Treasury to reimburse the two British banks for any loss incurred. Third, there would be an undertaking by China that during the life of the Fund, she would design her economic and monetary policy to maintain the stability of the dollar in terms of sterling, would buy and sell foreign exchange through the member banks, would pay over any foreign exchange acquired in excess of immediate commitments to the Fund as long as its sterling assets were less than £10,000,000, and when the Fund was wound up, would purchase the British banks' share of any Chinese dollar assets.[16]

Craigie broke the news to Vice-Minister of Foreign Affairs Sawada

Renzo on 8 March, and the next day (8 March in London) Sir John Simon made the decision public in the House of Commons.[17] The Japanese reaction was rather milder than expected, although privately Arita denied that Japan was attacking the Chinese currency, and complained that the Fund seemed rather large if it really were going to be used only for stabilization.[18] Generally speaking, the British business community, both at home and in China, welcomed the move.[19] No serious objection was voiced in the Commons, and the Bill authorizing the loan passed unanimously on 24 March.

Despite Arita's disclaimer of any intentions to harm the Chinese currency, Japan was clearly engaged in a major effort to destroy it, both to weaken Chinese military resistance, and to speed the integration of occupied China into the yen bloc. As a British adviser in Chungking wrote in late May,

[The] outcome of [the] present war will probably be decided by [the] 'currency war'. So long as Chinese currency can be maintained Japanese efforts to consolidate military gains will be in large measure frustrated. [The] collapse of [the] currency would lead to [a] breakdown of [the] guerrilla campaign which turns on the people's confidence in *fapi:* it would moreover open the way to [the] puppet currencies of North and Central China, thereby leaving trade and economic development at the mercy of Japan and making [the] occupied areas lost for ever.[20]

If this was a correct reading of the situation, then Britain had, through her granting of the loan, decisively abandoned her neutrality, and had fired a heavy opening salvo to announce her direct intervention in the economic sphere of the East Asian battle.

Put quite bluntly, she had to act as she did; by now it was evident that neutrality would only lead to the extinction of almost all British interests, first in the north, and then in central and south China as well. The new trade and exchange control measures could mean nothing else. They had already existed in Tsingtao, a city which had no foreign areas to hamper Japanese plans, and the result had been to divert a good deal of foreign shipping from that port to other northern cities. On 15 January the system of export permits was extended to Chefoo and Weihaiwei as well, and on 11 March trade control measures went into effect throughout the north. This meant that now most of the export trade of north China, both to points abroad and to the rest of the country, would be by permit only. Exports of listed goods would have to be covered by a F.R.B. certification that the foreign exchange against the goods to be shipped had been acquired at the official rate at a bank designated by the Government. Foreign exchange coverage of import bills was to be dealt with by the

F.R.B. at its discretion, giving priority to those articles needed for military operations and reconstruction.

North China was thus to be brought into the yen bloc with Japan and Manchukuo, while central and south China, outside it, would be treated from an economic standpoint as foreign countries. It meant that the trade of foreign firms would be driven from the north as it had already been driven from Tsingtao. In a letter to *The Times*, on 7 March, a representative of the London Chamber of Commerce complained that

When the new system, if allowed, has been established, permits for imports will be made discriminatory, or withheld altogether. If the Japanese succeed in obtaining complete control of trade and currency, they will be in command of a large supply of foreign currency with which to continue the war in China. This threatened control by Japan is another definite effort to destroy eventually all foreign trade with China other than her own.[21]

Foreign firms were faced with a choice of supporting the F.R.B. currency at a loss to themselves, or giving up their export trade altogether and quitting north China. Japan, of course, hoped that the desire for profits would triumph, and that rather than relinquish their position, Western firms would seek an accommodation. British banks would thus become in effect collecting agencies for the F.R.B., and would collaborate in imposing an alien currency at a time when Britain was committing herself to the support of the Chinese dollar.

A further threat to the national currency came from the establishment of a new bank in central China. On 27 April the Japanese embassy in Shanghai announced that this, the Hua Hsing Commercial Bank, would be opened in Shanghai under the aegis of the Nanking Reformed Government on 1 May. It would deal in foreign exchange as well as handle regular banking business, but unlike the F.R.B. would issue notes freely convertible into foreign and Chinese currencies. It was not another F.R.B., the Japanese insisted; Hua Hsing notes would be 'parallel' with national notes, would not be linked to the yen, and there would be no attempts to raid the Chinese currency. Nor was there any present intention of imposing trade controls. British cooperation, they hinted, would be welcome, and the success of the new currency might help revive commerce in the Yangtse Valley—a delicate way of saying that in return for British support, the river might be reopened.[22]

Halifax, however, blocked Craigie's suggestion that a limited cooperation might keep the Japanese from more drastic steps, and in Shanghai the British banks assumed an attitude of non-cooperation. So did the French, and later, it seems, the Americans.[23] Nevertheless the Japanese moves had their effect in the currency war, and during the summer it became clear that the Stabilization Fund was not going to be able to hold the Chinese dollar to the desired level of $8\frac{1}{4}d$. On 7 June the Fund temporarily withdrew its support to allow the dollar to seek its own level, an action which further undermined confidence, and within ten days over £1,000,000 had been sold. On 22 June, a moratorium was imposed limiting withdrawals for general purposes to Ch $500 per week, but it was confined to Shanghai, and the drain on foreign exchange continued, so that by mid-July, the original £10,000,000 had almost disappeared. For the second time the sale of foreign exchange was suspended, and the new $6\frac{1}{2}d$ rate abandoned. Chinese appeals for further support were fruitless, and after 19 July the exchange rate continued to fall sharply, slipping below $4d$ in August. It was the coming of war in Europe rather than any outside help which finally shored up the currency. As the pound sterling dropped in terms of the American dollar after 3 September, the Chinese dollar appreciated, and the Fund was able to add some £2,000,000 to its reserves to tide it over into 1940. Further support came late in that year, when in November and December the United States and Britain announced further credits of US $50,000,000 and £5,000,000 respectively for stabilization.[24]

If Britain could at least mount some sort of a counterattack in the currency war, she remained helpless in the face of the other restrictions on her trade. Despite a flurry of speculation early in 1939 that the Yangtse and Pearl Rivers might be reopened, Tokyo continued to insist that such a step depended upon 'local conditions', meaning, as the treasurer of the China Association put it, that both rivers would stay shut until Japanese business interests were firmly in control.[25] In addition, restrictions were now imposed in the Yangtse delta, a region hitherto generally unaffected by the occupation.[26] Meanwhile, the coastal blockade was tightened, and cases of interference with foreign shipping increased, as the Japanese sought to strengthen their control over the port cities of the Chekiang and Fukien coasts. Only in Tsingtao was any advance made in the restoration of trading facilities. Here, the harbour was reopened on a limited basis to foreign merchantmen on 25 March, but not until November was there any real improvement in the treatment of third powers.[27]

The process of integrating occupied China into the New Order also meant more trouble for Sir Frederick Maze, as he fought to maintain his rather precarious position between the Japanese and their puppets on the one hand, and the orders of Chungking on the other. When China announced her decision to discontinue the Customs-secured foreign loan services in January, some 78 per cent of the revenues were already being collected in occupied ports, and continued to be deposited in Japanese banks.[28] By 15 April an estimated Ch $199,056,000 was so held, the bulk of it in Shanghai and Tientsin, and except for one remittance from Shanghai in June 1938, none of these funds had been used for loan services. There is no clear evidence that any of the revenues were finding their way to the client régimes of Nanking and Peking, but the funds certainly strengthened the Yokohama Specie Bank in China and, as the Japanese admitted, Chinese dollars were being converted as fast as possible into foreign exchange.[29]

Besides his economic problems, Maze also had to face the stepped up Japanese attempts to have him augment the Japanese staffs of the Customs Houses in occupied areas, a move which Finance Minister Kung resolutely opposed. Since 1926, as part of the attempted Sinicization of the Customs, foreigners had been recruited for the administrative staff only when special skills were needed. Now, however, after considerable argument by Maze that he had to compromise, and considerable pressure from Clark Kerr, Kung agreed to the resumption of foreign recruitment 'on a broad international basis', thus tacitly allowing in more Japanese and temporarily solving the problem. More threatening perhaps than the staff question was Tokyo's plan to establish a new Central Government at Nanking under Wang Ching-wei, a government which might 'appoint' Maze as its Inspector-General, and when he declined, give the post to someone more compliant. Among the possible candidates was a former Officiating Inspector-General, A. H. F. Edwardes, who had resigned from the Customs in 1928, and several years later had become an adviser to the Government of Manchukuo.[30] The plans for Wang's future encountered a number of problems, however, and by the end of the year the threat still remained latent rather than real.

Meanwhile on 1 September, under the pressure of Japanese demands that the Shanghai revenues be collected in Hua Hsing currency, the Central Bank's collecting agency withdrew from the Customs House, to be replaced by one from the Yokohama Specie Bank. It was another victory for Japan in the currency war, but it went virtually unnoticed. Three days later Britain and France were at war with Germany, and with Europe in flames, suddenly only the United States seemed to stand in the way of a Japanese domination of East Asia.

Chapter XI

Shanghai, Amoy and Tientsin: 1939

Nowhere were the two issues of the economic and political control of occupied China so closely linked as in the foreign settlements of the coastal cities, and nowhere was there such a narrow focusing of all the difficulties and frustrations which plagued Japan in her protracted efforts to subdue China. After the fall of Hankow and Canton, the war against Chiang no longer produced any pitched battles or massive victories, and the brilliant campaigns of 1937 and 1938 gave way, by 1939, to an apparently never-ending stalemate. The Central Government had retreated to the comparative safety of Chungking, leaving behind only bands of guerrillas which were strong, well organized, and dangerous, yet which, in the fashion of guerrillas, melted into the north China countryside before they could be found out and destroyed. In such a situation, the treaty port concessions presented what was perhaps the nearest thing to a tangible enemy that the Japanese military could find, and accordingly it was against these areas that they turned in 1939.

A victory over the West would have a certain value as propaganda; it would offset both the stalling of the war against the Central Government, and the fact that, despite the victories of the past, the end of the fighting seemed as distant as ever. Chiang had spurned the peace terms of December 1938, and the defection of Wang Ching-wei had failed to produce any mass exodus of Kuomintang adherents from Chungking. Above all, of course, as long as the foreign settlements remained immune to Japanese regulations, there could be no real consolidation of control in occupied China. In Tientsin the British and French Concessions, by their very presence, hampered the efforts of the Federal Reserve Bank to force its new currency on the north. In Shanghai there remained a considerable amount of Chinese capital which was needed to make effective the Japanese domination over central China and the Yangtse Valley, but whose owners remained obstinately loyal to Chungking. In Tientsin, Shanghai, and Amoy there was the fear (often justified, it might be added) that the foreign settlements were being used by Chinese propagandists, terrorists, and underground organizations. In these enclaves, pro-Chungking newspapers could still be published, Kuomintang flags could be flown, and guerrillas might still seek sanctuary under what the Japanese regarded as the all too sympathetic eyes of the West.

In all three cities the problems were similar, but they demanded different solutions. In Shanghai and Amoy the Settlements were internationally controlled, and while Japan could work steadily to increase her influence in their administration, the day was bound to come when she would be powerful enough legally to dominate them, as Britain had dominated them in the past. This was impossible, of course, in the British and French Concessions of Tientsin (the Italian Concession, needless to say, presented no real problems), and while Japan could exercise no direct control here, she could try to neutralize and to isolate them. The campaign against the foreign areas concentrated on these three cities, and while there were minor incidents elsewhere, it was here that relations between Britain and Japan were subjected to the most severe strains they had yet encountered, in those long and desperate months of 1939, before war came in Europe. In the damp heat of a Chinese summer, unimportant squabbles threatened to blow up into international crises, and differences of language and custom were no longer petty vexations but became real dangers. Behind it all lay the fear of war: war in Europe, where the democracies were still too weak, and war in East Asia, where they were almost powerless.

Shanghai

When he saw Craigie on 22 September 1938, Ugaki had suggested a bargain: Japan would restore the Hongkew and Yangtsepoo areas to the authority of the Municipal Council, if that body would promise 'full cooperation' in maintaining order—meaning the appointment of more Japanese to the Municipal Police and the staffing of the Special District Court with Nanking's appointees. Craigie had favoured some concessions, but Clark Kerr objected strenuously, and London, although holding out the possibility of 'minor adjustments', generally backed him up.[1] By that time, however, Ugaki had resigned and the talks come to an end.

Nor were discussions in Shanghai itself any more fruitful. The British were particularly irked by the deterioration of conditions in the western extra-Settlement roads, and by the fact that the Japanese were not only said to be deriving revenues from the 'protection' they afforded to the local gambling houses, but were also trying to use the situation to extract concessions from the West.[2] To try to settle the problems of the northern areas, Consul-General Hidaka had, late in 1938, made a set of proposals to the Council which included the S.M.C.'s undertakings of the previous March, and added provisions which would give the Japanese substantially complete control in the northern Settlement. A lengthy meeting on 5 December between Japanese and Western officials achieved nothing; Hidaka carefully avoided any assurance that the northern districts would be reopened, and the Council promised only to give the matter further study.[3] Before any concrete steps were taken, however, a new wave of terrorism erupted, leading both sides to harden their positions. Shanghailanders had seldom had much occasion to be proud of their city as a haven of peace, but even they had never seen anything like the outbreak of violence which now occurred, as a series of political crimes, sponsored by the undergrounds of both sides, swept the city. The Japanese were quick to take advantage of the situation, and after the murder of Nanking's Foreign Minister in the Chinese city, Consul-General Miura (who had recently replaced Hidaka) pressed a new series of 'requests' on Council Chairman C. S. Franklin. They were made, he said, in a spirit of good will, since there were indications that the terrorists sought to promote a clash between Japan and Britain, and Britain should not allow herself to be trapped by such sinister strategy.[4]

Whether or not he was correct (and he may well have been), the crime wave put the Council in an awkward position, and Clark Kerr wired his Diplomatic Mission in Chungking to ask Chiang 'to persuade those responsible to "lay off".'[5] Meanwhile the Japanese and their puppets railed at the Council, and from Tokyo there issued dark warnings that if the Council were unable to keep the peace, 'appropriate and effective' measures would be taken.[6] All this was timed to go with Miura's requests, and touched off another round of charges and countercharges between the Council and the Japanese. In the face of threats from the military, the Council's attitude stiffened. Although a compromise was reached in March agreeing to a limited collaboration between the Japanese gendarmerie and the S.M.P., the Council refused to surrender the District Court to Nanking, or to turn over the Land Records of the Chinese municipality—these had been given to the S.M.C. for safekeeping during the fighting in 1937, and the puppet city government now demanded their return.[7] All that Miura was able to get thereafter, taking advantage of a further outbreak of crime in April, was the muzzling of a number of Chinese papers in the

Settlement, and the limitation of the display of Chungking's flags to the eight major national holidays.[8]

So far the main pressure on the Council had come from the military in Shanghai, using the consul-general as their mouthpiece, but in early May Tokyo intervened more actively, and the attack took on a more subtle and more persuasive aspect. On 18 May Vice-Minister Sawada Renzo handed Craigie a long memorandum, milder and more reasonable in tone than the statements which were issuing from army headquarters in Shanghai, but equally firm. Its burden was that the Land Regulations, which had been drawn up in the mid-nineteenth century, were 'incongruous with the new situation of today'. Japan lacked the full, fair, and just voice which would permit her active cooperation in the Settlement, and the time had come to make changes which would bring the machinery of administration into line with the realities of the twentieth century.[9]

There was no denying the accuracy of this charge. The Settlement's machinery was archaic, undemocratic, and still adapted to a period when Britain's had been the dominant voice in the determination of treaty port affairs. Yet there was some hope, perhaps, that the very truth of these accusations might keep Japan from resorting to force. Within about a year, it was estimated, the Japanese could secure control of the Settlement simply through an increase in their voting strength, with no need for any change in the Land Regulations. Although at this point they paid only about 9 per cent of the taxes on which the franchise was based, they controlled some 35 per cent of the vote—more than any other single country, and an increase of 79 per cent since 1936.[10] It was easy enough to protest that Japan had no right to use force against the Settlement, but it was less easy to counter the claim that the changes which Japan proposed would make the Settlement more democratic, and that it was unreasonable for Englishmen and Americans not to agree to them.[11]

Needless to say, the situation caused a good deal of concern among Shanghai's Anglo-American community. Fortunately, however, those with a sense of history might remember that Englishmen had a long tradition of manipulating votes based on a property qualification, and the same techniques which the Duke of Newcastle had used to rig elections in favour of the Whig oligarchy of the eighteenth century might be applied to the rigging of elections in favour of an Anglo-Saxon oligarchy in the twentieth century. An increase in the number of Western property owners would mean an increase in the number of Western voters, and since the British owned more land than anyone else, they could subdivide large lots among smaller owners, keeping each piece of land large enough to carry the franchise with it. Large firms could put their properties in other names, and sympathetic Chinese holders of unregistered land could transfer it to Western ownership. All these moves came under consideration in 1939 (and some were actually used for the Council elections of 1940), but unfortunately the same tactics were open to the Japanese—who, it might be added, also had a tradition of rigging elections in favour of an oligarchy—and it was unlikely that there could be any permanent settlement in favour of the West.[12]

The Japanese continued to press for a reorganization of the Council, and the Westerners continued to insist that the time was not ripe for any changes, but by late spring, Shanghai had survived the worst of the Japanese attacks. On 11 May 1939, the S.M.C. and French authorities issued another proclamation clamping down on political activities within the foreign areas,[13] while in Chungking further quiet pressure was brought to bear on the Central Government to call a halt to anti-Japanese terrorism.[14] By late May the city was comparatively peaceful again, and both Japanese and Western eyes turned to the troubles of Tientsin and Amoy, now beginning to dominate the headlines. There was a flurry of excitement in mid-August and September, when the puppet city police clashed with the S.M.P. in the region of the extra-Settlement roads, and Japanese troops moved into position around the Settlement, to 'bring the Council to its senses'. If they contemplated anything drastic, however, the Japanese were unwilling to push too hard, even after the outbreak of war in Europe, for the bombshell of the Nazi–Soviet Pact of 23 August had left them confused and isolated.[15] And if the closing months of 1939 saw no perceptible diminution of tension in the city, at least the situation grew no worse, and once again Shanghai took on the appearance of prosperity, as its merchants and manufacturers began to benefit from Europe's economic dislocations, with the coming of war in the West.

Amoy

The chief significance of the crisis at Amoy lay in the possibility that a surrender there might provide a precedent for Shanghai, for like Shanghai, Amoy had an International Settlement, governed by a Municipal Council on which Japan, as a treaty power, had certain rights. Located on the island of Kulangsu in Amoy harbour, the Settlement was not nearly as large nor as important as Shanghai's, but from the beginning the West was conscious of the parallel, and aware that any weakness shown in Amoy would lead to a renewal of pressure in the larger city.

On 11 May, Hung Li-hsiun, the chairman of the puppet Amoy Peace Maintenance Commission, was murdered on Kulangsu. The incident was the first of its kind in the Settlement, and came only after the Kulangsu Municipal Council had been forced to hire Japanese policemen. Immediately a detachment of 150 Japanese landed in the Settlement, and proceeded to make a number of arrests. Western protests, and the request that the landing party withdraw, were ignored and on 15 May the Japanese consul-general presented the K.M.C. with a list of demands for an increase of Japanese strength in both the Council and the police.[16] The West countered with a show of force, and the two British destroyers already in the harbour were joined by HMS *Birmingham*, flagship of the China Squadron, and by French and American cruisers. On the 17th, forty-two men each from the British, French, and American ships went ashore to join the Japanese force (now reduced to that number), explaining that since the Settlement was international, any landing force should be international too.[17]

Negotiations took place throughout the summer, while the situation was aggravated by a blockade on junk traffic with the mainland, leading to a shortage of food. All three Western landing parties remained ashore, despite waverings by both Washington and Paris, until the British and French withdrew on the outbreak of the European war. The Americans remained, and in mid-October an agreement was reached, providing for cooperation between Japanese and Municipal police and for the appointment of additional Japanese policemen. In return, traffic between the mainland and the Settlement was restored.[18] There was little given away, and on 18 October when the Japanese and Americans boarded their ships, Japan was not appreciably closer to control of Kulangsu than she had been before.

Tientsin

The most serious of all the crises of 1939, however, was that which broke out around the British Concession in Tientsin. The apparent Japanese promise to withdraw the order for the evacuation of the French and British Concessions in September 1938 had ended a potentially dangerous situation for the time being. But wherever foreigners lived in positions of relative autonomy next to the Japanese, there were bound to be clashes between them, and like Shanghai, Tientsin was too important a prize for either side to abandon. Even more important than Shanghai perhaps, in terms of 1939, for it was north China which the Japanese first wanted to incorporate into the New Order, and the foreign areas of Tientsin were proving to be major stumbling blocks on the road to Japan's imperial destiny.

The Japanese had five chief grounds of complaint against the British and French in the northern city. First, their Concessions were said to harbour Chinese guerrillas, and to be centres of anti-Japanese terrorism and propaganda. Second, the Japanese wanted control of their telephone systems for security purposes. Third, the Japanese alleged that within the Concessions there were secret radio stations in contact with Chinese forces. Fourth, the Japanese were angered at the refusal of the foreign banks to hand over the Chinese silver in their vaults. And last of all, they were angered at the refusal of the banks to deal in Federal Reserve Bank currency, and at the failure of the Concession authorities to prevent the circulation of *fapi*. The first three of these complaints dealt generally with the questions of terrorism and security, and were similar to those which were made in Shanghai and Amoy. The latter two concerned economics, and were indicative of the situation in which Japan now found herself in north China. Although technically the region was hers, strong guerrilla forces continued to operate, and the Border Governments controlled areas behind Japanese lines, so that all that was safely within Japanese control were the towns, rail lines, and main highways. Economically, much of north China's wealth was tied up in the Concessions, in Chinese and foreign banks and business houses. On 10 March 1939 *fapi* had ceased to be legal tender for the north, but it continued to circulate in the British and French Concessions in Tientsin, as well as in the Legation Quarter of Peking. Thus here, in China's second largest port, the Concessions refused to grant the new currency a preferential position, while in the countryside the Japanese army was unable to confirm its control because of the strength of the guerrillas. From both an economic and a political point of view therefore, it was necessary for Japan, if not actually to take over the Concessions, at least to neutralize them and make them serve as agents of her policy in China rather than as the symbols of Chinese resistance to the New Order which they had by now become.[19] Thus it was here that, in the summer of 1939, the British were forced to make a stand, and unfortunately for them, to make it on grounds considerably less secure than had been theirs in Shanghai or Amoy.

There is another, less tangible factor which made the Tientsin crisis different from those in Shanghai and Amoy. A study of these years yields the impression that the foreign communities of the north in general, and of Tientsin in particular, were somewhat more ready to come to terms with the Japanese and their puppets than were those of Shanghai and the south;

there was, for instance, the Tientsin Customs Commissioner's hasty settlement in 1937, and there was the determinedly non-political stand of the Kailan Mining Administration in its dealings with Japan. Well before 1937, it must be remembered, the north was beginning to move into Japan's orbit, while maintaining only a technical loyalty to Nanking, and Japan's power, from an economic, military, and political point of view, must have seemed considerably more real than that of the Central Government. Political authority and political allegiance in China came and went, and there were some at least who felt that Chiang's cause was in eclipse, and that realism demanded the maintenance of friendly relations with Japan and Wang Keh-min.[20] If the Concessions had become symbols of opposition to the New Order, in other words, it was probably due more to force of circumstances, and to the actions of home governments, than to any conscious desire on the part of the Tientsin foreign community.

In any case, some of the problems of Tientsin did not at first seem too far from solution. The Japanese were less interested in actually controlling the silver which lay in foreign vaults than in making sure that it stayed within the city, and in November 1938 the British and French worked out a plan to seal it where it was. Chungking agreed to this in March 1939, but negotiations with the Japanese dragged on, and the question continued to hang fire into the summer.[21] Nor did terrorism seem to be a dangerous issue. Inside the British Concession itself, there had been only one political crime, whereas a number had taken place in the Japanese controlled city.[22] Nevertheless, in Japanese eyes the Concession was an asylum for enemy agents, and this outlook seemed to be confirmed when the British police, acting on Japanese intelligence, arrested a guerrilla leader on 24 September 1938. This was Ssu Ching-wu, self-styled commander of the Fourth Army of the 'North China National Anti-Japanese Army', and although he denied that he had engaged in any political activities during his three weeks in the Concession, his very presence there seemed to indicate a tie between the Concession and the guerrillas.

The Japanese wanted his surrender, but Consul-General E. G. Jamieson refused, unless given proof that Ssu had actually taken part in criminal activities while in the Concession. The Japanese then seem to have produced evidence that he had used both the British and French Concessions as a base since September 1937, and had been counterfeiting notes in the Italian Concession.[23] On the British side, an argument now developed over how best to dispose of his case. Craigie and Jamieson, as well as the British Municipal Council, wanted to turn him over, either for trial by the Peking authorities, or by expelling him from the Concession, while privately informing the Japanese of the time and place; this latter plan, admitted Jamieson, had 'the disadvantage of not being straightforward'. Neither he nor the Council wanted to intern Ssu, as Clark Kerr and London suggested, but this was the solution adopted on 1 November.[24]

The Japanese had earlier warned that life would become more difficult if he were not surrendered,[25] and while there had been problems before— scuffles between British and Japanese soldiers, and the banning of the *Peking and Tientsin Times* in October[26]—it was the decision to intern Ssu which seriously worsened the situation. It now turned out that the Japanese never had rescinded their evacuation order, and by mid-November about half the Japanese residents of the French and British Concessions had left, and there was a possibility that the Chinese might be forced out also. In early December barricades were set up around the two Concessions, and between the 14th and 17th a rigorous traffic control system was instituted, resulting in serious delays.[27] Both Clark Kerr and Jamieson agreed that representations in Tokyo would not do much good, since the Japanese army was clearly in control of the situation, and would not consider itself bound by any guarantees given by the civil government. The British and French did formally protest to Consul-General Tashiro in Tientsin, who apparently disapproved himself of the military's actions, but was in no position to challenge them.[28] In early January Craigie was told that the traffic controls were 'urgent and unavoidable', and that until the Council authorities began to clean out the terrorists, and to act 'in conformity with the new situation in North China', there would be no change.[29] Two days later the military warned that stricter measures might be imposed unless all political prisoners were handed over.[30]

Craigie clarified the British position in a note of 23 January 1939, pointing out that the Concession authorities were doing their best to maintain a '*correct* attitude' in view of their neutral position,[31] but of course the difficulty lay precisely in the fact that a correct attitude, from a Japanese standpoint, favoured Chungking. Yet the situation at least grew no worse for a while. No official complaints were made, and early in January 1939 Lieutenant-General Homma Masaharu, who enjoyed a pro-British reputation, took command at Tientsin.[32] On 8 February the barricades were lifted and daytime searches ceased.[33] The respite did not last long, however, and on the 16th the Japanese refused a British suggestion to transfer Ssu Ching-wu to Shanghai, and warned further that the barriers would be reimposed unless four members of the British police were removed, including Deputy Commissioner Li Han-yuan, whom they accused of being Chungking's agent. To reinforce the point, heavy barbed and live wire entanglements were placed along the western edge of the Concession, and a bridge built from the Japanese to the Italian Concessions, enabling the British to be more effectively isolated.[34] Neither protests nor a series of meetings between Homma and the British and French consuls-general were any help, and accordingly in April Major-General F. S. G. Piggott, the military attaché in Tokyo, was sent to the city as peacemaker. He had gone on a similar mission to Shanghai in June 1938, and was on good terms with both Homma and General Sugiyama Hajime, the commander-in-chief in north China. After several meetings with the military, he warned that the situation was extremely serious, and said that he was satisfied that there were indeed anti-Japanese organizations at work in the Concessions. The Japanese, he continued, were bewildered and resentful at the lack of British cooperation, and since the internment of Ssu had given the British police no more information on criminal activities.[35]

Then, while Craigie, Jamieson, Clark Kerr, and the Foreign Office were carrying on a long debate by telegraph over what to do with political offenders,[36] the situation took a sudden turn for the worse. On 9 April, as General Piggott was leaving Tientsin, Cheng Lien-shih, an official of the Peking régime, was shot and killed in a movie theatre in the British Concession. In the ensuing scuffle, the assassins escaped, having first killed a Swiss who tried to stop them. There were no immediately serious repercussions and the next day Major Herbert, the superintending consul, told Tashiro that the British would welcome Japanese cooperation in solving the crime. Jamieson asked for Japanese gendarmes to be lent to the Concession police, for a joint raid on suspected guerrilla hideouts, and to arrest the murderer as well as any others believed to be guilty of anti-Japanese activities. After the raid, the murderer and his accomplices were to be turned over to the *de facto* (Peking) authorities. Others guilty of anti-Japanese activities would be detained only on orders from Clark Kerr, although the Japanese would be allowed to interrogate them.[37]

Just what happened then is not entirely clear. For some reason Jamieson did not give London a complete account of what took place, and it was only gradually that Clark Kerr and the Foreign Office began to learn the full story.[38] Naturally, this only further confused an already complicated situation, and in acting as he did Jamieson must have assumed that he would be free to follow his own judgment, and that a detailed report was unnecessary. However, from what can be pieced together from a vast number of telegrams over the next four months, the sequence of events

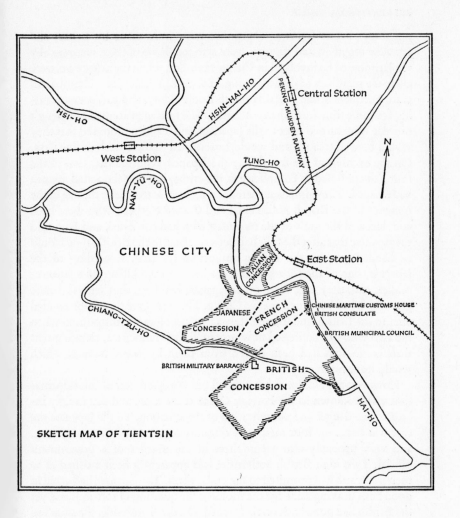

SKETCH MAP OF TIENTSIN

ran somewhat as follows. The police raids were made by British and Japanese together, and six men were arrested. Four of these were said by the Japanese to be involved in Cheng's murder, while the other two were allegedly members of the same gang, and were in possession of bombs. All were members of the guerrilla Ninth Route Army, and had been operating for some time from the Concession. The four men accused of Cheng's murder were turned over to the Japanese, and Tashiro promised that they would be well treated, and would be returned to the British in five days. On the evening of the fourth day the Japanese reported that two of the four had confessed to complicity in the crime, but that the actual assassin had escaped. The crime was thereupon reconstructed in the theatre in the presence of the British police chief and Consul Herbert, who were both convinced of the guilt of the two men who had confessed, and who told the Japanese that after the four had been returned to the British, they would be handed over to the Peking authorities for trial. According to the Japanese, one of the four had also confessed to the killing of a Japanese soldier, and, they said, three other Japanese had been shot with the same gun which had been used against Cheng. The men were thereupon handed over to the British, and immediately a new problem was introduced when the two who had confessed now protested their innocence, claiming that their confessions had been forced from them by water torture, which would leave no trace.[39]

However, as F. C. Jones has pointed out,[40] a good deal of this information was unknown to the Foreign Office at the time, and this greatly increased the danger and complication of the situation. To the Japanese the case was clear: the four men were certainly members of a terrorist gang, and very probably also accomplices in the murder of a government official. Two high British authorities had apparently been satisfied as to their guilt, and had promised to surrender them. The Japanese had acted in good faith (leaving aside for the moment the question of torture), and yet the British had gone back on their word. On the British side, the situation was confused by the fact that the Foreign Office had to act on such scanty information. The first dispatch on the case, on 13 May, told of the reconstruction of the crime, the confession of the two men, and their recantation, which apparently the Concession police had accepted. What it did not say was that the British had agreed to surrender the four men, and this point was not clarified until a month later, midway through June.[41]

On 13 May Jamieson asked Clark Kerr for permission to turn all four men over to the District Court on the production of a proper warrant. Whether or not their confessions were valid, he said, there was no doubt as to their being members of a criminal gang. He also warned that the Japanese felt that Britain was deliberately trying to help China through a policy of obstruction and, he continued, the local British community felt that the belief had 'considerable justification'.[42] Clark Kerr refused; he was probably still unaware of the promises made to the Japanese, and he saw in Jamieson's request simply the sacrifice of four men for expediency's sake. For him the issue was a moral one, and he wanted simply to expel the four, while awaiting further evidence against those who had possessed arms and propaganda. Other political prisoners, he said, were to be released with a warning.[43]

Another debate now followed between the British principals in Tientsin, Tokyo, Shanghai, and London. Craigie and Jamieson, the two men who had to negotiate and work with the Japanese, wanted to surrender the four men for trial by the local Chinese court; Clark Kerr opposed this, on the grounds that it would mean certain execution for them; and the Foreign Office, still unaware of all the facts of the case, opted for expulsion. Homma meanwhile pressed for action, and Jamieson, warning on 9 June that the Japanese 'mean business', advised all the British living outside the Concession to withdraw into its boundaries before the Japanese acted.[44] On the 10th, Clark Kerr, as a compromise, suggested that the four come before an *ad hoc* tribunal, composed of a British, a Japanese, and a neutral judge; if found guilty they would be surrendered. Halifax seized on this, modifying it to have the body act simply as an advisory committee to decide if there were a *prima facie* case against the four, and Washington agreed to have the American consul-general act as the neutral. Now it was Tokyo's turn to refuse;[45] almost certainly this was a tactical mistake, for judging by the tenor of both British and American dispatches from Tientsin, Japan would have won her case.

On 11 June Jamieson wired to London a long report which began to clarify the issues. For the first time he made it plain that the Concession authorities had agreed to hand over the four men, and he maintained that there was no legal right to refuse the execution of warrants issued by the Tientsin District Court. Both Clark Kerr and Halifax, he continued, persistently ignored the fact that apart from the murder, there was *prima facie* evidence that the men were members of a terrorist gang. Therefore, he argued, the men should be turned over, not because it was expedient, but because the Japanese were legally and morally justified in their demands. Much of this information was new to the Foreign Office, as were further details which followed a few days later.[46] Craigie added his voice to Jamieson's, warning that the whole British position in north China was being risked 'on account of legal niceties which I find myself unable to appreciate', an argument which drew a sharp retort from the embassy in Shanghai: 'The issue seems to be a nicety of morals rather than law.'[47]

Gradually London was being filled in on the facts of the case, but at this point, it would have been difficult for it to change its mind. A surrender of the men would look like a surrender to Japanese threats, something hard for the Government to do nine months after Munich. They stood firm, and generally their stand was backed by public opinion; all that the man in the street knew was that the Government did not consider that there was enough evidence to a make a *prima facie* case against the four, that the Japanese had refused to furnish any more evidence of guilt, and had refused to submit the case to an advisory committee. Incomplete as it was, it was a picture which did not differ much from that which the Foreign Office itself had had until recently. Moreover it was a picture confirmed by the Foreign Secretary's statement of 20 June, when he made no mention of the promise to surrender the four men, and implied that Britain in refusing to turn them over was acting in accord with her past practice. In fact, the opposite appears to have been true; according to Jamieson, warrants of the local Court had been executed in the past.[48]

Neither side was thus willing to back down. On 13 June the Tientsin military announced that the next day the British and French Concessions would be blockaded, and at the same time they issued a violent condemnation of British delay and prevarication. Nor was this all. Now, they said, the issue could no longer be settled simply by the delivery of the four suspects, but the British would have to 'reconsider' their whole attitude towards the protection of terrorists, the support of *fapi* and the obstruction of F.R.B. currency, and the use of 'anti-Japanese texts' in the Concessions' Chinese schools.[49] In other words the issue was no longer simply the murder of a minor official in a movie theatre, but now comprehended all the grievances, political and economic, which Japan held against the foreign settlements in China. Nor was this a purely military viewpoint; in Tokyo, Arita told Craigie that while surrender of the four would of course ease the situation, a number of other questions would remain. He also made it clear that the army had been given a free hand in Tientsin.[50]

The barricades went up on the 14th. Shipping on the river stopped, food and fuel supplies were suddenly subjected to interminable delays, while many Chinese, afraid of reprisals, refused to deal with the Concession. In Britain, anger mounted as the press headlined stories of the searching and stripping of British citizens at the Tientsin checkpoints. Official statements simply gave the Government's side of the picture,[51] and there were immediate demands for retaliation from both sides of the House. One Tory M.P. wanted to close Singapore, Penang and Hong-kong to Japanese ships, another to denounce the 1911 trade treaty, while Labour's Colonel Wedgwood urged immediate staff talks with Russia. The Government announced that retaliatory measures were being considered,[52] and in private the Foreign Office set to work to see how much support it could get from its friends.

Paris, approached on 16 June, was nervous: there must be no question of sanctions, everything would have to depend on America. Lindsay called on the State Department: would the United States mediate, or at least advise Tokyo of its concern? Perhaps, answered Sumner Welles on the 16th, and his Department went so far as to draft a strong note, but never sent it, because of the opposition of Ambassador Grew (then on home leave) and Eugene Dooman, his chargé in Tokyo. Instead, Dooman was instructed simply to express his country's concern at the growth of the anti-British agitation in north China, and Hull told the press that while America was not involved in the original incidents which had caused the blockade, she was concerned with the 'broader aspects' of the Tientsin crisis.[53]

This general lack of support was bound to weaken Britain's position. On 18 June Craigie proposed to London that he offer to negotiate a settlement with Arita, based on a lifting of the blockade, while promising all possible steps to ensure the Concession's neutrality.[54] He also wanted to be able to threaten retaliation if negotiation failed, but Halifax vetoed this, adding that Craigie need not even demand the end of the blockade as a preliminary.[55] If Britain's friends would not support London, London could not support Craigie, and the ambassador would have to do his best by himself.

On 23 June Arita did agree to negotiate, and with the help of Prime Minister Hiranuma Craigie and the Tokyo civilians won two small victories over the army at the outset: the talks would cover only local issues, rather than broader questions of British policy in occupied China, and they would be held in Tokyo, where the atmosphere was calmer and the presence of the North China Army not so easily felt. An agreed communiqué to this effect was made public on 28 June.[56] It was a step forward, but the real difficulties lay in the future; while an agreement on security and police matters would probably be easy enough to reach, the root problems, as Craigie warned, were the economic ones, and any serious discussions here would have to be cleared with Paris and Washington, whose interests were also involved.[57]

Both Arita and Hiranuma were under considerable pressure from the military to broaden the base of discussions, and the Tientsin soldiers had already left no doubt that what they really wanted was an outright revision of London's attitude towards Chiang. Furthermore, the Tientsin negotiations were linked—especially in the military's mind—with the question of the proposed German alliance. As Ambassador Ott reported to Berlin, an army success in Tientsin would commit Japan so heavily against Britain that the protagonists of the alliance would carry the day, and to this end the military would work for a breakdown in the talks. By the same token the anti-alliance forces in Tokyo were trying to play down the severity of the Tientsin crisis.[58] All this made Arita's position one of considerable delicacy. When he met Craigie for the first time on 15 July, the Foreign Minister proposed an agenda under three headings: 'general questions', questions relative to peace and order, and economic questions. The 'general questions', said Arita, would not deal with Britain's policy towards China as a whole, but would merely be a background for talks on the local issues in Tientsin. Craigie had no objection, as long as agreement here was not a condition for settlement of the other points. No, said Arita, 'condition' was not the right word, but it was essential that the 'general questions' be cleared out of the way first. On this somewhat ambiguous note the talks began.

Arita opened with his draft on 'general questions' which, interpreted broadly, would give the Japanese *carte blanche* to take whatever action they wanted, both in and out of the foreign settlements, anywhere in China. Craigie made a counter proposal,[59] and for the next few days stood firm against giving Japan any sort of a free hand. He had already suggested legislation at home to allow economic retaliation; now he suggested it again, but again nothing was done.[60] Then on the 21st the two men reached agreement on a formula to cover the 'general questions'. It admitted the necessity of measures by which the Japanese might safeguard their security, and continued:

His Majesty's Government have no intention of countenancing any act or measures prejudicial to the attainment of the above mentioned objects and they will take this opportunity to confirm their policy in this respect by making it plain to British authorities and British nationals in China that they should refrain from such acts and measures.[61]

Superficially, this was similar to Arita's earlier draft, but the final wording of the agreement would make it possible for the British, in policing their own Concession, to admit only as much Japanese 'cooperation' as they chose. Nevertheless the formula's announcement three days later provoked an uproar. *The Times*, the *North China Herald*, and the *Japan Weekly Chronicle* approved, holding that the agreement was no more than the recognition of an attitude generally adopted by the United States, France, and other countries with Chinese interests.[62] More significant however, was the widespread criticism of those who saw it as a surrender, as a sort of Far Eastern Munich. The Left, of course, repeated the old charge that Simon's chickens of 1932 were coming home to roost,[63] but they were not alone. The Shanghai monthly, *Oriental Affairs*, whose editor, H. G. W. Woodhead, was certainly no partisan of Chungking's cause, called it a 'lopsided . . . dangerous formula' which recognized the 'right of the Japanese to disregard all British interests'.[64] Also from Shanghai the British Chamber of Commerce and the China Association cabled a protest to London, warning of a 'deplorable betrayal of British rights, interests, and obligations in China', and complaining that 'legitimate British interests . . . appear to have been placed at the mercy of the Japanese Army'.[65]

To Craigie, commenting on it some years later, the formula did no more than recognize a situation of fact. Although Hiranuma, bowing to nationalist pressure, at first tried to suggest that it applied not just to Tientsin, but to all China, the formula never proved to be an embarrassment to Britain, and Japan never again sought to represent it as a fresh obligation.[66] Nevertheless the fact remains that Japan had won a clear propaganda victory. Not only was Chungking deeply worried,[67] but to many in the West it looked as if Chamberlain and Halifax had once again sacrificed principle for an illusory ideal of appeasement.

The most unexpected reaction came from Washington. The State Department, anxious to keep its distance from Britain while Congress was discussing changes in the neutrality laws, had refused a British proposal of 12 July to join the talks if the currency question were raised,[68] and this lack of support undoubtedly contributed to Craigie's acceptance of the formula. The announcement of 24 July provoked the expected criticisms of London's policy, but also helped push America towards the first significant measure of economic retaliation since the start of the war. The United States had been considering for some time the ending of her 1911 commercial treaty with Japan; now on 26 July Roosevelt, without consulting either Grew or Dooman (much less London or Paris) gave Tokyo the required six months' notice of abrogation. This meant that as of January 1940 the United States would be free to regulate its trade with Japan as it saw fit.[69] The British press cheered Roosevelt, but London was clearly in an awkward position. Once again America had moved uni-laterally, without consultation, and the juxtaposition of the Craigie–Arita formula on the one hand, and the American denunciation on the other, made a striking contrast in the diplomatic postures of the two countries. Since 1937 Hull had carefully insisted on 'parallel action', but after the *Panay* affair, the Customs negotiations, and now this, Whitehall must have been in considerable doubt as to just what the Secretary could mean.

In Tokyo the meetings continued on 24 July, with Craigie and Arita now joined by the other members of the negotiating teams: Major-General Piggott and Major Herbert, the consul at Tientsin for the British, Kato Sotomatsu, Minister-at-Large in China, General Muto Akira of the North China Army, and Major Ohta of the Tientsin gendarmerie for Japan. Kato submitted a list of twelve points, covering both security meas-ures and economics; they sought, among other things, the surrender of 'anti-Japanese criminals', stronger steps against subversive organizations, the prohibition of *fapi* in the Concession, the surrender of the Chinese silver, and the inspection of Chinese monetary establishments in the Concession. From the beginning it was obvious that these latter points would be the stumbling block; Tokyo insisted that the Concession auth-orities suppress *fapi*, and the British were equally insistent that they could not do this as long as they recognized Chungking, and that in any case the question concerned other countries.[70] For the moment, however, neither side wanted a deadlock, and the discussions which dealt with police matters were more fruitful.[71] Meanwhile further evidence was produced in the April murder case, and Craigie recommended the surrender of the four men; at the same time Ssu Ching-wu was to be interned by the Peking authorities, and visited periodically by a British representative to make sure that he was well treated.[72]

Paris, and after some hesitation, Washington, told Tokyo that they could countenance no bilateral Anglo-Japanese currency arrangement,[73] and by 1 August when it was apparent there would be no further progress on economic questions, Craigie suggested a separate police agreement. The Japanese refused, as they refused a compromise on the *fapi*, angered by what they considered to be an obvious attempt to bring in other countries. Behind the scenes the army kept up its pressure against an agreement, worried (as the German ambassador pointed out) that diplomatic success here would hurt the chances of an alliance.[74] The military delegation re-turned to Tientsin in a huff on 14 August, and on the 20th the talks were adjourned *sine die*, each side issuing a communiqué to set forth its own point of view.[75] In early September the four men of the murder case were finally turned over to Peking, but they had long since ceased to be important factors, and their surrender produced no improvement in the situation.

The blockade continued, and Tientsin's troubles were made worse by a series of disastrous floods which swept through the city in late August and early September. A cheerless north China winter set in: cold rain, sleet, grey skies, and a shortage of food and fuel. The American ambassador, who visited the city just before Christmas, sent back a vivid report of what life was like in the besieged Concession.

Getting in and out of the British Concession is like going in and out of a beleaguered city. Crowds of Chinese stand for hours at the barriers waiting their turn to pass. . . . Examination facilities are inadequate and when a truck loaded with goods . . . is permitted to proceed it is stopped halfway through the barrier and required to unload its entire contents. . . .

Apparently a form of graft has grown up around the barriers with considerable profit to those conducting the examinations and . . . it has been found possible to expedite the passage of goods by the payment of fees. . . .

The British community apparently is resigned to its situation and asks little and receives little. One has the impression that the whole barrier system is an embarrassment to the Japanese as well as to foreigners but that face has become involved and that the Japanese do not know how to rid themselves of it in spite of the fact that its maintenance acts as a wet blanket on trade in Tienstin and to the detriment of the Japanese as well as foreign business.[76]

Perhaps it was no more than face which kept the two sides from reaching a compromise that winter. Tientsin continued to suffer, but the crisis was over and this was the most important accomplishment of the Tokyo talks. As Craigie emphasized, they had taken up time and had allowed tension to die down; by the end of August it was clear to Tokyo that no strike against the Concession would have had the necessary measure of public support.[77] This had been the most severe crisis by far in the history of Anglo-Japanese relations, and as the negotiations dragged on through the oppressive, stagnant heat of a Tokyo summer, there had been talk of war, a war which neither side wanted, but which would have been forced by the North China Army and the nationalists, who were busily stirring up massive anti-British demonstrations throughout north China and Japan. When the talks ended, war no longer seemed possible, and Britain gained an unexpected advantage when the Nazi-Soviet Pact made it strikingly clear that Japan had been isolated, not by her enemies, but by her friends.

Craigie did his best to fight a holding action in the talks, but despite all his efforts, he was forced to give ground. Again the lack of Anglo-American solidarity had been made glaringly apparent; little support had come from Washington, and the denunciation of the American trade treaty, which could have been of extraordinary value if it had come a few days earlier, had been done in the most harmless way possible. Sir Robert's obstinate refusal to give in on the currency question had shown a determination in British diplomacy whose existence many had doubted, but generally this was overlooked. The formula, and the ultimate surrender of the four men—these were the publicized issues, and these spelled appeasement. Yet the latter case summed up one of the dilemmas of British policy. The men were patriots; the Concession was neutral territory. Clark Kerr was right in seeing the case as a moral one, and Craigie and Jamieson were right in regretting the fact that Britain had elected to make a stand on a point where legally she was so vulnerable. Where should foreign authorities—British, French, and American—stand in relation to Japan in the occupied areas? How far could they compromise? How could official neutrality be maintained in a war (and an undeclared war at that) where moral rights and wrongs seemed so clear? It was left up to Britain to seek a solution to these questions on behalf of the West; she was given little enough help by her friends, and it was no surprise that the Tientsin formula ultimately did nothing more than confirm the *status quo* in the official language of diplomacy.[78]

Chapter XII

War in Europe, I: New Problems, September – December 1939

In the summer of 1939, while the Tientsin crisis was at its height, a three-cornered debate took place between the Foreign Office and the ambassadors in Shanghai and Tokyo, on the future of Britain's Eastern policy. Craigie regarded the crisis as the occasion, not the cause, of an outburst of Japanese feeling against Britain, whose 'open partisanship' for China had hurt her. The four men in Tientsin should have been handed over, and the case of Colonel Spear should never have been allowed to happen: this was a reference to the arrest of the British military attaché in China, who had been caught behind the Japanese lines in undeniably suspicious circumstances, and whose release had been effected by the indefatigable General Piggott. Instead of her 'often excessive benevolence' to Chungking, said Craigie, Britain should hew to a line of stricter neutrality, such as America had maintained.[1] Clark Kerr disagreed. If America were better treated than Britain, he argued, this was less because of her stricter neutrality than because of a greater Japanese fear of what Washington might do.[2]

Here were two conflicting viewpoints: Craigie arguing against a stand strong enough to drive Japan into the arms of the Axis, and Clark Kerr arguing for a stronger stand yet, for the sake both of China and of British interests in China. The real point at issue, of course, was whether or not the distinction which Craigie drew (along with Grew and others) between Japanese 'moderates' and 'extremists' was a valid one, and if it was, whether the moderates still had any control over the making of policy. Halifax raised this question, pointing out that the moderates could continue to demand concessions, in order to avoid strengthening the extremists; so the civil government in Tokyo, while disapproving of the military's behaviour in China, did not hesitate to use that behaviour as a means of weakening Britain.[3] Sir George Sansom, the great historian of Japan, who was at the time commercial counsellor for the Tokyo embassy, took an even stronger view in a memorandum which he wrote for the Foreign Office:

... it is open to serious doubt ... whether in present conditions we have any really useful friends in Japan. All Japanese want a 'new order' in Asia, and a 'new order' involves the ultimate displacement of Great Britain in the Far East.

If Britain did indeed have any friends, he said, she could best help them by resisting the extremists, and he went on to recommend a 'carefully planned and well-timed programme of economic measures against Japan'.[4]

Craigie, however, continued to believe that an agreement must be sought, and continued to believe that Hiranuma, for all his reputation as a fire-breathing nationalist, might be the man to conclude it. He knew something of the secret letter which Hiranuma had sent to Roosevelt, entrusting it to Grew when the latter went on home leave in the late spring of 1939, a letter which proposed a joint effort to halt the oncoming European war. Yet even this had its potentially dark side; Japan might want to solve her problems with America, yet while she made advances to Washington, she was stepping up her campaigns against the Tientsin concession, against British shipping, and against those foreign interests to which America seemed indifferent. Might this not simply be a deliberate attempt to separate America from Britain, and to kill the burgeoning 'united front' which had been struggling to develop since the Yangtse notes of the previous November?[5] In any case, in early August Craigie reported that Hiranuma, together with moderates like Kato Sotomatsu and Admiral Yonai, were leading a movement for rapprochement with the democracies. When Hiranuma secretly told the ambassador that his position as Prime Minister was weakening, and that he needed some good news to be able to hold his present course away from the Axis, Craigie took the warning seriously, dismissing the idea that it was simply a pressure tactic.[6] His arguments achieved little, however; he was able only to win a delay in the conclusion of a new agreement which granted China £2,800,000 in credits, and to make sure that when it was signed (on 18 August), it was given no publicity.[7]

Undoubtedly there was some truth in Craigie's picture of Arita and Hiranuma trying to restrain the ultra-nationalists from taking any precipitate action in favour of the Axis, while the army was apparently doing its best to embroil Japan with Britain.[8] But events were fast moving beyond the control of either Whitehall or the Gaimusho. The announcement of the Nazi-Soviet Pact of 23 August not only stunned Europe, but also struck Asia with an impact sufficient to bring the Hiranuma cabinet toppling down. Since May, what was a war in all but name had been raging in the disputed territory between Japan's client states of Manchukuo and Inner Mongolia, and the Soviet Union's satellite of Outer Mongolia. Here Russian and Japanese troops faced each other, backed by armoured divisions and aircraft, and here the crack Kwantung Army had sustained a severe defeat, just three days before the pact's conclusion. Thus while the Japanese were being beaten in the field, it seemed to them that their Western allies were allowing the enemy to move fresh troops to the East.[9] It was hardly a secret that Tokyo frankly regarded Germany's action as treachery. Japan was not the sort of totalitarian state which could reorient its public opinion overnight, and Hiranuma was no Mussolini who could quickly adapt himself to the new situation. Japan's press and public figures freely made known their disenchantment with the Nazis, and the German assurances that Berlin would work for an amelioration of Russo-Japanese tensions were cold comfort, as was the rather transparent Italian argument that anything which, like the pact, weakened the democracies represented an advantage to Japan.[10] On 26 August Tokyo announced its intention to pursue an independent foreign policy, 'based on morality and irrespective of the international situation', and to abandon all plans to join the Axis.[11] The Hiranuma cabinet resigned in disgrace on 28 August, compromised by its relations with Germany, and was replaced by a new government under General Abe Noboyuki. He was another moderate, a man who would offend no one, a soldier not identified with any army faction, and clearly a figurehead who would run the country only until Japan had recovered her breath.

For all the claims of its defenders, at the time and since, that the Nazi-Soviet pact was an instrument of peace, it cleared the way for a new partition of Poland and for the outbreak of the Second World War. Nevertheless, in East Asia it had a quite opposite effect, for by isolating Tokyo and throwing Japanese policy into a tailspin, it temporarily removed the threat of conflict which had been hanging like a heavy cloud in the Japanese summer sky. Craigie immediately sought to grasp the opportunity for a settlement, advising the Foreign Office to reopen the talks on Tientsin, and lead them towards a Far Eastern agreement, 'by which we might have to recognize Japanese preponderance in a nominally autonomous North China . . . but by which the economic position in Central China may be saved from further deterioration.' He insisted that the next few days would be critical in either driving Japan into the Axis camp for good, or in turning the situation to Britain's advantage.[12] In

London the Japanese embassy made an exploratory approach, and on 29 August Halifax outlined his own ideas to Craigie. A solution in Tientsin might be followed by informal talks (with American and French partici- pation), on the economic situation in the north, and eventually by Sino- Japanese peace negotiations. Halifax also admitted that any settlement thus reached would probably have to include 'recognition in some form of Japan's special interests at least in North China'.[13] In Washington, Lord Lothian (who had replaced Lindsay as ambassador on 29 August) dis- cussed the proposal with Stanley Hornbeck, who did his best to pour cold water on it, warning that there could be no useful compromise with Japan.[14]

Hornbeck's attitude was indicative of a current of suspicion in both Washington and Chungking that Britain might take advantage of the situation to patch up her quarrels with Japan at China's expense, and Halifax's assurances to the contrary did little to allay this feeling. Chiang professed fear of a revival of the Anglo-Japanese alliance, and wanted Roosevelt's help in blocking it.[15] Certainly Hitler's diplomacy had given the West a magnificent opportunity, and a further inducement for action now lay in the fact that Japan might follow Berlin's advice, and negotiate a non-aggression pact with Russia herself, thus freeing more men for operations in China and perhaps eventually in Southeast Asia. Although the policy of appeasement came to an end in Europe on 3 September, there remained a lingering suspicion that it had not yet run its course in the Far East, and it was to cause concern among China's friends in the next few months.

The coming of war in Europe brought no major reorientation of Brit- ain's policy in the East, but it did bring a change in the relative importance of the problems facing her. Until then her prime concern had been to protect her rights and interests in China, and incidentally to try to mitigate the Japanese demands on that country. But now the questions which had caused so much concern before—the maintenance of Customs integrity, the reopening of the Yangtse, the status of the foreign settlements—were obviously very low on the list of wartime priorities. The major problem had become, and was to remain, that of imperial defence, and the major policy aim was to keep Japan peaceful until a defensive position—hope- fully with American participation—had been built up in the East. Con- nected with this were a number of factors, both political and strategic.

The Japanese occupation of Hainan on 10 February 1939 had brought home clearly the danger of having a potential enemy firmly established on the southwestern coast of China. A year earlier both Paris and London had warned Tokyo against such a step,[16] but when it came nothing was done save for the French decision to reopen the Indochina rail line to arms shipments into Yunnan. The Japanese tried to play down the importance of the move, as they did in March, when they announced their occupation of the Spratly Islands. Nevertheless, a quick glance at the map would suffice to show that from Hainan, Japan was in a position to command the Gulf of Tonking, and to harass Singapore's communications with Hongkong, Hanoi, and Saigon, as well as to stage air and naval attacks against Indochina. And the occupation of the Spratlys, southwest of Manila, and midway between Saigon and British North Borneo, seemed more in keeping with a drive into Southeast Asia than with the needs of the war in China.

Hainan's occupation coincided with a new review of imperial defence by the Chiefs of Staff in London. As they had in 1937, they realized that a fleet would have to be sent East to meet threats to India and Australia, but they spoke only in vague terms of its strength, and a report of 2 May 1939, by the Committee of Imperial Defence, pointed out that Japan had now been demoted as potential enemy to third place behind Germany and Italy.[17] Nor were discussions of fleet movements restricted to military circles. The fact that Singapore was a first class base with no ships was too obvious to be ignored, yet despite press reports of the formation of a large Pacific fleet, over a year after its opening, it remained empty.[18] In November 1938 Sir Josiah Crosby, the minister in Bankgok, had wanted a squadron to visit Singapore to bolster British prestige, and to keep Thailand away from the Japanese orbit. Craigie enthusiastically seconded the motion, and went further by suggesting that the ships be based permanently on Singapore; this would carry some weight in Japan, especially if an American fleet were to go to Hawaii. Clark Kerr, of course, concurred, and the Foreign Office accordingly put the idea up to the Admiralty, in a memorandum of 27 January 1939. Envisaging a squadron of from five to seven capital ships at Singapore, they claimed, rather optimistically, that as long as the Anglo-German Naval Agreement of 1935 were adhered to, Britain would have the necessary margin for operations in the East.[19] The Admiralty killed the plan, by replying that the Royal Navy was too weak to do anything of the sort, although perhaps in three years a single capital ship might be spared. Meanwhile, unless Japan actually struck at Western possessions, British naval strength would have to stay in European waters. And, the Admiralty concluded acidly, the diplomats should realize that foreign policy and naval strength were related, and that 'a reduction in the number of our potential enemies is as definite an accretion to our strength as is an increase in the number of our battleships'.[20]

This then was official British policy: no fleet to Singapore until war broke out. Even then there was a good deal of doubt. In February 1939 London had for the first time said explicitly that if the Commonwealth were to be involved in war simultaneously in Europe and the Pacific, a fleet would be sent to Singapore, but added nothing definite about its timing or composition. Even this could hardly have been meant as a real promise. From London the American ambassador reported that Halifax had told him on 21 March that despite the pledges to Australia, the darkening situation in Europe meant that there was little chance of a fleet going from the Mediterranean to the East. Halifax added the suggestion that at the right psychological moment, America might send her fleet to the Pacific. In May, Commander T. C. Hampton of the Admiralty, on a secret mission to Washington, told the Navy Department that if Britain found herself at war with both Germany and Italy, she might have to keep her fleet in Europe, and control of the Pacific would devolve on America. Apparently the Dominions were kept in the dark on this. At a Pacific Defence Conference in Wellington in April, the British delegation stated that nothing in the Mediterranean could prevent the dispatch of reinforcements to Singapore, and when during the Tientsin crisis Prime Minister Lyons of Australia sought reassurance on this point, Chamberlain told him that the plan was still to send the fleet.[21] In fact, however, the only tangible comfort for Australia and New Zealand lay in Roosevelt's order of 15 April for the American fleet to return to its Pacific bases.

In March British and French staff officers in London had discussed the naval problem, and while they agreed that the security of Singapore was 'the key to the strategical situation' in India and the East, the dispatch of a fleet would seriously weaken the eastern Mediterranean. An Anglo-French conference in Singapore that June made known its serious concern over the weakness of local naval and air forces. At the same time, at French urging, a decision was taken to bring pressure to bear on Thailand, whose premier, Luang Pibul Songgram, was engaged in a flirtation with Japan.[22] The C.I.D. agreed to do what it could to find reinforcements, and in August a number of troops disembarked in Singapore; they were followed by sixteen Blenheim bombers in September. At the same time, however, the Committee decided to raise the period for the relief of Singapore from the seventy days originally held necessary to ninety days, and ordered a study to be made for the stocking of Malaya with reserves for six months. But Singapore remained empty, and when Craigie pleaded for ships during the Tientsin crisis he found sympathy, but nothing else.[23]

One of Britain's friends was willing to send help—only too willing in fact. Chungking was anxious to be included in London's military planning, and at the end of March submitted a four-point programme for 'practical consultation and effective joint action' in the East. This called for a series of military and economic measures against Japan, with China supplying the manpower, and France and Britain the air and naval force. Of course this was far too transparent, and the only question was how to kill the plan tactfully. The French conveniently remembered that the United States would have to be consulted, and the Chinese proposal was accordingly passed to Washington where, as was generally the case with such plans, it died. In May Chiang tried to interest Clark Kerr in a force of 20,000 trained men for the defence of Hongkong, but this was vetoed by the Singapore conference; the War Office dared not compromise British neutrality.[24]

Thus by the time that war came in Europe, British strategic planners realized that the project of moving the main fleet to Singapore was no longer feasible. Not only was the Royal Navy up against a powerful German underseas and surface force in the Atlantic, but as long as Italy maintained her malevolent neutrality, the Mediterranean could not be entrusted to the French alone. A strong fleet had to remain there to answer the demands of the British position in Africa and the Near East, and to give some meaning to the British guarantees of eastern Europe. Thus, far from strengthening her forces on the China Station, Britain actually weakened them, and withdrew a number of warships in September for service in Europe.

In this situation there was no real alternative to trying to keep Japan out of the war, and Britain was going to have to do her best to exploit Tokyo's disillusionment with Hitler, and to try to prevent a rapprochement with the Soviet Union. According to a German report, Shigemitsu told Halifax in early September that the Royal Navy need make no preparations in the Far East, because Japan planned no action there,[25] but if in fact such an assurance were given, it must have done little to calm London's fears. Japan would obviously attempt to profit from the situation by bringing the 'China Incident' to a swift and successful conclusion. The crucial question would be whether or not America would be willing to play an enlarged role in the East, and the success of Britain's efforts to keep Japan from overrunning China while still avoiding war, would depend upon the amount of support she could gain from Washington, and her ability, with France, to keep Germany at bay.

It would be a long time before America actually took the lead in the

Pacific however, and in September 1939 she was giving few indications of any willingness to jump headfirst into those troubled waters. On 5 September the Japanese had sent an *aide mémoire* to the British, French, German, and Polish Governments, declaring their intention not to become involved in the European war, and asking, in a spirit of 'friendly advice', for the 'voluntary' withdrawal of all of the troops and warships of the belligerents from China. Since Germany and Poland had no forces in China, this advice, however friendly, was obviously onesided, and Sawada made it more so by adding to Craigie that it of course meant that no more aid should be given to Chiang.[26] As usual in a situation like this, London looked west to the new world for help, warning that the British garrison in north China would be evacuated unless a clear statement of support in the event of an Anglo-Japanese war were forthcoming. As usual too, the State Department, while trying to talk London (and the French, who made a similar threat) out of such a step, remained unwilling to commit itself to any future policy.[27] Eventually London and Tokyo compromised. By the end of the year eight of the Yangtse gunboats had been withdrawn (Winston Churchill, now at the Admiralty, vociferously denied that Japanese pressure had anything to do with this),[28] and in December the north China garrison was pulled out, while a token force of 175 men was transferred from Shanghai to stay in Tientsin and Peking. Japan hailed this as a 'friendly gesture', while in private Stanley Hornbeck glumly warned Lord Lothian that the United States had no intention of becoming the guardian of British interests in China.[29]

Even the most suspicious could see little of British appeasement here. It is true that Craigie had twice expressed to the Gaimusho his hope that a new solution to Anglo-Japanese problems could be found, and that in Parliament, R. A. Butler had announced that the Government was willing to reopen the Tokyo talks. It is true also that the appointment of Admiral Nomura as Foreign Minister in late September seemed to indicate Japan's desire to mend her fences with the West, although this gesture was directed more towards Washington (where Nomura had once served) than to London.[30] But a number of serious stumbling blocks remained. There was, for instance, the plan to set up a new Central Government at Nanking under Wang Ching-wei; if established, it would mean that the West would be faced with the prospect of having to deal with a much stronger and more viable régime than the present Nanking and Peking puppet governments. Halifax had told Craigie on 1 August that there was to be no question of British recognition of Wang, although two months later Sir Robert seems to have been impressed enough by Wang's chances (and perhaps also by the signs of his relative independence from Tokyo) to recommend that the democracies should not judge him too hastily, and thereby debar themselves from dealing with what might become the Government of China.[31]

Of more immediate importance were the problems raised by the continuation of trade under wartime conditions. No one was prepared for a situation in which Japan was neutral in an Anglo-German war, and consequently the only existing plans envisaged sanctions, reprisals, or full-scale war against Japan as well as Germany. Nor, naturally, had the Nazi-Soviet pact been foreseen, yet here were Japanese shipments of war materials going unmolested, over the Trans-Siberian Railway to Germany.[32] After 3 September it was evident that any measures of economic war against Germany were also bound to affect Japan. Until the end of the year, talks took place in London between the Japanese embassy, the Board of Trade, and the Ministry of Economic Warfare, but they had no tangible result, largely because of American opposition to any concessions.

These trade problems, and the negotiations which accompanied them, have been fully dealt with in W. N. Medlicott's masterful official history of the economic aspects of the war, and here it needs only to be noted that neither Tokyo nor London was willing to push the other into a complete rupture of commercial relations. At the behest of the Foreign Office, trade with Japan continued on a hand-to-mouth basis, with no long term contracts. The Japanese, for their part, had the shadow of the abrogation of their commercial treaty with America hanging over them, and did not want to risk halting the flow of supplies from Commonwealth countries. They held up implementation of a recent trade agreement with Germany, despite the vociferous protests of the Wilhelmstrasse, while Britain pledged herself not to interfere with German exports to Japan, a pledge by which she abided until Chamberlain's announcement of the Reprisals Order of 27 November. Tokyo protested that this order (which was made in retaliation against German mine warfare and which clamped down on German exports) violated the British promise, but in fact it was never fully applied to Germany's shipments to Japan.[33] Thus, although there was no written agreement, the situation was such that Britain was unwilling to apply to Japan the strict letter of the law in exercising her belligerent rights in economic warfare. And Japan, despite public bluster about British violations of international law, was satisfied by the concessions which Britain granted. Trade remained more a potential than an actual cause of friction.

No issue, perhaps, provoked quite as much anxiety in London during the autumn of 1939, as the possibility that after the Nazi-Soviet Pact, a Japanese-Russian agreement might be in the making. Although Japan was clearly unwilling to follow Germany in a quick about-face towards her erstwhile enemy, there were enough signs of a thaw in relations between the two countries to cause Whitehall a considerable amount of apprehension. Abe had no reason to want to see a general war develop out of the fighting on the Manchurian frontier, and neither did Stalin, as he watched the swift advance of the *Wehrmacht* into eastern Europe. An armistice was signed on 16 September, the day before the Red Army's invasion of Poland, and a commission set up to demarcate the frontiers. Meanwhile Constance Smetanin arrived in Tokyo, the first Soviet ambassador to Japan in sixteen months, and presently talks were under way for the conclusion of a new commercial treaty, and a new agreement on the question of disputed fisheries.[34]

Secure for a while in the East, Russia turned her attention to Europe. The Polish partition was followed by a crisis with Finland, which erupted into war on 30 November, threatening Britain with the possibility of hostilities in a new quarter and against a new enemy. Never had she been under such pressure to come to terms with Japan, not just to protect her interests in China, but because there now began to loom before her the awful possibility that while she fought desperately to stave off Germany in the West, the whole of Asia might go up in flames. Lothian tried to get the point across to Sumner Welles on 21 November: if the Japanese struck at the British and French colonies in Southeast Asia, London was not going to be able to spare any troops for their defence, and consequently, although she feared its effect on American opinion, Britain badly wanted an agreement with Tokyo. Welles dismissed the danger, and in early December the State Department tried to cheer up Lothian by pointing out that Tokyo was aware of the threat which a possible Japanese-Soviet agreement posed, and was simply exploiting it. With or without Russia, she was determined to oust the West from the Orient, and appeasement would serve no purpose. Lothian, although clearly unhappy with the reply, could obtain no change of attitude from Washington[35] and a gloomy winter set in—a stalemated war in the West, and the seeds of new conflicts in the East, seeds which would begin to sprout and develop as the spring came.

Chapter XIII

War in Europe, II: The Fall of France, January - July 1940

When winter came in 1939 the war in the West had not yet taken shape. Still unable to tell what the outcome would be, the combatants eyed each other warily, feinting and probing, while the neutral powers—Russia, Italy, America, and Japan—sat by as onlookers, trying to gauge the strength of the antagonists. For them too, it was a period of waiting and watching; except for America, which would have liked nothing better than to be able to retreat into its isolationist shell, none of the neutrals was strongly committed to either side, and each waited only to see which way the wind would blow before it made its move. Germany had overrun Poland in a matter of days, but no one expected the western front to collapse quite so easily, and until either Germany or the Allies seemed to be winning, no one—certainly not Japan—was going to risk offending a potential victor.

Consequently the winter of 1940 in the Far East saw a number of exercises in carefully polite diplomacy; neither Britain nor America nor Japan was willing yet to engage in what has since come to be called brinkmanship. Tokyo remained worried about its ruptured trade treaty with America, and to placate the West even went so far as to hint, in December 1939, that the Yangtse might be reopened to foreign merchantmen, at least as far upstream as Nanking. This was the sort of move, however, which only earned for General Abe a reputation as an appeaser of the West, and in mid-January 1940 his government fell. Although the extremists had helped to bring it down, it was succeeded by another moderate cabinet, this time under Admiral Yonai, a former Naval Minister, with Arita Hachiro back at the Foreign Ministry. Yonai continued the policy of cautious watchfulness which had characterized his predecessor's régime, although for the benefit of the warhawks he did abandon the plan for a reopening of the Yangtse.[1] Then, in January, he had to meet his first severe test.

The outbreak of war had left a number of German reservists and technicians in the Americas with no means of getting home across an Atlantic controlled by the Royal Navy. Some tried to cross the Pacific in Japanese ships, and continue their journey through Siberia, and it was in an attempt to stop this traffic that the British decided to make a test case by holding up the *Asama Maru*, which was carrying some fifty Germans. On 21 January HMS *Liverpool* stopped her about thirty-five miles off Tokyo, and removed twenty-one of her German passengers, allowing the rest to continue.

The incident aroused what Craigie described as the worst anti-British outburst he had yet seen. Undoubtedly it was embarrassing that the interception had taken place so close to Japan. 'The issue is not the twenty-one Germans', complained a naval spokesman, 'but the fact that the affair occurred at Japan's front gate. . . . It is very disagreeable to see British warships prowling along our coasts.'[2] Neither side wanted to push the matter too far, however. Japan protested on 22 January; Britain defended her action; Japan repeated her protest, this time citing the *Trent* case as a precedent. Behind the scenes Craigie and Arita met, and reached a compromise for the release of nine men who were of no special importance, while the rest were kept in custody. A confidential agreement followed whereby Japan thereafter refused passage on Japanese ships to German reservists and technicians homeward bound from the Americas. It was not entirely upheld, Craigie later observed, but nevertheless the return of hundreds of Germans was blocked or delayed.[3]

Grew criticized the British strongly in his Diary,[4] but London had won a diplomatic success. The bargain meant that Britain needed to keep no significant naval force in the Pacific to intercept returning Germans, and more important, the settlement of the case was indicative of the outlook of the new Government in Tokyo. Neither Yonai nor his Foreign Minister wanted to force a British retreat, and instead they had made a peace without victory. The nationalists grumbled, but no serious trouble followed, and the issue was allowed to die down.

Tokyo's unwillingness to blow the incident up may have been partly due to its search for Western backing for the establishment of Wang Ching-wei at the head of a new Central Government of China. The project was meeting with some difficulty; Wang's Cantonese background did him no good in the north, and he was unable to find many statesmen of any standing to join him. Abe's fall also caused a temporary setback, but in January Chu Min-yi, a former Chungking official, called on the British and French ambassadors in Shanghai in a search for support. He explained Wang's policies for a new China, and claimed to have received assurances in return for their willingness to promote peace,[5] although probably nothing more definite than this pious hope was expressed. Yet Japan was willing to go to some lengths to make Wang appear respectable, and as long as she remained under no illusions as to the strength of her move, her attitude to the West remained conciliatory. Wang's installation as head of a new National Government of China, at Nanking on 30 March, was accompanied by promises to recognize the legitimate rights and interests of foreign powers,[6] and Tokyo was not yet ready to force the West to deal directly with the new régime. In Shanghai, Sir Frederick Maze, using his Chief Secretary—a Japanese—as mediator, managed to talk the new Government out of appointing him Inspector-General for Nanking, and thereby forcing the Customs Service to have to choose between free and occupied China.[7]

Probably Whitehall had no intention of recognizing Wang, yet Britain apparently was covering her bets, for when Ambassador Shigemitsu called on R. A. Butler on 21 March, the Under-Secretary was benevolently non-committal on the subject. After listening to an explanation of the Japanese position he replied (according to Shigemitsu) that while Britain could not immediately abandon Chungking, he hoped that the new Government would succeed. He added that that very day he had sent off instructions for a solution of the Tientsin question, as a 'gesture' to express Britain's desire to be of service on the occasion of Wang's inauguration.[8]

This, it must be emphasized, was how Shigemitsu told the story, and he may well have been over-optimistic. However, two days before Wang's inauguration, Craigie had spoken before the Japan-British Society in Tokyo, and rather pointedly avoiding the difficulties in Anglo-Japanese relations, had stressed instead the similarities in outlook between the two island empires, ending on a note of hope.[9] His speech, widely reported, aroused a storm of criticism in both Britain and America, where many took it as evidence that London was preparing to sell out to Japan. The Government was forced to deny that there were any plans to recognize Wang, but Butler admitted to the American chargé that the speech had not received the Foreign Office's *imprimatur* before delivery. Craigie himself professed to be surprised at the stir which he had caused, and wrote to Grew that he had not only told the Gaimusho that Britain would not recognize Wang, but had even told them that in his opinion, Japanese recognition would be a mistake.[10]

In one sphere only was Craigie able to see his wishes for a settlement fulfilled, and that was in the ending of the Tientsin dispute. Talks had continued through the winter, and on 19 June, just after the fall of France, Craigie and Arita had signed the notes which embodied the final agreement. At six o'clock the following evening, a year and a week after their erection, the barriers came down. The terms called for the sale of a tenth of the disputed silver for the benefit of flood and famine relief, while the remainder was to be sealed in the British Concession. Within the Concession, *fapi* and F.R.B. notes would circulate together, and the police agreement of the previous summer would go into effect.[11] China protested, but Craigie was in no position to press for better terms; nor were the French, who immediately concluded a similar agreement.[12] All this, needless to say, caused very little stir in the world at large; the very moderation of the terms when compared with the original Japanese demands was evidence enough that such local disputes had long ceased to be of any great importance. Japan's relations with Britain and the West were now going to be determined by concerns of a global nature.

On these greater issues, there was to be no easy agreement. April saw the Norwegian campaign end swiftly in a German victory, and in May and June Hitler's armies overran the Low Countries, and forced the French to capitulate in the Forest of Compiègne. In Tokyo Axis supporters were jubilant, convinced that a British surrender was imminent, despite the warnings of men like Yonai and Shigemitsu who maintained a healthy respect both for the Royal Navy and for Churchill's qualities as a wartime leader.[13] Furthermore the very suddenness of the French collapse brought Japan face to face with new problems. Before she could benefit from the discomfiture of the Allies by turning south, she would first have to free herself from her China tangle. Moreover she would have to be in a position to deal with Germany if Hitler decided that having conquered the nations of the West, he could assume the title to their empires, and claim Indochina, the East Indies, Malaya, and Burma for his own. With a growing anxiety Japan now looked towards Southeast Asia, and from now on it was this part of the world, rather than China, which became the main theatre for her confrontation with the West. Heretofore, it had only been in China that the Western position was threatened; now, however, the whole Asian colonial empire seemed suddenly to be in jeopardy.

From this point until the attack on Pearl Harbor there followed a series of Japanese moves towards Southeast Asia, and while publicly all sides

pledged themselves to neutrality, to non-aggression, and to the maintenance of the status quo, in private Japan stepped up her pressure against
the Dutch, against the French, and against the British. The British response
took the form sometimes of firmness, sometimes of surrender, together
with a constant effort to increase the degree of American commitment to
the defence of the Far East. The issue was first raised in the Netherlands
East Indies, where on 15 April, even before Holland's involvement in the
war, Arita had warned that Japan would be 'deeply concerned' over any
change in the islands' status. He repeated this to the British, French, and
German ambassadors on 11 May, the day after the invasion of the Low
Countries.[14] Roosevelt managed to prevail upon the Allies to adopt a
conciliatory stance, while the State Department discouraged an Australian
proposal to concentrate ships and troops at Darwin, ready to meet a
Dutch call for help.[15] On 12 May Craigie and Arita exchanged assurances
of their peaceful intentions towards the Indies and Tokyo's fears—which
were largely economic—were temporarily allayed by a Dutch promise
to try to continue the export of normal supplies of raw materials and oil
to Japan.[16]

Now Britain, having agreed to the American request for a hands-off
policy towards the East Indies, wanted America to take up a position of
firmness in the East. Richard Casey, the Australian Minister in Washington
who worked closely with Lothian, would have liked the United States
to announce that no intervention would be allowed, but this implied the
use of force, and Welles quickly vetoed the idea.[17] Churchill, in his first
message to Roosevelt on becoming Prime Minister, offered the use of
Singapore 'to keep the Japanese quiet', but the President was not ready to
undertake the defence of Malaya, and he indicated that the American
fleet was doing quite well enough at Pearl Harbor.[18] America was going
to formulate a Pacific policy in her own good time, and no amount of
British prodding—and there was a good deal in the next few months—
would influence her.

Italy's entry into the war, and the collapse of France on 17 June, meant
that Japan was more anxious than ever to be on the move, and despite
Shigemitsu's assurance to London on the 11th that his country would stay
neutral,[19] it was clear that her weight was now shifting decisively to the
side of the Axis. A threat of intervention was enough to induce the Indochina Government to stop the transport of all cargo to China on 17 June,
to close the frontier on the 20th, and to allow the stationing of a Japanese
inspectorate on French soil.[20] Then it was Britain's turn. On the morning
of 19 June, the British military attaché in Tokyo was summoned to the

office of the Director of Military Intelligence, and treated to a fiery lecture on the proper course for future British policy. Britain's weakness and hostility, he was told, had driven Japan into Germany's arms, and by now an overwhelming majority of the people and of the military were anti-British. The Japanese would earn the disdain of their ancestors if they failed to seize the opportunity presented by a defeated France and an impotent Britain. Nothing, no one, could now stop Japan from taking Indochina, the Netherlands Indies, and Hongkong. Britain must fulfil three conditions: first, she must close the China–Burma frontier; second, she must close the Hongkong frontier; and third, she must pull her troops out of Shanghai. Only instant and decisive compliance could avert war. This was what the Japanese people wanted, and the British embassy should not be fooled by the soothing words of the Foreign Office, which were only those of a weak government.[21]

Craigie, of course, immediately demanded an explanation of this startling *Diktat* from Arita, who replied blandly that the demands 'should not be taken too seriously', and that Japan would continue to conduct her foreign relations through the orthodox channels of the Gaimusho. But, he added, Tokyo was indeed thinking of presenting some of the same points to Britain, although of course, in an entirely different way.[22] Whether the initiative came from the army or the civil government, the episode marked the beginning of a serious drive to force Britain to shut down the Burma Road; with this and the Indochina railway sealed off, only the Soviet Union would remain open for any quantity of supplies for China.

On 22 June a considerable Japanese force landed in south China to take up positions along the frontiers of the New Territories, and on the 24th Vice-Minister Tani called on Craigie to demand the closing of the Hongkong frontier, and a halt in the flow of arms, ammunition, and transport supplies over the Burma Road. He admitted that his demand could not be justified by international law, and that Britain was being asked to commit an unneutral act, but added that this was just a 'friendly communication' on a matter which was hurting the relations of the two countries.[23] The violence which had marked the earlier interview with the military attaché was lacking, but the demands, whether they came from 'extremist' army men, or 'moderate' civilians, were substantially the same. The British were powerless to resist, and they knew it. In London the Chiefs of Staff insisted that war with Japan must be avoided, and the Government, after consulting the Dominions, decided to accede to the demands, unless some clear assurance of American help were forthcoming. Twice this was sought, on 19 June and 25 June, and twice refused; Lothian was given no more than lectures against the illusory gains of a policy of appeasement.[24] It was the Tientsin situation all over again; everyone was encouraging Britain to stand fast, and no one was offering any help.

Now London tried a new approach. On 27 June an *aide-mémoire* was given to the State Department, pointing out that Britain had had to reconsider her entire Eastern policy in the light of the French collapse. For the last year she had sought agreement with the Japanese on minor issues, while resisting the general plans for the New Order, when they harmed either the integrity of China or Western interests. Now, however, she faced Germany alone, and while she knew that if she yielded to Tokyo, other demands would follow, she could not resist if it meant war. Therefore two courses were open. The first would be an increase in American pressure on Japan, either by a 'full embargo' or by sending ships to Singapore, 'in full realization that if these steps do not suffice to stop aggression, it may result in war with Japan'. The alternative was to 'wean' Japan from aggression by an offer to negotiate a settlement in the Far East.

London was confident that the first course would work, and was willing to take the necessary steps. However, should America refuse, Craigie had suggested that the time might now be ripe for an Anglo-American effort to bring an end to the 'China Incident' on the basis of a restoration of China's 'independence and integrity'. America and Britain would co-operate to give Japan financial and economic aid, both now and after the war. In return Japan would give a formal undertaking of neutrality in Europe, and would respect Dutch, French, and British possessions in the Pacific so long as their present status were preserved. The question of settlements and concessions in China would be left in abeyance until the fighting was over both in Europe and the Far East.

Without the British correspondence it is difficult to know exactly what lay behind this. Presumably the approach was based largely on the opinions of Craigie, who was then arguing against any attempt to try to involve America in an eastern war for the benefit of Britain, on the grounds that this would divert American aid and attention from Europe, and thus do more harm than good. Apparently in line with this reasoning the British *aide-mémoire* maintained that the military clique was gaining in strength in Tokyo, and unless a 'concrete alternative' to aggression were offered, the army would triumph, overthrow the Yonai cabinet, and set up a government more determined to exploit Allied misfortunes.[25] But was it at all realistic to suppose that Japan, after three years of fighting, would agree to a peace granting China terms which would satisfy the

United States? Such proposals could hardly attract Tokyo at a moment when an Axis victory seemed to be just a matter of time, and one may wonder whether Craigie's original terms were quite so innocuous as those that found their way to the State Department.

Was this really the agonizing reappraisal of policy which it purported to be? More likely it was an ultimatum to the United States, either to support a strong British stand, not only on the issue of the Burma Road, but throughout Southeast Asia, or to help reach a settlement which would at least temporarily appease Japan and keep trouble away from the East. In any case, Hull refused to be drawn, replying that no ships could be sent to Singapore, and that after the collapse of France there was not much hope of a peace settlement in China. If Britain and Australia wanted to try to work something out, let them go ahead, but he warned that in the first place the New Order 'would need negativing or at least serious modifying', and that in the second place America could countenance no peace made at the expense of China, or of the principles which the Secretary had set forth in his statement of 16 July 1937.[26]

How far would Britain have been willing to go to buy off Japan? The answer to this must remain a mystery, although Lothian certainly stated an extreme view when on 1 July he made the surprising suggestion to Sumner Welles that Indochina (whose government had just opted for Vichy) might be a sufficient reward to keep Japan from striking at the British or Dutch colonies.[27] In any case, despite America's non-committal stand, Britain was not ready to capitulate completely. Craigie had been instructed to play for time, and though he was convinced that war would follow a refusal of Tokyo's demands, he saw Arita on 8 July to try to whittle down the Japanese terms. The Foreign Minister as usual pleaded that he was under pressure from the extremists, and asked for a quick reply. When Craigie mentioned the possibility of a peaceful end to the 'China Incident', Arita agreed that Chiang might be persuaded to enter into secret talks, but that any final settlement would have to be fully in accord with the Konoye statement of 3 November 1938.[28] Someone in Whitehall must have had a moment of wry amusement in seeing Britain faced with the problem of reconciling the two high declarations of principle of Cordell Hull and Prince Konoye, both of which now seemed to be hoary with tradition, and neither of which could be in the least compromised.

On the lesser question of the Burma Road, however, Arita was ready to compromise, and on 18 July Prime Minister Churchill announced to Parliament that an agreement had been reached. Both the China-Burma border and the Hongkong frontier would be closed to the transit of arms, ammunition, gasoline, trucks, and railway materials, but, he added, the closure was to last only for three months, during which time there was to be a search for 'a solution just and equitable to both parties to the dispute and freely accepted by them both'.[29]

Just how the closure of the Road was to contribute to a settlement of the war was never made clear, but the Japanese undertaking to seek peace was more than a face-saving device for Britain, for it gave her a reason (which she used three months later) to terminate the agreement and reopen the Road when no progress to peace had been made. But at the time it sounded ominous, especially when coupled with a statement on 15 July by the Acting Governor of the Straits Settlement that Britain was doing all she could to end the war and bring about an honourable peace.[30] Chiang, sensing the worst, said that linking the closure of the Road with the question of peace 'would practically amount to assisting Japan to bring China to submission', and Chungking condemned the closure as 'unfriendly and unlawful', contrary to international law, Sino-British treaties, and the League's resolutions.[31] In Washington Cordell Hull, despite an appeal by Lothian for support, told the press on 16 July that the United States had a 'legitimate interest in the keeping open of arteries of commerce in every part of the world', and observed that the Road's closure would 'constitute an unwarranted obstacle to world trade'. *The Times* observed politely that this seemed to be aimed more at Tokyo than at London, a point of view confirmed by Hull to Lothian.[32] If true, it was unconvincing, and in Britain Hull's statement was once more taken as proof that the Government had acted unilaterally without consulting the United States.

Did Britain really expect anything to come of the three months' search for peace? On 14 July Craigie had wired London his views of a general Eastern settlement, stressing that what Japan really wanted was not so much territorial gains as access to the products and markets of South-east Asia.[33] In retrospect this sounded too hopeful. A year earlier, she might have been more interested in economic than territorial concessions, but it is doubtful if this was still true in the summer of 1941. Whatever hope London may have had of a settlement, the move to close the Road was primarily a calculated risk, a play for time at a moment when Britain found herself fighting Germany and Italy alone, and when America had yet to pass the Lend-Lease Act, or to supply the Royal Navy with destroyers for the Battle of the Atlantic. How much the move hurt China materially is a matter for conjecture: Craigie pointed out that the closure took place during the rainy season in southwest China, when traffic was in any case reduced to a tenth of its normal figure.[34] Yet the moral effect was unfortunate, and Churchill's critics in the press and in Parliament cannot be blamed too much for seeing in the agreement a repetition of those steps which in their view had brought their country to war in Europe.

Chapter XIV

War comes to the East:
July 1940 – December 1941

With the fall of France and the opening of the Battle of Britain, London finally abandoned its role as chief spokesman of the Western powers in the Orient. Now, at last, it was the United States which took the lead in dealing with Japan; gradually, and then decisively, she stepped forward, and by 1941 the final negotiations preceding the Pacific war were carried on with little reference to Britain. The story of the eighteen months from the Burma Road agreement until Pearl Harbor belongs chiefly to the history of American foreign policy. Britain moved on the outside, offering advice, furnishing intelligence, seeking aid, but never in a position to make policy. She continued to try for a firm American commitment in the East, fearing above all, as Churchill has written, that Japan might strike only at British and Dutch possessions, while the United States, hampered by constitutional restrictions, would not declare war. In 1914 she had stood on the periphery of Europe, unable to give France a certain promise of help if Germany marched, but now it was she who sought the promise, and despite a series of Anglo-American staff talks, both in Washington and the East, there was never a definite undertaking by the United States to come to the aid of Malaya, Burma, or the East Indies.[1]

The fall of France, the threat of invasion at home, and the danger to the British position in the Middle East had stifled whatever hope there once had been of sending an adequate force to Singapore. The Commander-in-Chief, China, sought an agreement whereby French naval units would operate with the British, but Indochina and its military forces, after some hesitation, chose to follow Vichy.[2] In the autumn of 1940 there were staff conversations with the Dutch for the cooperation of the small but well trained units of the Royal Netherlands Navy in the East Indies, and these continued through 1941.[3] And some progress was made in the vital question of coordination with America. In January 1941 Anglo-American staff talks in Washington produced the agreement known as ABC-1, which made Germany's defeat the primary objective of wartime strategy. If war came, America would concentrate her ships in the Atlantic in order to allow the British to send their own to the Far East.[4] Then, however, a conference from 22 to 26 April 1941 between British, Dutch, and Americans in Singapore failed to reach an Eastern war plan satisfactory to Washington, and little had been accomplished here by 7 December.[5]

During the Washington and Singapore talks a basic strategic division had arisen between British and American planners on the importance of Singapore and on the cost to be paid for its defence. To the British it was the keystone of their position in the East, and they wanted American ships stationed there as a deterrent, a step which the United States resolutely opposed.[6] Not until late 1941 was there a definite plan adopted for the dispatch of any British capital ships, and after some disagreement between Churchill and the Admiralty on the composition of the Eastern Fleet, the plans were passed by the Defence Committee. On 25 October 1941 Admiral Sir Tom Phillips broke his flag aboard HMS *Prince of Wales* and on 2 December that ship, with HMS *Repulse*, arrived in Singapore.[7] The carrier *Indomitable* which was to have accompanied them, had earlier run aground at Jamaica, thus leaving the two ships without air support when the attack came which sank them a few days later. And slowly—too slowly—the Malayan air and ground forces were being augmented, while in Hongkong two Canadian battalions arrived to strengthen that Colony's slim forces.[8]

By now the problem of Western interests in China had become an issue of secondary importance. Vital as the question of the status of the International Settlement may have seemed to its British and American inhabitants, neither the Foreign Office nor the State Department had much time to devote to Shanghai, and the officials of the S.M.C. found themselves trying to hold their ground alone, with little diplomatic support from abroad. Terrorism remained a major factor, particularly in the western extra-Settlement roads, where on 6 January 1940 an attempt was made on the life of G. Godfrey Phillips, the British Commissioner-General of the Council.[9] The Council did manage to hammer out two agreements with the puppet municipal government in February and March 1940, for the policing of the western roads, and the northern and eastern areas of the Settlement, which were still under Japanese control. Yet neither of these was implemented for the time being,[10] and the assassination of the puppet Mayor Fu Siao-en on 11 October did nothing to help the situation, although in the following February his successor did agree to the creation of a special police force for the western roads.[11]

A crisis came and was passed in April 1940, with the elections for the Municipal Council, when for the first time the Japanese seriously challenged the unwritten agreement on the Council's foreign membership, and offered five candidates, three more than usual. Had they won, they would have been in almost complete control of the Settlement's machinery, and a determined drive was launched to bring out the Western vote, accompanied by the splitting of large properties to increase the number of those enfranchised. It was a desperate measure, but it worked; the Anglo-American community turned out *en masse*, and in the largest poll ever recorded managed to keep the Council's balance of nationalities the same, returning five Britishers.[12]

If there were some victories, however, there were also some retreats. The French, while letting it be known that they would forcibly resist any attempt to seize their Concession after the surrender of Paris did allow Nanking to take control of the two Chinese courts in their territory, on 7 November 1940.[13] The two British battalions left Shanghai at the end of August 1940, and Japanese troops moved into 'D' Sector in the western roads. 'B' Sector, which had also been held by the British, included an important part of downtown Shanghai, and presented a more difficult problem, since the Japanese wanted it and the Americans objected; finally it was taken over by the Shanghai Volunteer Force, while the contending sides held inconclusive talks on its future.[14]

On 22 January 1941, at a special meeting of the Settlement's ratepayers, the Chairman of the Japanese Ratepayers' Association (who had just seen his motion voted down) advanced to the speaker's platform, and shot and wounded W. J. Keswick, the Council Chairman.[15] There was a prompt apology, but the incident was indicative of the tension caused by the Japanese conviction that they were inadequately represented in the Settlement's Government. Two Council members, one British and one Japanese, thereupon began a series of private conversations, and by mid-February they had evolved a plan to suspend the land regulations, and to replace the S.M.C. by a commission, to last for two years, while a new constitution was drawn up. After long discussions, the ratepayers accepted the idea in April, and while Chungking refused to countenance the arrangements, the Provisional Council took office.[16] With this problem out of the way, the Settlement continued its uneasy existence until the outbreak of war. One more important concession was made to Japan, when Sir Frederick Maze was forced to appoint a Japanese as Customs

Commissioner for Shanghai in November; but Pearl Harbor was then less than a month away, and after 7 December, Maze himself was removed from his post and interned.[17]

Britain's agreement to close the Burma Road had been a move made from weakness, and it represented the low point of her Eastern policy. A good deal happened in the three months following Churchill's announcement in Parliament, and by October, the British position was beginning to improve. The Battle of Britain was being won, and the immediate threat of an invasion had passed. Nor had the Japanese done much, in keeping their part of the bargain, to demonstrate a desire for peace. On 16 July Prince Konoye had once again become Prime Minister, replacing Yonai, and bringing in Matsuoka Yosuke to the Gaimusho. The new Government increased the Japanese demands on Indochina, and in two agreements of 30 August and 22 September, Japan extracted permission to station troops in the north of the colony, allowing its use as a base for operations against Yunnan. On 27 September Tokyo had at last joined the Axis in the long delayed Triple Alliance, which now seemed to be directed less against the Soviet Union than against the United States, in an effort to frighten Washington into neutrality. Thus, when in mid-September Craigie asked Matsuoka what positive steps to peace had been made, the Foreign Minister could only reply that his country was doing her best to reach a settlement through the Government of Wang Ching-wei.[18] Consequently on 4 October the Cabinet agreed to reopen the Road when the three months' period had expired two weeks later. Craigie informed Matsuoka of the decision on the 8th, and on the following day (8 October in London) an announcement was made in Parliament.[19]

A new conflict now began to develop, diverting Western attention from the problems of Burma and China. Although France and Japan had temporarily solved their difficulties in Indochina, Thailand now took advantage of Vichy's weakness to press her claims to territory along the Mekong. These manifestations of Thai irredentism seemed at the time to be inspired by Tokyo, and Britain at first so far forgot her enmity towards Vichy as to urge both Tokyo and Bangkok to ease their pressure on the French.[20] Then however her policy changed, and this led to a split with the United States. Sir Josiah Crosby, the minister in Bangkok, was deeply worried by Thailand's gravitation towards Japan, and afraid that if the Thais could not make good their claims themselves, the Japanese would do it for them, thereby increasing Tokyo's influence in that part of the world. Accordingly he wanted the French to yield on the question of the frontier, a recommendation strenuously opposed by the American minister, Hugh

Grant, and (somewhat less strenuously) by the State Department.[21] From London's point of view, Thailand was chiefly important as a staging area for strikes against Malaya, Singapore, and Burma, and if the disputed territory were the price necessary to prevent Japan's entry into the country, it could be paid without too great a violation of principles—and, it might be added, at the expense of a country which was no longer an ally. Thus, although in public both Crosby and London took a line in favour of the maintenance of the *status quo*, it was obvious that they did not plan seriously to oppose Bangkok's claims.[22]

Japan at first declared her neutrality and later decided to extend a limited assistance to Thailand.[23] In January 1941 fighting broke out between French and Thai forces, and on the 21st the Japanese offered to mediate, determined to prevent a settlement for which Crosby and the British would get the credit, and suspecting that the French and British were conniving behind their backs. An armistice was signed aboard a Japanese cruiser in Saigon on 30 January, and the cessation of hostilities enforced by an influx of Japanese troops into northern Indochina. Negotiations continued for another five weeks until Vichy, under pressure both from Tokyo and Berlin, yielded, and in an agreement of 11 March gave Thailand about a third of Cambodia, as well as parts of Laos on the west bank of the Melong.[24]

There is considerable mystery surrounding Crosby's activities in this affair. From the point of view of the American minister, his policy represented appeasement pure and simple, in the worst sense of the word, a desperate effort to buy off Thailand in order to keep her from becoming a Japanese satellite, and Grant's point of view was one which of course the Indochina authorities shared. And certainly Britain made no secret of her fears for Thailand, or of her willingness to pay a price to prevent Bangkok's loss.[25] Yet the picture that emerges from this, of Britain and Japan both courting Thailand by promising chunks of French territory to Prime Minister Luang Pibul Songgram, may not be entirely accurate; on 26 February 1941 Matsuoka treated Grew to a long diatribe against Crosby's intrigues, accusing the British of inciting the Thais to unreasonable demands, and asking Grew to try to have London publicly urge moderation on Bangkok.[26] Whatever Crosby was up to, he had by now managed to convince French, Americans, and Japanese that he was the guiding spirit behind Luang Pibul's demands, and yet in the end the only result was a significant increase in Japanese influence in that country.[27] Nor did the Anglo-American disagreements over a Thai policy end with the settlement of the territorial dispute; the British made it clear that they would keep trying to buy Thailand off as long as there seemed a chance to do so. London also wanted to keep Thai tin and rubber out of Japanese hands, particularly since at this point the tin was still being shipped through the Soviet Union to Germany. Economic strategy eventually provided a common ground for Anglo-American action; in June the Americans decided to try to buy all the Thai tin and rubber they could, and for the rest of the year the British and Americans on the one hand, and the Japanese on the other, engaged in a tug of war to win both Thailand's favour and her raw materials.[28] The whole subject deserves adequate treatment by itself, as a case study in the ability of a small and weak country to play off two powerful rivals against one another.

Japan's successful intervention in the Franco-Thai dispute did much to increase British fears of an impending move to the south, and helped give rise to a serious war scare in February 1941. In an interview with R. A. Butler on 1 February Shigemitsu had protested that Japan would never allow Germany to dictate her policy, but the British remained deeply concerned at reports from the Far East that Tokyo was planning to penetrate still more deeply into Indochina and possibly into Thailand as well. On 3 February the American naval attaché in London reported Britain's fears to Washington, and London itself warned of a coming strike at Singapore and the Netherlands East Indies.[29] Eden called in Shigemitsu on the 7th to read him a long and severe criticism of Japan's behaviour in the Franco-Thai fracas, adding that Craigie had recently warned of a crisis impending within the next two or three weeks. He insisted that the worried ambassador transmit the message in full to his chief, but Matsuoka, when he received it, dismissed Craigie's ideas as a 'ridiculous fantasy', and the Gaimusho tried to calm Sir Robert's fears.[30] Harry Hopkins, who was then in London, seemed to hold out some hope of strong American support, and Eden, encouraged by this, wired Lord Halifax (who had succeeded as ambassador in Washington after Lothian's death in December) to press the United States for a statement. Halifax would have liked a joint Anglo-American declaration pledging war in the event of an attack on British or Dutch possessions, and while he did not go as far as that, Roosevelt did give the newly arrived Ambassador Nomura a sharp warning on 14 February. In Tokyo Eugene Dooman went further, and told Vice-Minister Ohashi that an attack on British territory would be likely to bring America into the war.[31]

Craigie saw Matsuoka again on the 15th, and the Foreign Minister disavowed any ideas of aggression. He also denied that Japan sought any compensation for her mediation in Indochina; the greatest reward, he remarked piously, would be the restoration of peace. The tension was somewhat eased, and Craigie appeared more convinced by Matsuoka's protestations.[32] On the 17th Shigemitsu handed the Foreign Office a personal message from Matsuoka, denying that there was any cause for alarm in the Far East, defending the Triple Alliance as a move to limit the European war, and justifying Japan's intervention in the Franco-Thai dispute on the grounds that she was prepared to do whatever was necessary to restore normal conditions 'not only in Greater East Asia, but anywhere the world over'.[33]

With this, the February war scare subsided, and now the British seemed even more willing than America to accept Tokyo's professions of peace.[34] What lay behind the curious episode? At the time the Germans were in fact discussing plans for an attack on Singapore,[35] but Tokyo was by no means ready to allow Hitler to dictate its policy. Perhaps, as has been suggested, the British seized on the Japanese moves in Indochina and Thailand to manufacture a crisis in an effort to get Washington to issue a warning to Japan, or to send ships to Singapore.[36] If this is true they were partly successful—Dooman's careful statement to Ohashi was the closest America had come to guaranteeing support for Britain—and to encourage Washington, Churchill told Roosevelt that the Japanese retreat had been caused largely by American firmness.[37] Certainly almost all the warnings of imminent Japanese action came through London, and if the British did not manufacture the crisis, it was they who pointed to its existence.[38]

Churchill, when he wrote the President on 20 February, also suggested that the recent announcement of Matsuoka's forthcoming trip to Europe might be intended as a cover for the failure to take action against Britain. The Foreign Minister's trip did inspire some nervousness in London, and Craigie had tried to talk him out of it, but what Britain really feared was not so much Matsuoka's talks with the Nazis as the possibility of a Japanese pact with the Soviet Union. Both Craigie and Sir Stafford Cripps, then the ambassador in Moscow, were very much concerned with this,[39] and, as it turned out, they had every reason to be. Matsuoka's trip to Germany took him through Moscow, where he had an inconclusive meeting with Stalin on 24 March. He did not see Cripps, who was not on speaking terms with the Japanese embassy at the time, and unable therefore to arrange an interview, but he did assure the American ambassador that Japan had no intention of attacking Allied possessions. In Berlin Matsuoka held a series of secret conversations with the Germans, and succeeded in avoiding the commitment to attack Singapore which Hitler and Ribbentrop sought from him. He also listened carefully to the German emphasis on the fluidity of relations with the Soviet Union, and the warning to be ready for 'any eventuality'.[40]

On 7 April Matsuoka was back in Moscow, where he found a letter from Churchill asking eight questions on Japan's relationship to the European war. They were so worded as to be an outright challenge to the Japanese link to the Axis, and a statement that Japan's best interests would be served by turning toward the democracies.[41] More important, he found Stalin in a changed mood, and although he was unable to win the dictator over to the idea of a non-aggression pact, on 13 April the two agreed on a pact of neutrality. That evening, Stalin quite unexpectedly appeared at the railway station to bid his new-found friend farewell.[42] The two men embraced; it was, said the *Manchester Guardian* on 30 April, the 'most touching [scene] since the Walrus and the Carpenter wept like anything before they ate the oysters'. Again Russia had managed to maintain her neutrality in an imperialist war, and as Germany had been set free to strike in Europe by the Nazi-Soviet Pact, now Japan was set free to move towards the south.

Meanwhile, Nomura's arrival in Washington as ambassador initiated a new series of Japanese-American negotiations which were to continue until Pearl Harbor. They have been fully treated elsewhere, and need not be described here. They were conducted by the United States, and Britain was hardly consulted on them until much later in the year. Gone was any remnant of the old idea of parallel action; Cordell Hull, in fact, was indignant at a suggestion made in late May that his talks were causing some concern in London, apparently seeing this as a reflection upon his good faith and diplomatic sagacity, and it took a conciliatory message from Eden to appease him. After another attempt to find out what was happening, Halifax could only report that 'matters looked hopful'. 'I left it at that', he wrote home, 'rather than try to pull out unwilling teeth'.[43]

The talks continued into the summer, and were one of the causes of Matsuoka's ouster on 16 July, and of the re-formation of the Konoye cabinet with Admiral Toyoda as Foreign Minister: a man not hampered by the sort of antipathy to the Allied cause that Matsuoka had shown. On 24 July, after an agreement with Vichy, a Japanese force landed in southern Indochina. The move came as no surprise to the British and Americans, who by now were able to read certain of the Japanese diplomatic communications, and who had in any case been warned by Admiral Darlan in Vichy on the 16th.[44] On the 25th the two countries froze Japanese funds and made all trade subject to official permits. The Netherlands Indies followed suit on the 28th and at the same time the talks between Tokyo and Washington were temporarily broken off.

Here was the first example since Lukouchiao of concerted strong measures against Japan; the next would be the declaration of war. The freezing orders were the final moves in a series of economic sanctions which had gradually been imposed by both Britain and America through 1940 and 1941, and they resulted in an almost complete cessation of trade with Japan. Tokyo was now caught between having to capitulate to America's demands or resisting, and if she decided to resist, she would have to overrun the rich oil and rubber producing lands of Southeast Asia before the exhaustion of her own stockpiles. The Western moves did not dictate to Tokyo what decision to make, but they did force Japan into making a decision, and from now on events moved rapidly towards Pearl Harbor. Eden, among others, realized that sanctions would force a choice on Japan, but did nothing to restrain Washington, conscious once again, as he wrote, of 'the risk of creating another Simon-Stimson incident'.[45]

In any case Eden was by now becoming more convinced that America could not stand by in an Anglo-Japanese war. Nevertheless, his Government still sought from Washington a commitment stronger than any they had received in the past. In early August, shortly after the issuance of the freezing orders, Roosevelt and Churchill met aboard HMS *Prince of Wales* at Argentia. Cadogan and Welles, who had accompanied the two leaders, met on the 9th to discuss the problem of an American guarantee of British and Dutch possessions, and Cadogan pointed to the fact that Churchill had reluctantly promised to support the Dutch and now wanted a similar American commitment. Churchill drafted a warning to Japan, threatening war in case of further aggression, and pressed Roosevelt to issue it, and the President, although he wanted to continue the talks with Nomura, agreed.[46] It would have been the strongest of its kind, and the Prime Minister, in a letter to Attlee, said that he had laid special stress on this. 'One would always fear the State Department trying to tone it down— but the President has promised definitely to use the hard language'.[47] His fears were well founded; Hull felt that the warning was too harsh, and had his way. When Roosevelt saw Nomura on 17 August he read him a watered down version, and at the same time proposed a reopening of the talks.[48] Disappointed, Churchill and the Dutch never made their own statements, although the Prime Minister on his return broadcast a speech which referred to the Washington talks, expressing the earnest hope that they would succeed. 'But this I must say', he continued, 'that if these hopes should fail we shall, of course, range ourselves unhesitatingly at the side of the United States.'[49]

The negotiations were begun again, briefly touching on the possibility of a meeting between Konoye and Roosevelt. Washington refused a set of Japanese proposals on 2 October, and two weeks later Konoye resigned, to be replaced by General Tojo Hideki. On 29 and 30 October Foreign Minister Togo Shigenori warned Craigie that the Americans were moving too slowly, and made an indirect request for British intervention. On 5 November, an Imperial Conference approved a plan to make one last attempt for a settlement with Washington, and to fight if it failed.[50] Presumably Togo had hoped that Britain would prevail upon Washington to moderate its stand, but this was a miscalculation of Churchill's attitude. Both publicly and privately he was urging a strong position.[51] His confidence by now was increased by the fact that the Eastern Fleet was at last on its way to Singapore, and in early November in answer to an appeal from Chiang Kai-shek, he suggested to Roosevelt a joint warning against an attack on Yunnan, which might cut the Burma Road. Roosevelt refused.[52] However, on 20 November, when the Japanese made their final offer, Churchill suggested that it might be well to ease the economic restrictions to permit Japan to live from hand to mouth for a little while longer. 'I must say', he wrote, 'I should feel relieved if I read that an America-Japanese agreement had been made by which we were to be no worse off three months hence in the Far East than we are now.'[53] Washington suggested a *modus vivendi* with the Japanese, which would grant them somewhat more generous terms, and on 24 November informed the British, Dutch and Chinese of its terms. The next day Churchill replied that it would seem to provide a 'very thin diet' for Chiang Kai-shek, and this, together with the strong Chinese opposition, led Hull to reject the plan.[54] Thus, when Nomura and Kurusu Saburo, who had joined him as a special representative for the negotiations, met Hull on 26 November, they were presented not with the *modus vivendi*, but with a new proposal for a comprehensive settlement. Under its terms, Japan would join in a multilateral non-aggression pact among Pacific powers, would recognize the territorial integrity of Indochina, would withdraw her forces both from that country and from China, would support no Chinese régime other than that of the legitimate Central Government, and would surrender her extraterritorial rights in China. Furthermore, she would undertake to interpret the Tripartite Pact of September 1940 in such a way as not to interfere with this settlement. In return for this, she would get a new commercial agreement with America and be granted other economic concessions. Hull made it clear that the terms would not be modified, and that unless they were accepted, the trade restrictions would continue unchanged.[55]

To have accepted this would have meant abandoning most of what Japan had fought for since 1937. Now she could only choose war or full retreat, and on 6 December Togo sent the Japanese refusal to Washington, so scheduling it as to be presented by Nomura twenty minutes before the attack on Pearl Harbor. However, for a while it looked as if Churchill's fears of a strike directed only against British possessions might be realized, for on 6 December (Malayan time) patrol aircraft from Singapore spotted two convoys of troopships under escort steaming towards the Kra Isthmus, the narrow neck of land joining Thailand to Malaya.[56] Meanwhile Roosevelt had decided to make a final appeal to the Japanese emperor, and on 8 December, at fifteen minutes after midnight, Ambassador Grew sought an appointment to deliver his message. Just a few minutes earlier a party of Japanese soldiers crossed into the International Settlement in Shanghai, occupying the Bund. At one forty Kota Bharu was shelled, and shortly afterwards the first troops came ashore in Malaya. At three-twenty carrier aircraft swept over Pearl Harbor, and three hours later the air raid alarms sounded in Singapore.

Chapter XV

Conclusion

A century after her warships had forced the opening of the first treaty ports, at the end of the Opium War, Britain found herself in full retreat from China. She had come to that country for purely commercial reasons; the British ships which nosed their way into Canton, Ningpo, and the other ports of the south and central coast, came only to tap the vast markets of the Middle Kingdom, and if it was an imperialist spirit that drove them, it was the spirit of what has recently been called 'the imperialism of free trade'. By the late nineteenth century, Britain's was the dominant foreign voice at the court of the Manchu Emperor, but she never directly controlled, or sought control of, more than a tiny fraction of China's huge bulk: Hongkong, Weihaiwei, and some concessions in the treaty ports. When J. H. Hobson wrote his *Imperialism: A Study* in 1902, he had feared a coming partition of China—China cut up like a melon, K'ang Yu-wei had said—as Africa had been partitioned in the closing years of the nineteenth century. He was a bad prophet; the year which saw his book appear also saw the signing of the Anglo-Japanese alliance, by which Britain in effect relinquished her position of primacy at Peking, and took the first step in her long withdrawal from Asia. The alliance has long been recognized as the ending of Britain's period of splendid isolation, but it meant something far more important than a minor diplomatic revolution. For four centuries, Europe had been expanding throughout the world, but if one seeks a date from which to begin Europe's contraction, the day on which Lord Lansdowne and Baron Hayashi set their signatures to the alliance will serve the pupose. On 30 January 1902 the new order in East Asia had dawned, and unconsciously, the greatest imperial power in the world was the first to ratify it.

She signed the alliance largely for strategic reasons, as indeed she had gone into Africa largely for strategic reasons. What made Britain an imperial nation, Curzon had said, was her possession of India, and the security of the routes to India was her paramount interest. She had to concentrate her forces in those parts of the world from which the threats to India were most likely to come, and that meant the eastern Mediterranean, the Middle East and Central Asia, rather than the western Pacific, where the Japanese could be trusted to police the seas after the withdrawal of the Royal Navy. Not until after 1918 was the threat from this direction apparent, and then the recognition of the change led to the construction of the Singapore naval base, when for the first time a defensive position was erected east of India. This act did more to end the ties between Britain and Japan than did the formal conversion of the alliance into the Four Power Pact of Washington in 1921. With Singapore as the main line of defence, the anomaly of Britain's Chinese interests—including Hongkong—in the imperial scheme of things grew more evident, and they became simply hostages to an Asia which was beginning to claim its own. In the 1920s the new forces of the aroused continent were seen in Chinese nationalism acting through the Kuomintang and the Communists; in the thirties Japanese imperialism came to the fore, and remained dominant until 1945.

Slowly, sometimes blindly and often reluctantly, Britain realized that she had to come to terms with the implications of Asia's rebirth, with revolutionary nationalism like that of Gandhi, Nehru, and Chiang Kaishek, and this involved a fundamental change in outlook, a realization that the days of Napier and Curzon were gone, and the days of empire numbered. It is a tribute to Lord Halifax that he was able to see this when he was Viceroy in New Delhi, that he could make the change and dismiss the attacks of the imperialists who were emotionally unready to see 'a seditious Middle Temple lawyer ... striding half-naked up the steps of the Vice-regal palace ... to parley on equal terms with the representative of the King-Emperor'.[1] But the heirs of the Meiji revolution seemed to present a different problem, for their vision of a new order postulated an East Asia under the leadership of Japan. Their programme was frankly imperialistic, a manifestation of power which perhaps power alone could oppose. In so far as power was the answer to Japanese expansion, there was no need here of an emotional change, a conversion of heart, as there had been when dealing with the All-India Congress or the Kuomintang; all that was needed was the old Tory rallying cry of the Empire in danger. But who would respond to such a cry in the thirties? Not the pacific members of Chamberlain's government, with their Little England outlook, trying desperately to avoid war on all fronts, and not the leaders of the Left, embarrassed as they were both by the existence of empire and the need of force to defend it.

In any case, events in the Far East were of secondary importance throughout this period. The imperial idea was dying, and apart from the Anglo-Indians, Britain had few Asia-firsters to turn her attentions away from Europe. Furthermore, it was of course from Europe that the greatest immediate threat came. What could Britain do but try to separate her Eastern problems from her European ones and, after 1939, try to keep the European war from speading to the East?

Was such a course possible? Craigie, it appears, remained convinced to the end that it was, or at least that the war could have been postponed, and to him the final American proposals, amounting virtually to an ultimatum, were simply a spur to drive Japan to war. He felt that the Japanese points of 20 November at least provided a basis for negotiation, and he repeated this in his final dispatch on 4 February 1943, but at neither time did the Foreign Office agree.[2] Churchill has made no secret of his desire to have America as an ally, and of the relief which he felt, even knowing as he did of the dreadful unpreparedness of Singapore, when the news of Pearl Harbor broke.[3] Yet what if Craigie's advice had been taken, and a temporary agreement with Japan patched up? She would have remained in China, and the West would have had to face the problem of coexisting with this situation. To assume that the Allies, victorious over Italy and Germany, could later have dictated their own terms to Japan, is to beg the question by introducing so many variables as to be unrealistic.

The business of the policy maker in an imperfect world is not to perfect it, but sometimes simply to try to prevent the intolerable from arising, the situation with which no coexistence is possible. To define the limits of the tolerable after they have been reached, or passed, is a dangerous course, suitable only to a nation strong enough to dictate her will to an adversary, or to a nation *in extremis*, taking a stand on principle before the inevitable collision occurs. Yet this is precisely what the West did in these years. The American note of 26 November 1941, which called for an evacuation of China and a denial of Japanese support to any government other than that of Chiang, presumably defined the limits of what the United States considered tolerable, and this, Churchill has said, was quite in accord with Britain's outlook.[4] Yet these were limits which Japan could not have then accepted, for to agree to them would have been to cast aside the fruits of four years of fighting.

When had the limits of the tolerable been reached? Perhaps in 1931–32 with the seizure of Manchuria. Yet this alone did not make inevitable a future conflict between Japan and China, or between Japan and the West. The world had silently acquiesced in the establishment of Manchukuo, taking refuge in the doctrine of non-recognition, and while it was a severe blow to Chinese nationalism, it was a blow which China might have weathered, as she had already weathered the loss of Outer Mongolia to the Soviet orbit a decade earlier. The reduction of China proper to the status of a Japanese puppet, politically and economically, was something else again. Here Japan outlined a situation which neither the Chinese nor the West could tolerate; Britain, America, and France might be able to come to terms with Chinese nationalism, maintaining something of their economic position even while giving up the unequal treaties, but Japanese supremacy was intolerable for reasons which were economic, political, strategic, and ideological.

A year after Lukouchiao, Japan was so deeply committed in China that withdrawal would have been extremely difficult, and an admission of defeat. Yet before that a settlement could have been achieved, although it would have needed a higher order of statesmanship than was evident in either Japan or the West at the time. After the peace efforts of 1937 and 1938 had failed, there came Konoye's enunciation of the New Order for East Asia, redefining and expanding the ideas which Amau had set forth four years before. Now it was clear that if Tokyo meant what it said, the limits of the tolerable had been reached. Yet the West did no more than protest.

To understand this, a number of factors, both practical and psychological, must be kept in mind. There was, of course, Britain's outright military weakness in the Pacific. There was a lack of interest in the broader questions of security and imperial defence. And most important perhaps, yet the hardest to gauge in its effect, was the British commitment to the policy of appeasement, a policy which was tried in the East as well as in Europe.

Yet appeasement did not mean the same thing in the East as it did in Europe. Look first of all at the nature of the Anglo-American relationship here. From these years there emerges the record of a fairly consistent British attempt to win the support of the United States for common action against Japan, and it is a record that has no parallel with British policy in Europe. Despite the doubts and hesitations which London showed, particularly on the question of sanctions, the British posture in the Far East was decidedly different from that which Chamberlain's government assumed in Europe. There were good reasons for this. In pursuing collective security in China, Britain would be working with a relatively known quantity—the United States—rather than with the unstable Third Republic or the uncertain and frightening Soviet Union. And while a firm policy in Europe was hampered by the deep ideological cleavage which developed during the thirties (and which was manifested above all in the reactions to the Spanish civil war), in the East the situation was different. There were some who supported Japan's cause out of tradition, commercial interest, or the feeling that Japan was saving Asia from Bolshevism, but their numbers were few, and they had only a handful of spokesmen in press and Parliament. Feeling was overwhelmingly on China's side, and it was a feeling with strategic and economic bases, as well as moral and ideological ones.

Furthermore, Britain felt that while little could be expected from America in Europe, Washington might assume a more active role in the East, due to her own interests there and her interest in seeing China develop into a viable state with links to the West, dominated neither by Russia nor Japan. If a Republican administration had once almost seemed willing to form an Anglo-American bloc, a Democratic administration should be ready at least to consider such a policy. But it was not, and it took some time for this apparent change in front to be made clear.

One reason for this has already been suggested: the very contrast between her European and Asian policies left Britain's sincerity open to some doubt. As Eden, Lindsay, and Craigie were arguing with the Americans for joint action against Japan in the autumn of 1937, Halifax was visiting Germany, and Chamberlain was trying to associate the United States in his negotiations with Mussolini, negotiations which led to the recognition of the Italian conquest of Abyssinia, and the violation of Stimson's doctrine of non-recognition. At the same time many in Washington retained the old fear of having to fight for British interests—to 'pull British chestnuts out of the fire'—a fear compounded of isolationism and a dislike of British imperialism. Above all there was the obvious drawback that in any partnership of the two countries, it was the United States that would have to take the lead. On the other side, all this was matched by the British feeling that they were bearing the brunt of the diplomatic action on such issues as the Customs and the status of the foreign settlements. It was London, not Washington, they thought, which was earning Japan's enmity, by being forced to handle the negotiations on questions which concerned America as well as Britain.

In addition there was a basic difference in outlook as to the policy which should be followed towards Japan. In June 1937 the State Department had insisted upon 'parallel' rather than 'joint' approaches in the East, and said that such action should be taken 'concurrently', following 'consultation between and among the powers most interested'.[5] Since then Washington had frequently avoided discussions with Britain before proceeding on its own, and the British were unprepared for this. Furthermore, while both countries were from the first conscious of the rivalry between the military and the civil government in Japan, they sometimes differed over how best to exploit the split. In December 1937 Craigie suggested that a show of force would bolster the 'moderates' against the military, while Grew felt that it would simply weaken them. And, the American ambassador added privately to Hull, America should not have to share the 'consequences of British ineptitudes, both of action and of statement' which had exacerbated feelings between London and Tokyo.[6] In Grew's mind, the United States had managed to make its views known just as effectively as had Britain, but without stirring up Japanese passions as much, simply by acting independently and by not 'encouraging other powers to take a stronger position *vis-à-vis* Japan than that which they would be disposed independently to take'.[7] A year later both sides held to the same views. In September 1938 Craigie told Halifax that, bad as the situation was in China, it could have been worse, and British pressure had been necessary to mitigate it, especially in view of the 'supineness of the United States'.[8] In October Grew told Washington that while America had not been able to secure her rights in all respects, American approaches had at least commended themselves to the Japanese Government, and consequently there was less feeling against Washington than against London[9]—an estimate which was undeniably true. Eugene Dooman summed it up in a talk with Craigie during the Tientsin crisis: the main reason, he said, why Britain was having more trouble with Japan was because from the beginning the United States had declared its intention of defending American rights by its own exertions, while the British, both in China and London, had shown that they relied on a Chinese victory to protect their position, and had thus led the Japanese to believe that British and Chinese interests were the same.[10] He might also have added that in Japanese eyes it had been Britain who from the beginning seemed intent on building up an anti-Japanese coalition.[11]

What made the situation even worse from the British point of view was the ironical fact that by her very inaction, the United States looked as if she were doing more than Britain to meet the Japanese threat. Thus the world heard Hull's statement of principles in July 1937; it heard the 'quarantine speech' and misunderstood it as a call for sanctions;[12] it noted the American abstention from the Customs agreement of May 1938; it saw the American treaty denunciation in July 1939 as a contrast to the

Craigie-Arita formula; and it welcomed Hull's defence of free trade routes when the Burma Road was closed in 1940. At the same time Britain appeared to be temporizing with aggression in the East as in Europe, and the Government came under attack from its critics of both the Right and the Left, the lobbyists for British trade and financial interests, and the Labour benches in the House of Commons. So in late 1937 a Labour M.P. could even say that it was clear that at Brussels America had pressed for decisive action, while Britain had held back.[13]

Yet Britain never quite understood why America was unwilling to join her, and while she realized the American desire to keep an independence of action, she never really grasped its depth, nor did she ever quite understand Hull's faith in the possibilities of educating public opinion. Hence the American rebuffs to British overtures, and the fact that the overtures themselves occasionally embittered relations between the two countries. Hence Chamberlain's cynical comment on American policy: 'It is always best and safest to count on nothing from the Americans but words.'[14] It was a view matched by Washington's outlook on British policies, its insistence upon seeing Britain primarily in terms of a power bent on upholding a privileged economic position in China. There was much to be said for this view; what was missing was the realization that the defence of the Western treaty position often helped China's war effort, and the realization that for reasons of domestic politics as well as foreign policy there were clear differences between British actions in Europe and in the Far East. Washington wanted independence, and in its insistence upon 'parallel' action was able to preserve the illusion of neutrality; joint action for Britain would have meant the sort of collective security measures which Labour and the Liberals were demanding, yet a collective action not overly dependent upon the League (or the Soviet Union) and therefore more in keeping with Conservative preferences. Not until a year after the fall of France did concerted action come on a vital issue, when Japanese assets were frozen, and then the war was just over four months away.

In one sense then it may be said that it was the failure to agree on collective security in the East, as in Europe, that stifled any effective action which might have prevented the intolerable from arising. In the East however, unlike Europe, Britain actively sought to take the lead in the formation of an alliance that could have blocked the aggressor, and she failed partly because it was obvious that once the alliance was formed she would become the junior partner, and America was unwilling to assume the senior role. Yet this diagnosis, while true, is incomplete for the same reason that most of the similar diagnoses of the other failures of the thirties were incomplete, for they make the assumption that only force could have stopped aggression. What was lacking was not only the willingness to form an alliance which might stop Japan, but also the willingness to probe more deeply into the problem, to study the reasons why Japan behaved as she did, to make some concrete proposals to meet Japanese needs, and thus to divert her from the course of her imperialism. In 1939 the historian E. H. Carr published a book, *The Twenty Years' Crisis*, in which he argued persuasively for a recognition of the process of change by the rich, satisfied nations of the world, and a realization that they would have to come to terms with the new forces which were arising to challenge the old conceptions of pre-eminence still held by the Anglo-Saxon countries. His book has since been called (by A. J. P. Taylor) 'a brilliant argument in favour of appeasement', and it is certainly open to the criticism that it did not define the direction in which change was proceeding quite as clearly as it might have; how far should America and Britain, for instance, come to terms with the sort of change embodied in the New Order or the Third Reich? But Japan's New Order, and the new imperialisms of Germany and Italy were examples of the sort of change that, left to themselves, nations might follow once they had the power to assume what they considered to be their rightful economic and political positions in the world—and the economic nationalism which they embodied, it might be added, was a feature common also to the policies both of the United States and the British Empire after the Great Depression. These too were symptoms of the sort of change that the League of Nations was unequipped to deal with, and which Japan's adversaries refused to face up to.

To 'stop Japan' might mean two things: either by sanctions and military force to block her (and this was the solution adopted in 1941); or to remove the reasons for her desire to advance, by measures of what was then called 'economic appeasement', perhaps in judicious combination with enough military force to induce her to accept the measures. The British sometimes seemed willing to try both of these, but the Americans objected. If British appeasement had really meant the 'methodical removal of the principal causes of friction in the world', perhaps something might have been accomplished, but too often it simply meant surrender, and British force, in the Far East at least, was virtually non-existent. In such circumstances, no basis for peaceful change which would take Japanese needs into consideration while protecting China, was likely to be arrived at. It was all very well for the British to say, as they did in their note of 14 January 1939, that they were willing to entertain constructive Japanese proposals for the modification of the Nine Power Treaty, but the constructive proposals themselves should have come from the West. Left to herself, Japan's response was bound to be that of the New Order, a Japanese political and economic hegemony over large parts of East Asia. Western statesmen did occasionally discuss such proposals among themselves, but generally they were too little, too late, and never communicated to Tokyo. The Foreign Office's unofficial essay of February 1938 was one such example, and Craigie, Halifax, and Lothian, all turned their attention to the problem of a general East Asian solution in the years before Pearl Harbor. But the proposals remained private— they were not among the matters discussed by the League, or by the Brussels Conference—and after that it was too late, for by 1938 Japan would have accepted nothing less than a firm foothold on the mainland, south of Manchuria, and this was a solution which had to be rejected, on political and strategic grounds, both by the West and by China.

By 1938 then, stopping Japan could only mean stopping her directly by force and making her back down. Here again the Western democracies refused to face the facts, and furthermore in examining the situation in the East they made two great errors. In the first place they failed to realize the strength of Japan, and in the second place they did not foresee the results of the European war. Both Britain and America appear to have believed from 1937 on that Japan was not strong enough economically to sustain a long war in China, and that sooner or later she would be forced to withdraw. This simply was not so, and as the concept of the New Order was developed, it began to grow obvious that Japan would not be distracted from her goals, no matter what sacrifices were necessary at home. And the longer the war continued, the less likely became the chances of a settlement reasonable by either Western or Chinese standards. Firm measures, together with a genuine attempt to understand and to meet Japan's needs, might have brought a Japanese retreat in 1937 or 1938, but when firm measures alone were applied in July 1941, they helped drive Japan to war. It would never have been easy to block her, despite the predictions of those who foresaw a swift collapse of the imperial armies after the imposition of sanctions. To talk about Japan's feet of clay was evidence of wishful thinking, as harmful in its way as were the beliefs of those—an ever dwindling number—who felt that Britain could continue to work with a China dominated by Japan.

The other mistake was the failure to foresee the course of the European war. If Chamberlain's sort of appeasement can be said to have had any justification, it lies not in the illusion of a year of rearmament bought at Munich, but in the fact that when Britain went to war on 3 September 1939, she faced only Germany. Japan and Italy were neutral. It would be a mistake to give Chamberlain and Halifax too much credit for this; Italian unpreparedness and the political confusion in Tokyo which followed the Nazi-Soviet Pact were of the utmost importance. Yet British concessions to the two countries had helped. To keep Japan's neutrality Britain would have had to prevent the rise to power of the pro-Axis military clique, and that she had a degree of success here is attested to by the succession of governments in 1939 and 1940. Abe and Yonai were both 'moderates', and Hiranuma, though himself a strong nationalist who favored a tie to Germany, pursued a cautious and conservative policy as Prime Minister. It was quite true that these men were not above using the indiscipline of the extremists as a lever against Britain, but they took no overt action until June 1940.

This was the decisive date, and here the second error emerges. British policy was not based on a French collapse after two months of fighting, and when this event occurred it radically altered the situation in Europe and the East. It brought Mussolini into the war, and it was the signal for the beginning of Japan's advance into Southeast Asia, and her direct confrontation with the West. Konoye and Matsuoka followed Yonai and Arita in July. The French surrender, in other words, wiped out the only positive gain for which the appeasement policy could take any credit. This is not to justify British action during this period, in Europe or in the East. The maintenance of peace in the Orient would still have left the West to face the fact of deep Japanese penetration into China. It is merely to suggest that until June 1940 it was not obvious that the situation was irrevocably lost. To secure a Japanese evacuation of China, even just south of Manchuria, would have been difficult enough after late 1937, and became more difficult as time went on. This is the fact which was never clearly faced until 1941, and by then it was too late.

Notes

Abbreviations

DBFP   *Documents on British Foreign Policy, 1919–1939*
DGFP   *Documents on German Foreign Policy, 1918–1945*
FRUS   *Foreign Relations of the United States: Diplomatic Papers*
FRUS Japan   *Foreign Relations of the United States: Japan: 1931–1941*
H.C.Deb.   *Parliamentary Debates: Official Report (House of Commons)*
H.L.Deb.   *Parliamentary Debates: Official Report (House of Lords)*
I.G.   Inspector General, Chinese Maritime Customs
IMT, IMTFE   International Military Tribunal, Far East
Jap. Archives   Archives of the Japanese Ministry of Foreign Affairs, Library of Congress
NCH   North China Herald
RIIA   Royal Institute of International Affairs.

CHAPTER I

1. The fighting at Lukouchiao and its aftermath is described most fully in James B. Crowley, 'A Reconsideration of the Marco Polo Bridge Incident', *Journal of Asian Studies*, XXII, No. 3 (May 1963), 277–91; also in F. C. Jones, *Japan's New Order in East Asia: Its Rise and Fall, 1937–1945* (London, 1954), pp. 30–38; G. Richard Storry, *The Double Patriots: a Study in Japanese Nationalism* (Boston, 1957), pp. 216–18; Robert J. C. Butow, *Tojo and the Coming of the War* (Princeton, 1961), pp. 94–99; and in the Royal Institute of International Affairs, *Survey of International Affairs, 1937*, ed. Arnold J. Toynbee and Veronica M. Butler (London, 1938), I, 181–87. (This series henceforth referred to as RIIA, *Survey*.)

2. Viscount Templewood (Sir Samuel Hoare), *Nine Troubled Years* (London, 1954), p. 374.

3. A. J. P. Taylor, *The Origins of the Second World War* (London, 1961), pp. 45–46, 104–5.

4. A. P. Thornton, *The Imperial Idea and Its Enemies: a Study in British Power* (London, 1963), p. 233.

5. A. L. Rowse, *Appeasement: a Study in Political Decline, 1933–1939* (New York, 1961), p. 52.

6. In a speech of 5 February 1939; quoted in Hugh Dalton, *The Fateful Years: Memoirs, 1931–1945* (London, 1957), p. 213.

7. For Anglo-Chinese relations in this period see Irving S. Friedman, *British Relations with China, 1931–1939* (New York, 1941), chaps. i–ii; John T. Pratt, *War and Politics in China* (London, 1943), and the Foreign Office Memorandum of 8 January 1930, printed in Great Britain, Foreign Office, *Documents on British Foreign Policy, 1919–1939*, ed. E. L. Woodward and Rohan Butler (London, 1946–), Second Series, VIII, No. 1. (This collection of documents hereafter cited as *DBFP*; all future references, unless otherwise stated, are to the Third Series, which covers the period from Munich to the outbreak of World War II.)

8. The extent to which the following disagree indicates the sort of misunderstanding and suspicion to which the Manchurian crisis gave rise: Henry Stimson, *The Far Eastern Crisis* (New York, 1936); Friedman, *British Relations with China*, chap. iii; Pratt, *War and Politics*, chap. xiii; Reginald Bassett, *Democracy and Foreign Policy: A Case History: The Sino-Japanese Dispute, 1931–1933* (London, 1952); Sara Smith, *The Manchurian Crisis* (New York, 1948); Armin Rappaport, *Henry L. Stimson and Japan* (Chicago, 1963). For a typical view of British guilt see Sir Norman Angell, *The Defence of the Empire* (New York, 1937), pp. 93–123.

9. The Amau statement is in United States, Department of State, *Papers Relating to the Foreign Relations of the United States, Japan: 1931–1941* (Washington, 1943), I, 223–25. (Hereafter cited as *FRUS, Japan.*) For comment on this, as for the whole period from the end of the Manchurian crisis, I am indebted to Dr Dorothy Borg, who allowed me to read in manuscript her *The United States and the Far Eastern Crisis, 1933–1938* (Cambridge, Mass., 1964). Chap. ii deals with the Amau statement.

10. Borg, pp. 132–37; United States, Department of State, *Foreign Relations of the United States: Diplomatic Papers, 1935* (Washington, 1952–1953), III, 619, 631–32. (This series hereafter cited as *FRUS*, followed by year and volume number.)

11. There is no way of telling how far Leith-Ross influenced the Chinese move. He told the American ambassador that he had tried to restrain the Ministry of Finance, feeling that they were acting prematurely (*FRUS, 1935*, III, 631–32). It was also reported that while he was working on a reform programme, the Chinese had acted before he was finished (*The Economist* [London, weekly], 25 April 1936, p. 204).

12. *The Times* (London), 23 June 1936. For an official view of China's increasingly favourable prospects, see the Department of Overseas Trade, *Report on Economic and Commercial Conditions in China, April 1935–March 1937* (London, 1937).

13. Friedman, *British Relations with China*, pp. 81–87. The railway loans were never issued because of the war. For other railway loans, see Chang Kia-ngau, *China's Struggle for Railway Development* (New York, 1943), pp. 100–26. Kung and Maze discussed the £20,000,000 loan with Montague Norman, Governor of the Bank of England, who found the sum too high for China's still uncertain credit. Details are in the papers of Sir Frederick Maze (in the Library of the School of Oriental and

African Studies, London University); see the Record of Interview with the Governor of the Bank of England, in Confidential Letters, etc. of Sir Frederick Maze, vol. XIII (1936–1939), pp. 180–86; Maze to Norman, 8 July; Norman to Maze, 14 July; and Maze's later record of the interview, pp. 188–95. The sum, however, was modest in comparison to the £150,000,000 loan which Kung had asked Maze to seek in 1934; details of this are in Confidential Letters, etc., vol. X (1934–1935), pp. 1–268, *passim*.

14. China, Maritime Customs, *The Trade of China* (Shanghai, published annually), 1934–1937. In retrospect the picture looks less bright; see Douglas S. Paauw, 'Chinese National Expenditure during the Nanking Period', *Far Eastern Quarterly*, XII, no 1 (Nov. 1952), 3–26; and 'The Kuomintang and Economic Stagnation, 1928–1937', *Journal of Asian Studies*, XVI, no. 2 (Feb. 1957), 213–20.

15. Great Britain, *Parliamentary Debates: Official Report (House of Commons)*, Fifth Series, CCCXXIII, 6 May, col. 1253.

16. *FRUS 1937*, IV, 607; III, 126. According to some press reports, Japan wanted at least *de facto* recognition of Manchukuo, and a recognition of her position in north China; in return she would recognize British advances in south and central China; presumably the railway loans and currency reforms were meant (*Japan Weekly Chronicle* [Kobe], 27 May 1937, p. 653).

17. *FRUS 1937*, I, 98–106; Borg, *Far Eastern Crisis*, pp. 270–74.

18. Great Britain, Accounts and Papers, Session 1936–1937, XII, Cmd. 5482: *Imperial Conference, 1937: Summary of Proceedings*, p. 15. Lyons's proposal echoed a similar suggestion of the previous autumn; see Paul Hasluck, *The Government and the People, I, 1939–1941* (Canberra, 1952) (*Australia in the War of 1939–1945*. Series 4 [Civil] vol. I), p. 61.

19. Private information; but see also Yoshida Shigeru, *The Yoshida Memoirs: The Story of Japan in Crisis*, trans. Yoshida Kenichi (Boston, 1962), pp. 17, 118. It was at this point also that Sir Nevile Henderson went to Berlin.

20. S. Woodburn Kirby, et al., *The War Against Japan*, I, *The Loss of Singapore* (London, 1957) (*History of the Second World War, U.K. Military Series*, ed. J. R. M. Butler), p. 17; J. R. M. Butler, *Grand Strategy*, II, *September 1939–June 1941* (London, 1957) (same series), p. 325.

21. *The British Commonwealth and the Future: Proceedings of the Second Unofficial Conference on British Commonwealth Relations, Sydney, 3rd to 17th September, 1938*, ed. H. V. Hodson (London, 1939), p. 39.

22. *DBFP*, Second Series, VIII, no 1. Maze himself described the Customs as 'really a sort of unofficial "outpost of Empire" ' in a letter to W. O. Law, 17 Oct. 1938 (Maze Papers, Personal Correspondence, July–Dec. 1938). For a fuller treatment, see Nicholas R. Clifford, 'Sir Frederick Maze and the Chinese Maritime Customs, 1937–1941', *Journal of Modern History*, XXXVII, no. 1 (March 1965), 18–34.

23. E. M. Gull, *British Economic Interests in the Far East* (New York, 1943), p. 119; C. F. Remer, *Foreign Investment in China* (New York, 1933), pp. 397, 403.

24. *The Times*, 19, 20 August 1937.

25. Kate Mitchell, 'Revitalizing British Interests in China', *Far Eastern Survey*, VI, no. 13 (23 June 1937), p. 141; 'Japan's Challenge to the West', *Round Table*, XXVIII, no. 110 (March 1938), p. 236; E. A. Ch.-Walden, 'The Sino-Japanese War and the Open Door', *International Affairs* (London), XVII, no. 5 (Sept.–Oct. 1938), p. 631.

26. Mitchell, p. 141. In 1936 British imports from China amounted to £7,642,655, compared to £9,804,510 from Japan (Great Britain, Accounts and Papers, Session 1936–1937, XII, *Accounts Relating to Trade and Navigation of the United Kingdom, January 1937*).

27. *The Trade of China, 1936*, I, 119.

CHAPTER II

1. *FRUS 1937*, III, 154. For a detailed examination of American policy during July and August, see Borg, *Far Eastern Crisis*, chap. 10.

2. *FRUS 1937*, III, 157.

3. *Ibid.*, pp. 158–61.

4. *Ibid.*, p. 164.

5. *FRUS Japan*, I, 325–26.

6. *FRUS 1937*, I, 102–6; Cordell Hull, *The Memoirs of Cordell Hull* (New York, 1948), I, 533.

7. Dodds had advised London that 'in certain eventualities' he might tell Hirota that there could be no amelioration of Anglo-Japanese relations if Japan tried to turn north China into another Manchukuo. Eden, however, told Dodds to take immediate action, overlooking the chargé's qualifying phrase, by which he meant 'as a last resort' (*FRUS 1937*, III, 164–66, 178–79). On 15 July, in accordance with Eden's instructions, Ambassador Sir Hughe Knatchbull-Hugessen urged moderation on Nanking.

8. *FRUS 1937*, III, 178. The orders had been given some days earlier; see Jones, *New Order*, pp. 34–35, and Storry, *Double Patriots*, pp. 219–20.

9. *FRUS 1937*, III, 187–88, 206–7.

10. Royal Institute of International Affairs, *Documents on International Affairs, 1937*, ed. Stephen Heald (London, 1939), p. 645. (This series hereafter cited as RIIA, *Documents*.)

11. *FRUS 1937*, III, 214–15.

12. *Ibid.*, p. 207, pp. 216–18.

13. *Ibid.*, pp. 248–49.

14. *Ibid.*, p. 232.

15. *Ibid.*, pp. 226–28, 236.

16. United States, Department of State, *Documents on German Foreign Policy, 1918–1945* (Washington, 1949–1964), Series D, I, No. 468. (This series hereafter cited as *DGFP*.)

17. *FRUS 1937*, III, 287–90, 319–20, 340–42, 350–51.

18. *Ibid.*, pp. 368–69, 372–73, 384–85, 388.

19. They are listed in Jones, *New Order*, pp. 42–43.

20. *FRUS 1937*, III, 254.

21. *Ibid.*, pp. 288–89, 301. In late June Soviet and Manchukuoan troops had clashed over the ownership of certain islands in the Amur; by early July, a settlement was reached; see RIIA, *Survey, 1937*, I, 151–53.

22. Jones, *New Order*, p. 46; F. C. Jones, *Shanghai and Tientsin, with Special Reference to Foreign Interests* (London, 1940), pp. 58–59; *FRUS 1937*, III, 320–22, 332–33.

23. *FRUS 1937*, III, 386–87.

24. *Ibid.*, pp. 356–57, 375–76, 390, 396–97, 399–400.

25. *FRUS Japan*, I, 346–47; *FRUS 1937*, III, 404–5.

26. *FRUS 1937*, III, 445–46.

27. *Ibid.*, pp. 440–41, 448–50.

28. *FRUS Japan*, I, 354–55; *FRUS 1937*, III, 449, 455–56, 464–65.

29. *The Times*, 26 Aug.; *FRUS 1937*, III, 480.

30. *FRUS 1937*, III, 244–45. For a description of foreign defence plans in Shanghai, see *Oriental Affairs* (Shanghai, published monthly), Oct. 1937, pp. 175–83. See map, p. 25.

31. For the correspondence on these subjects, see *FRUS 1937*, III, 451–52, 550–78, 642–43; *FRUS 1937*, IV, 265, 276, 280–81, 304–14, 342–43, 436; *FRUS Japan*, I, 487–88.

32. Among other things, Japan accused the British of supplying provisions to a Chinese battalion cut off from the main body of retreating troops; they later withdrew the charge. They also claimed that British warships were spotting for Chinese artillery fire. In September, the American consul-general reported that wounded Chinese soldiers were being hospitalized in the Settlement, and then passed out to Chinese lines; see F. S. G. Piggott, *Broken Thread: An Autobiography* (Aldershot, 1950), pp. 295–96; *FRUS 1937*, III, 55.

33. Earl of Avon, *The Memoirs of Anthony Eden, Earl of Avon: Facing the Dictators, 1923–1938* (Boston, 1962), pp. 603–4.

34. Joseph C. Grew, Papers, Diary, 1937, III, 3259. In the Houghton Library, Harvard University.

35. See on this *FRUS 1937*, III, 485–88, 505–8, 529; Borg, *Far Eastern Crisis*, pp. 296, 311.

36. *FRUS 1937*, III, 401–4.

37. *Ibid.*, pp. 475–78; see also Roger Levy, Guy Lacam, and Andrew Roth, *French Interests and Policies in the Far East* (New York, 1941), pp. 21–57, for a general discussion of the French position.

38. *FRUS 1937*, III, 460, 484–85. For Russian aid, see Arthur N. Young, *China and the Helping Hand, 1937-1945* (Cambridge, Mass., 1963), pp. 18–22, 54–59. This work, by a former Financial Adviser to China, is the fullest treatment of foreign aid to that country.

39. Ernst L. Presseisen, *Germany and Japan: A Study in Totalitarian Diplomacy, 1933-1941* (The Hague, 1958), pp. 125–26; *DGFP*, I, No. 463, No. 472. See also Herbert von Dirksen, *Moscow, Tokyo, London* (Norman, Oklahoma, 1952), p. 177.

40. There is a reference in the German documents to a $3,000,000 credit for goods to be delivered to a British firm in Singapore, in Danish ships, all in 'strictest secrecy' (*DGFP*, I, No. 504; Presseisen, *Germany and Japan*, p. 155.

41. Italy has not been dealt with here; apart from a concession in Tientsin, she had few important interests in the East. There was an Italian Financial Adviser in Nanking, and an Air Mission in Nanchang, which was withdrawn late in 1937. From the first, Italy made no secret of her pro-Japanese sympathies. See Frank Tamagna, *Italy's Interests and Policies in the Far East* (New York, 1941), p. 28.

CHAPTER III

1. 326 *H.C.Deb.*, col. 1800.

2. *Ibid.*, cols. 1811–14.

3. *Ibid.*, col. 2182.

4. *North China Herald* (Shanghai, weekly), 28 July, p. 157. (Hereafter cited as *NCH*; the *Herald* was the weekly edition of the *North China Daily News*.)

5. *The Times*, 22 July.

6. In Shanghai the Japanese ambassador called on Knatchbull-Hugessen in the hospital, to express 'sympathy', but no regrets, and was treated to a lecture on the civilities of international behaviour. From Peiping, a Japanese diplomat flew to the summer resort of Peitaiho to inform the ambassador's wife of the incident; she had, however, already left for Shanghai. As the ambassador recorded it: 'My children received the Secretary and gave him luncheon. I understand the meal was somewhat icy. The Japanese Secretary brought it to a close by rising and explaining that he must be in Peking early that afternoon as the aeroplane was required to go and bomb Nant'ai' (Sir Hughe Knatchbull-Hugessen, *Diplomat in Peace and War* [London, 1949], p. 123.

7. RIIA, *Documents, 1937*, pp. 665-69.

8. *FRUS 1937*, IV, 34-35, 37-38; League of Nations, *Official Journal* (Geneva), Special Supplement No. 177, No. 13.

9. *New Statesman and Nation* (London, weekly), 25 Sept., pp. 433-34. She also made the point (absent from the organs of more conservative opinion) that those who feared the increasing influence of the U.S.S.R. in the Far East should consider the wisdom of forcing China into the arms of the only power that seemed inclined to help her.

10. *Spectator* (London, weekly), 1 Oct., p. 533; *Time and Tide* (London, weekly), 4 Sept., p. 161; 2 Oct., pp. 1284-85.

11. *The Times*, 25 Aug.

12. *The Times*, 4 Oct.

13. *The Times*, 5 Oct. The debate on rearmament had not yet come.

14. *The Times*, 25 Sept., 13 Oct., 6 Oct.; Freda Utley's letter in the *New Statesman*, 2 Oct., pp. 483-84.

15. *New York Times*, 6 Oct.

16. Borg, *Far Eastern Crisis*, chap. xiii, esp. pp. 382-86.

17. *The Times*, 8 Oct., 13 Oct.; *Manchester Guardian* and *Daily Herald* quoted in *Keesing's Contemporary Archives* (London), 5 Oct., p. 2766.

18. RIIA, *Documents, 1937*, p. 49.

19. Keith Feiling, *The Life of Neville Chamberlain* (London, 1947), p. 325.

20. *The Times*, 15 Oct.

21. *The Times*, 5 Oct.; *NCH*, 6 Oct., p. 1; 13 Oct., p. 43.

22. *FRUS 1937*, IV, 35, 51. One result, however, was simply to convince Japan that Britain was trying to form an anti-Japanese bloc. Especially irritating was the fact that the Archbishop of Canterbury, whom the Japanese regarded as having a quasi-official position, had presided at a newspaper's protest meeting; the Anglican Bishop of South Tokyo (a Canadian) had wired him, deploring his intention to take part (Piggott, *Broken Thread*, p. 295; *The Times*, 4 Oct.).

23. By the Advisory Committee on Trade Questions in Time of War (A.T.B.), which had been established shortly after World War I (W. N. Medlicott, *The Economic Blockade* [London, 1952-1959] [*History of the Second World War, U.K. Civil Series*, ed. W. K. Hancock], I, 12-14).

24. The I.I.C. had been formed in 1931 under the Committee of Imperial Defence. One reason for the need of American cooperation was the fact that 83 per cent of Japanese raw silk exports went to the U.S., and only 5 per cent to Britain. Although the industry represented only 18.6 per cent of Japanese exports, it required no raw materials, and was therefore a prime earner of foreign exchange. From the point of view of an economic boycott, there were no Japanese exports other than textiles worth considering (Medlicott, I, 384).

25. *FRUS 1937*, III, 560, 582–83; Avon, *Facing the Dictators*, p. 606.

26. *FRUS 1937*, III, 600–2.

27. Borg, *Far Eastern Crisis*, pp. 386–98. Some American statesmen (notably Norman Davis) did not share this view, and were coming to favour American participation in a plan for collective security. But Dr Borg concludes that the Chicago speech had actually lessened the chances of a strong American stand (p. 398), and Hull wrote that the speech set back 'by at least six months' the education of public opinion toward international cooperation by the United States (*Memoirs*, I, 545).

28. *FRUS 1937*, III, 465–66.

29. Borg, *Far Eastern Crisis*, pp. 319–25.

CHAPTER IV

1. League of Nations, *Official Journal*, Aug.–Sept. 1937, pp. 653–55.

2. *FRUS 1937*, IV, 9–10. For American dealings with the League, see Borg, *Far Eastern Crisis*, chap. xii.

3. Borg, p. 455; League, *Official Journal*, Dec. 1937, Annex, 1670, p. 100. Under Article X members undertook to protect each other from external aggression; Article XI stated that any war or threat of war was the concern of the entire League.

4. *FRUS 1937*, IV, 20–21; League, *Official Journal*, Special Supplement No. 169, p. 50.

5. *Official Journal*, Special Supplement No. 169, p. 76; Special Supplement No. 177, pp. 17–18.

6. *FRUS 1937*, IV, 29–30.

7. *Ibid.*, pp. 48–50, 55–56, 63–64; *Official Journal*, Special Supplement No. 177, pp. 22–23.

8. *Official Journal*, Special Supplement, No. 177, pp. 37–44, New Zealand, Russia, and China were overruled in their attempts to strengthen the wording.

9. *FRUS 1937*, IV, 62–63. Hull had the news of the quarantine speech telephoned to Geneva, perhaps as an encouragement to the League to act (Borg, *Far Eastern Crisis*, p. 365.

10. Avon, *Facing the Dictators*, p. 608.

11. *FRUS 1937*, IV, 69–72, 74, 79–82; Jay Pierrepont Moffat Papers (in the Houghton Library, Harvard University), Diary, vol. 39, 7 Oct., 9–10 Oct., 13 Oct. Moffat was a member of the American delegation to Brussels, and his papers are one of the chief sources for the Conference. They have been published in part as *The Moffat Papers: Selections From the Diplomatic Journals of Jay Pierrepont Moffat*, ed. Nancy H. Hooker (Cambridge, Mass., 1956); pp. 156–88 cover the Conference.

Moffat remained suspicious of the British and determined to prevent any forceful action by his country; he was preoccupied, he wrote, 'to prevent at any costs the involvement of the United States in hostilities anywhere, and to that end to discourage any formation of a common front of the democratic powers' (Diary, 13 Nov., p. 5). The fullest treatment of the Conference is in Borg, *Far Eastern Crisis*, chap. xiv.

12. 327 *H.C.Deb.*, cols. 44, 75–77.

13. *Ibid.*, cols. 88–89.

14. *Ibid.*, col. 65.

15. *Ibid.*, col. 174.

16. Great Britain, *Parliamentary Debates: Official Report (House of Lords)*, Fifth Series, CVI, cols. 1077, 1087, 1106, 1110.

17. *FRUS 1937*, IV, 89–91.

18. *Ibid.*, pp. 92, 115. The State Department itself was divided on the issue of sanctions, and consequently the instructions given Norman Davis (who headed the American delegation at Brussels) were unclear; when the question arose at the Conference, there was some friction between him and Washington (Borg, *Far Eastern Crisis*, pp. 407–8; Moffat Diary, 1 Nov., p. 3).

19. *FRUS 1937*, IV, 74, 80, 96.

20. RIIA, *Documents, 1937*, pp. 706–9.

21. *FRUS 1937*, III, 126–8; see also pp. 135–36 for another example of Yoshida's wishful thinking.

22. *FRUS 1937*, IV, 124–25.

23. Avon, *Facing the Dictators*, p. 611.

24. 328 *H.C.Deb.*, 1 Nov., col. 583.

25. *FRUS 1937*, IV, 145–47; Moffat Diary, 2 Nov.; *Moffat Papers*, pp. 162–65.

26. United States, Department of State, *The Conference of Brussels, November 3–24, 1937* (Washington, 1938), pp. 27–45.

27. *FRUS 1937*, IV, 157–59, 163–65; Moffat Diary, 3 Nov., pp. 4–11; 4 Nov., pp. 1–3; *Moffat Papers*, pp. 169–70.

28. Moffat Diary, 10 Nov., pp. 2–5, 10–13; 12 Nov., p. 1; *Moffat Papers*, pp. 174–179. See also Borg, *Far Eastern Crisis*, pp. 425–26.

29. *Conference of Brussels*, pp. 55–58; the Japanese refusal is on pp. 53–54.

30. *Ibid.*, pp. 65–68.

31. *FRUS 1937*, IV, 152–54.

32. *Ibid.*, pp. 186–91; *Moffat Papers*, pp. 184, 186; Borg, *Far Eastern Crisis*, pp. 432–33.

33. *FRUS 1937*, IV, 219–21; Moffat Diary, 19 Nov., pp. 1–2; 20 Nov.

34. *Conference of Brussels*, pp. 69–80.

35. Avon, *Facing the Dictators*, p. 613.

36. *350 H.C.Deb.*, 21 Dec., col. 1809.

37. *DBFP*, VIII, No. 440.

38. Sir Robert L. Craigie, *Behind the Japanese Mask* (London, 1946), p. 51.

39. Jones, *New Order*, p. 56; International Military Tribunal, Far East, Record of Proceedings (Tokyo, 1946–1948, mimeographed), pp. 37692–93, Exhibit 3738A. (Hereafter cited as IMTFE.)

40. Craigie, *Behind the Japanese Mask*, pp. 50–51; IMTFE, Record, pp. 37697–98, Exh. 3785A. According to Horinouchi at the Tokyo trials, Britain had proposed Anglo-German-American mediation, but both Berlin and the Japanese army opposed this (IMTFE, Record, pp. 2970–71; Jones, New Order, p. 61).

41. Borg, *Far Eastern Crisis*, p. 458. This might explain Yoshida's insistence that Tokyo was ready to talk peace with London and Washington; see *FRUS 1937*, III, 135–36.

42. *FRUS 1937*, III, 687–89, 699–701, 714–15. The British view (not shared by Washington) was that if too many conditions were imposed on Japan at the beginning, the opportunity might be lost, and that it would be more helpful to have Anglo-American understanding made the basis for action, rather than a mandate from the League or the signatories of the Nine Power Treaty.

43. *FRUS 1937*, III, 775–76.

44. *Ibid.*, p. 752.

CHAPTER V

1. *FRUS 1937*, IV, 434, 436–37, 446.

2. *Ibid.*, pp. 430–31, 471–72.

3. This account is based on the British note to Tokyo of 15 December (RIIA, *Documents, 1937*, pp. 767–79); see also *The Times*, 13 and 14 Dec.

4. *FRUS 1937*, IV, 490n.

5. Craigie, *Behind the Japanese Mask*, pp. 52–53; Storry, *Double Patriots*, p. 227. Storry points out that the naval air force, which attacked the *Panay*, was the most 'insubordinate, chauvinist wing of the navy'. However, the leader of the strike has since said that the bombing was an accident, although he claims that Hashimoto knew of *Ladybird*'s identity. See Okumiya Masatake, 'How the *Panay* was Sunk', *United States Naval Institute Proceedings*, LXXIX, no. 6 (June 1953), p. 589. At the Tokyo trials Hashimoto said that his orders were to 'sink all vessels proceeding towards Nanking without regard to nationality' (IMTFE, Record, p. 15679).

6. *FRUS 1937*, IV, 498–99, 767–79.

7. *Ibid.*, pp. 490–91, 494–95; *FRUS Japan*, I, 523–24; Avon, *Facing the Dictators*, pp. 615–16.

8. *FRUS 1937*, IV, 499–500, 503–4; Avon, *Facing the Dictators*, p. 617. See Borg, *Far Eastern Crisis*, pp. 488–92, for the American viewpoint. Roosevelt did not react strongly at first, unconvinced that the attack was intentional. It was not until a few days later, when further news came in, that he began to consider retaliation.

9. *FRUS 1937*, IV, 724–25; Avon, *Facing the Dictators*, pp. 613–14.

10. Avon, p. 618.

11. John M. Blum, *From the Morgenthau Diaries: Years of Crisis, 1928–1938* (Boston, 1959), pp. 485–92; the story is told more fully in Borg, *Far Eastern Crisis*, chap. xvi, esp. pp. 493–501. The State Department played no part in the episode, and the American diplomatic papers, as well as the memoirs of Hull, Eden, and Simon are all silent on it.

12. For the Ingersoll mission, see Avon, *Facing the Dictators*, pp. 619–20; Captain Tracy S. Kittredge, USNR, 'United States-British Naval Cooperation, 1939–1942', MS in the custody of the Director of Naval History, Washington, Section I, chap. iii, pp. 37–38; Mark Skinner Watson, *Chief of Staff: Pre-war Plans and Preparations* (Washington, 1950) (*The United States Army in World War II: The War Department*), pp. 92–93; Samuel Eliot Morison, *History of United States Naval Operations in World War II*, vol. III, *The Rising Sun in the Pacific, 1931–April 1942* (Boston, 1948), p. 49; United States Congress, *Hearings Before the Joint Committee on the Investigation of the Pearl Harbor Attack*, 79th Congress, First Session (Washington, 1946), Part 9, pp. 4273–77. (Hereafter cited as Pearl Harbor Attack.)

13. Grew Papers, Conversations, 1937–1938, pp. 182–87, 196–99.

14. *Ibid.*, pp. 208–9. For the Customs talks, see pp. 58–61.

15. Borg, *Far Eastern Crisis*, p. 501.

16. Grew Papers, *Conversations*, 1937–1938, p. 184.

17. *Ibid.*, pp. 227–28; *The Times*, 17 Jan. 1938; Eden, *Facing the Dictators*, p. 620.

18. Jones, *New Order*, pp. 69–70; *FRUS Japan*, I, 437–38.

19. RIIA, *Documents, 1938*, I, 342–44.

20. *Finance and Commerce* (Shanghai, weekly), 17 Nov., pp. 377–78.

21. *NCH*, 23 Feb. 1938, p. 303.

CHAPTER VI

1. *FRUS 1937*, III, 858–59. For more detailed treatments of the Customs negotiations, see Arthur N. Young, *China's Wartime Finance and Inflation, 1937–1945* (Cambridge, Mass., 1965), pp. 39–46, and Clifford, 'Sir Frederick Maze', pp. 21–27; see also Young, *Helping Hand*, pp. 45–48, 85–96.

2. Maze to J. H. Macoun, 13 Nov. 1937, Maze Papers, I. G.'s Personal Correspondence, March–Dec. 1937.

3. *Finance and Commerce*, 19 Jan. 1938, pp. 41–42.

4. These figures were, of course deceptive. Customs revenues in 1937 amounted to Ch $342,899,539, a 5.5 per cent increase over the 1936 figure of $324,633,291. The following breakdown more accurately reflects the war's effect.

	1936	1937
Jan.–July	$165,157,844	$262,261,262
Aug.–Dec.	$159,475,447	$80,638,477

Figures from Maritime Customs, *The Trade of China, 1937* (Shanghai, 1938), I, part I.

5. Myers to Japanese consul-general, Tientsin, 22 Oct. (extract); Myers to Maze, 29 Oct., Maze Papers, I.G.'s Personal Correspondence, Sept.–Dec. 1937; Maze to Hall-Patch, I Nov.; Maze to Macoun, 7 Dec.; Maze to Lawford, 28 Dec., I.G.'s Personal Correspondence, March–Dec. 1937; *FRUS 1937*, III, 877–78; *FRUS 1938*, III, 654–55.

6. Lawford to Maze, 29 Nov., I Dec., Personal Correspondence, March–Dec. 1937; Craigie to Foreign Office, 27 Nov., 28 Nov., Personal Correspondence, British Embassy, I, Jan.–April 1938, No. 0; *FRUS 1937*, III, 881–84, 886–87, 889–90; *FRUS Japan*, I, 730.

7. *FRUS 1937*, III, 898–903.

8. Howe to Maze, 28 Jan., Personal Correspondence, British Embassy, I, No. 11; Maze to Kung, 25 Jan., *ibid.*, No. 8; *FRUS 1938*, III, 634–40.

9. Maze to Naggiar, 8 Jan., Personal Correspondence, British Embassy, I, No. 4; Howe to Maze, 19 Jan., *ibid.*, No. 5; *FRUS 1938*, III, 627–28, 632–33.

10. 'The "China Incident" to "Pearl Harbour"', 1937–1941', in Confidential Letters, etc., of Sir F. Maze, vol. XV (1941–1943), pp. 180–81; Kung to Maze, 10 Feb. 1938, Personal Correspondence, British Embassy, I, No. 36a.

11. *FRUS 1938*, III, 661–63, 671–74, 676, 678–81.

12. The text of the agreement is in *FRUS 1938*, III, 678–81; see also pp. 683–84, 692–94. The communiqué may be found in *NCH*, 11 May, p. 218.

13. *FRUS 1938*, III, 684–85, 687–89; *NCH*, 11 May, p. 218.

14. *FRUS 1938*, III, 690.

15. *NCH*, 11 May, p. 218.

16. Grew Papers, Diary, 1938, V, 3742.

17. Clifford, 'Sir Frederick Maze', pp. 27–28. It was later alleged that the Yokohama Specie Bank granted loans from Customs revenues to the puppet governments, and that some Japanese military expenses were also financed from the revenues; see W. Y. Lin, 'The Future of Foreign Investment in China', *Problems of the Pacific*;

Proceedings of the Study Meeting of the Institute of Pacific Relations . . . November 18–December 2, 1939, ed. Kate Mitchell and W. L. Holland (New York, 1940), p. 217.

18. E. A. Ch.-Walden, 'Sino-Japanese War and the Open Door', p. 632.

19. The Border Governments were set up in early 1938, and existed side by side in the north China countryside with the puppet régimes, whose control was generally restricted to important towns and lines of communication. Although subordinate in theory to the Central Government, the Border Governments were largely dominated by the Communists. See also Young, *Helping Hand*, pp. 65–69; *China's Wartime Finance*, pp. 165–88.

20. Jones, *Shanghai and Tientsin*, p. 164.

21. *The Times*, 5 May 1938.

22. *FRUS 1938*, IV, 6–7, 10.

23. Jones, *Shanghai and Tientsin*, p. 165.

24. *NCH*, 25 May, p. 317; 26 Sept., p. 536; 29 Oct., p. 187; Jones, *Shanghai and Tientsin*, p. 165.

25. Gull, *British Economic Interests*, pp. 191–95. *Finance and Commerce*, 26 Jan. 1938, p. 73, gives a breakdown of the railway loans as they stood at the beginning of 1938; see also Young, *China's Wartime Finance*, pp. 338–40.

26. Chairman's Reports at annual meetings of the British and Chinese Corporation, in *The Times*, 26 May 1938; *NCH*, 21 June 1939, p. 511; China Association, *Annual Report, 1937–1938* (London, 1938), p. xlvii; *Annual Report, 1938–1939* (London, 1939), pp. xiv–xv.

27. *NCH*, 28 Dec. 1938, p. 529.

28. *NCH*, 19 Jan. 1938, p. 87; *FRUS Japan*, I, 760–61; 337 *H.C.Deb.*, 20 June 1938, col. 683; *FRUS 1938*, IV, 149–50. Some idea of the loss suffered from the river's closing may be gained from the following figures of the value of British trade at the three largest river ports.

IMPORTS (in Customs Gold Units)

	1936	1937	1938	1939	1940
Chungking	78,706	182,534	432,705	42,434	172,978
Hankow	2,951,467	1,335,235	82,784	5,913	23
Nanking	540,329	493,616	—	—	—

EXPORTS (in Standard Dollars)

	1936	1937	1938	1939	1940
Chungking	40	—	—	—	—
Hankow	5,281,771	3,518,982	48,078	—	—
Nanking	306,702	706,755	—	—	—

Chungking could be reached overland via the Burma Road after its opening in late 1938; some trade with Hankow was possible over the railway from Canton until both cities fell in October 1938. Figures compiled from Maritime Customs, *The Trade of China*, 1937–1940.

29. *FRUS 1938*, IV, 329–30, 466–68.

30. *NCH*, 23 March, p. 462; 333 *H.C.Deb.*, 25 March, col. 1383.

31. *NCH*, 3 Aug., p. 191, which also charged that the Japanese guards refused to stay aboard when the ship was in guerrilla territory.

32. *The Times*, 29 July; *NCH*, 3 Aug., p. 191; *Finance and Commerce*, 25 May 1938, p. 409. See also John Ahlers, *Closing the 'Open Door' in China* (Shanghai, 1940), pp. 56–58.

33. RIIA, *Survey, 1938*, I, 556; China Association, *Annual Report, 1938–1939*, pp. xix–xx; *DBFP*, VIII, No. 30.

34. *FRUS 1938*, IV, 13–14, 29–30, 38–39, 41–42, 46–53.

35. RIIA, *Survey, 1938*, I, 524–25.

36. Compiled from Great Britain, *Accounts and Papers, Trade and Navigation Accounts, Session* 1938–1939, XXIV; Board of Trade, *Accounts Relating to the Import Trade and the Re-export Trade of the United Kingdom, 1938–1944* (London, no date); Gull, *British Economic Interests*, p. 179.

37. Gull, p. 190.

38. Compiled from Maritime Customs, *The Trade of China*, 1936–1939. The figures are compiled without taking into consideration Japanese commercial shipments under the guise of military cargoes.

39. Gull, *British Economic Interests*, pp. 190, 197.

40. *DBFP*, VIII, No. 99.

41. *The Times*, 30 Dec. 1938.

42. *NCH*, 12 April 1939, p. 65; 5 April, pp. 25–26; 3 May, p. 205.

43. Grew Papers, Conversations, 1937–1938, Memo. of 28 June, pp. 303–4; *NCH*, 9 Nov. 1938, p. 232; 30 Nov., p. 366; 14 Dec., p. 449.

44. *The Times*, 30 Dec. 1938.

45. Ch.-Walden, 'Sino-Japanese War and the Open Door', p. 644.

CHAPTER VII

1. As introductions to Shanghai, see F. C. Jones, *Shanghai and Tientsin*, and Rhoades Murphey, *Shanghai: Key to Modern China* (Cambridge, Mass., 1953), especially chap. i.

2. Jones, *Shanghai and Tientsin*, pp. 1–2.

3. *Ibid.*, p. 37.

4. *Ibid.*, pp. 88–89; *Finance and Commerce*, 20 Oct., p. 297; 24 Nov., p. 409. In October, however, *Finance and Commerce* reported that the destruction of British capital assets had been 'surprisingly small' (6 Oct., p. 257).

5. *The Times*, 20 Aug. 1937; China Association, *Annual Report, 1937–1938*, p. xxxi.

6. China Association, *Annual Report, 1937–1938*, pp. xxx–xxxi.

7. 329 H.C.Deb., 24 Nov., col. 1197; *Japan Weekly Chronicle*, 18 Nov., p. 666; *FRUS 1937*, III, 684; *NCH*, 17 Nov., p. 245.

8. *FRUS 1937*, III, 704–5, 708; *The Times*, 22 Nov.

9. *NCH*, 17 Nov., p. 247; *Finance and Commerce*, 17 Nov., pp. 377–78.

10. *FRUS 1937*, III, 707; Jones, *Shanghai and Tientsin*, p. 66.

11. *FRUS 1937*, III, 705, 742, 747, 749–50, 754.

12. *Ibid.*, pp. 756–57.

13. *Ibid.*, pp. 760–61, 770, 779–80.

14. *NCH*, 5 Jan. 1938, p. 12.

15. *FRUS 1938*, IV, 116–17. There was no second in command as such to the S.M.P. Commissioner, but rather a number of Deputy Commissioners of different nationalities and equal rank.

16. *Ibid.*, pp. 123–28; 107 H.L.Deb., 15 Feb., col. 667.

17. *FRUS 1938*, IV, 129–31.

18. *Ibid.*, pp. 152, 175–76, 178, 184–85.

19. Lawford to Maze, 8 Jan., 18 Jan., 31 Jan. 1938, Maze Papers, I.G.'s Personal Correspondence, British Embassy, I, Jan.–April 1938.

20. *FRUS 1938*, III, 186–87.

21. *Oriental Affairs*, Dec. 1938, pp. 306–7; *NCH*, 29 March 1939, p. 544.

22. *FRUS 1938*, III, 184–85.

23. *Ibid.*, pp. 215–17.

24. RIIA, *Survey, 1938*, I, 560.

25. *DBFP*, IX, Appendix III, pp. 536–38; *DBFP*, VIII, No. 10.

26. *NCH*, 10 Aug., p. 232.

27. *Ibid.*, 7 Sept., p. 402. At the time there were 1,113 Japanese in the French Concession and 151 in the British.

CHAPTER VIII

1. Avon, *Facing the Dictators*, pp. 621–45; Sumner Welles, *The Time for Decision* (New York, 1944), pp. 64–69; Hull, *Memoirs*, I, 573.

2. *FRUS 1938*, III, 139–40; *FRUS Japan*, I, 463–64; 337 H.C.Deb., 21 June, cols. 905–6; *NCH*, 29 June, p. 526.

3. *FRUS 1938*, III, 491–503; League of Nations, *Official Journal*, Feb. 1938, p. 120.

4. *FRUS 1938*, III, 80.

5. League, *Official Journal*, May–June 1938, p. 378.

6. *FRUS 1938*, III, 104.

7. *The Times*, 22 Jan. 1938; *FRUS 1938*, III, 108, 111, 119.

8. *FRUS 1938*, III, 89–93; for the American reply which took a somewhat more optimistic view about the future course of Japanese policy and of the growing strength of the West, see pp. 142–53.

9. 332 *H.C.Deb.*, cols. 367–70; 109 *H.L.Deb.*, cols. 653–73.

10. Medlicott, *Economic Blockade*, I, 384; *FRUS 1938*, III, 153, 172–73.

11. 338 *H.C.Deb.*, col. 2728.

12. 337 *H.C.Deb.*, 24 June 1938, col. 1408; 347 *H.C.Deb.*, 16 May 1939, col. 110; *DBFP*, VIII, No. 379. Meanwhile on 1 July 1938 Washington announced a 'moral embargo' which discouraged the sale to Japan of aircraft which could be used to bomb civilians.

13. *FRUS 1937*, III, 769–70; Young, *Helping Hand*, p. 212.

14. Young, *China's Wartime Finance*, pp. 192–205; *Helping Hand*, pp. 34–42, 62–65; Chang Kia-ngau, *The Inflationary Spiral: The Experience in China, 1939–1950* (Cambridge, Mass., 1958), pp. 287–88; Chou Shun-hsin, *The Chinese Inflation, 1937–1949* (New York, 1963), pp. 119–20.

15. *NCH*, 6 April, p. 21.

16. *FRUS 1938*, IV, 3–4; *Economist, Commercial History and Review of 1938*, in issue of 18 Feb. 1939, p. 64.

17. *FRUS 1938*, III, 525.

18. Young, *Helping Hand*, pp. 73–74; Friedman, *British Policy in China*, pp. 142–43; see also Lord Lytton's letter in *The Times*, 5 July 1938.

19. *FRUS 1938*, III, 535–37. Craigie had agreed that a loan of this sort would not be open to the same objections by the Japanese as would a grant of general credits, although he recommended that they should be warned beforehand, and assured that the loan would not simply allow the Chinese to release their own currency reserves for arms purchases (*DBFP*, VIII, 257n).

20. 338 *H.C.Deb.*, col. 1524; *FRUS 1938*, III, 540; Alfred Duff Cooper, *Old Men Forget: The Autobiography of Duff Cooper* (London, 1954), p. 222; see also Feiling, *Neville Chamberlain*, p. 354, and Chamberlain's statement in Parliament on 26 July (338 *H.C.Deb.*, col. 2961).

21. *Japan Weekly Chronicle*, 21 July, p. 62; *DBFP*, VIII, No. 7.

22. *New Statesman*, 16 July, p. 101; see also issue of 6 Aug., p. 211; *Finance and Commerce*, 20 July, pp. 41–43.

23. *FRUS 1938*, III, 551–53, 560–61; *DBFP*, VIII, No. 67.

24. Craigie, *Behind the Japanese Mask*, p. 61; David J. Lu, *From the Marco Polo Bridge to Pearl Harbor: Japan's Entry into World War II* (Washington, 1961), p. 36.

25. *DBFP*, VIII, 5n–6n.

26. 110 *H.L.Deb.*, cols. 1528–63; *Japan Weekly Chronicle*, 4 Aug., p. 117; Friedman, *British Policy in China*, pp. 152–53.

27. 338 *H.C.Deb.*, 26 July, col. 2962. This statement is unhappily reminiscent of Chamberlain's famous characterization of the Sudetenland question two months later as 'a quarrel in a far away country between people of whom we know nothing' (broadcast of 27 September, quoted in Martin Gilbert and Richard Gott, *The Appeasers* [London, 1963], p. 170). America was not the only country where isolationism influenced the making of foreign policy.

28. *FRUS 1938*, III, 238–39, 250–51, 254–55, 257–58, 262–64; *DBFP*, VIII, No. 2, Nos. 4–5, Nos. 11–12, No. 18, Nos. 22–23, No. 25, No. 27, No. 36. Unknown to the West, Ugaki was already in secret correspondence with Chungking; see Ugaki Kazushige, 'Sino-Japanese Peace Talks, June–September 1938: Extracts from the Diary of General Ugaki', trans. E. H. M. Colegrave, *St Antony's Papers, No. II: Far Eastern Affairs, No. I*, ed. G. F. Hudson (London, 1957), pp. 94–104; Chonghan Kim, 'Konoye Fumimaro and Japanese Foreign Policy: 1937–1941', Ph.D. diss., Indiana University, 1956 (Ann Arbor.: University Microfilms, publication no. 17,964), pp. 103–5.

29. *DBFP*, VIII, Nos. 31–32; *FRUS 1938*, III, 265–66.

30. *DBFP*, VIII, No. 38, No. 41.

31. *Ibid,*, Nos. 45–46, No. 52.

32. *Ibid.*, Nos. 84–86, No. 96, No. 108; *FRUS 1938*, III, 280–81.

33. *NCH*, 12 Oct., p. 57; *DBFP*, VIII, No. 122.

34. Ugaki Kazushige, *Ugaki Nissei (Ugaki Diary)* (Tokyo, 1954), pp. 334–35. I am indebted to Mr Kosaka Masataka of Kyoto University for this reference.

35. *DBFP*, VIII, No. 95, No. 102; Lu, *Marco Polo Bridge*, p. 43.

36. *FRUS 1938*, III, 297; Jones, *New Order*, p. 78.

37. *DBFP*, VIII, No. 67, No. 77; *FRUS 1938*, III, 510; League, *Official Journal*, Nov. 1938, p. 865; Annex 1726, p. 988.

38. *DBFP*, VIII, No. 106; *FRUS 1938*, III, 514–15, 517; League, *Official Journal*, Nov. 1938, pp. 878–79.

39. *Japan Weekly Chronicle*, 6 Oct., p. 393.

40. *DBFP*, VIII, No. 233; see also No. 234 and No. 265, and *FRUS 1938*, III, 380–81.

41. *DBFP*, VIII, No .305.

42. *Ibid.*, No. 142. No. 158, No. 211.

43. *FRUS Japan*, I, 785–90; *DBFP*, VIII, No. 125.

CHAPTER IX

1. *DBFP*, VIII, No. 188, No. 198.

2. 340 *H.C.Deb.*, col. 82.

3. *Finance and Commerce*, 9 Nov., p. 368; Friedman, *British Relations with China*, p. 167; *The Times*, 11 Nov.; *DBFP*, VIII, No. 205, No. 213.

4. See below, p. 91.

5. In fact the Japanese turned out to be somewhat more liberal in their regulations on the Pearl River; see *FRUS 1938*, IV, 542–49; *NCH*, 8 March 1939, pp. 397, 406.

6. *FRUS 1938*, IV, 194–96.

7. *DBFP*, VIII, No. 214.

8. *Ibid.*, No. 239, No. 241, No. 259; *FRUS 1938*, IV, 203–4. See also *DBFP*, VIII, No. 278, No. 282, No. 287; *NCH*, 30 Nov., p. 360. *NCH*, 23 Nov., pp. 309, 319–20, carried articles exposing the Japanese trade on the river.

9. *FRUS Japan*, I, 477–78.

10. *Ibid.*, pp. 478–81.

11. *NCH*, 9 Nov., p. 231.

12. *DBFP*, VIII, No. 216, No. 249, No. 294; *FRUS Japan*, I, 801–6.

13. *DBFP*, VIII, No. 323, No. 333.

14. *The Times*, 8 Dec.

15. RIIA, *Documents*, 1938, I, 353–54.

16. *DBFP*, VIII, No. 124, No. 197, No. 254, p. 239n; Jones, *New Order*, pp. 102–8.

17. 340 *H.C.Deb.*, col. 33.

18. *DBFP*, VIII, No. 57. These ideas seem to have come from a conference between government representatives and members of the China Association in London (*ibid.*, p. 191n). Undoubtedly some business circles favoured such action; in January 1939 a member of the American embassy in London was told that large firms generally wanted retaliation, preferring it to slow strangulation. The smaller concerns did not agree, but they had less influence in Whitehall (*FRUS 1938*, III, 638–39).

19. *DBFP*, VIII, No. 175, No. 208.

20. *FRUS 1938*, III, 400–2.

21. *DBFP*, VIII, No. 382.

22. *Ibid.*, No. 384.

23. *Ibid.*, p. 278n, No. 298; *FRUS 1938*, IV, 194. For the varying views held by members of the State Department, see *FRUS 1938*, III, 406–9, 425–27, and *FRUS 1939*, III, 483–85, 489–90, 496–97.

24. *DBFP*, VIII, No. 298, No. 379.

25. *DBFP*, VIII, No. 440; *FRUS 1939*, III, 490–93. The same note was sent to Paris (*DBFP*, VIII, No. 452).

26. *FRUS 1939*, III, 646.

27. *DBFP*, VIII, No. 453.

28. *Ibid.*, No. 462, No. 465.

29. *Ibid.*, No. 280.

30. *Ibid.*, No. 354, 362.

31. 341 *H.C.Deb.*, 16 Nov., cols. 843–44; *NCH*, 21 Dec., p. 513. For the future history of the line, see Chang, *China's Struggle for Railway Development*, pp. 256–74.

32. For the background to the American credits, see Young, *Helping Hand*, pp. 75–85; also *China's Wartime Finance*, pp. 102–3, 106.

33. *DBFP*, VIII, No. 355.

34. *FRUS Japan*, I, 820–26.

35. Text of final note in *DBFP*, VIII, No. 431.

36. *Ibid.*, No. 407, No. 422.

37. *The Times*, 17 Jan., 25 Jan., 1939; *NCH*, 18 Jan., p. 100.

CHAPTER X

1. *DBFP*, VIII, No. 308.

2. *Ibid.*, No. 433, No. 441.

3. *Ibid.*, No. 473, No. 491; *FRUS 1939*, III, 15; see also Storry, *Double Patriots*, p. 242.

4. *DBFP*, VIII, No. 526, No. 536. For the Triple Alliance negotiations, see the RIIA, *Survey of International Affairs, 1939–1946: The Eve of the War*, ed. Arnold J. and Veronica M. Toynbee (London, 1958), pp. 666–74; Presseisen, *Germany and Japan*, chaps. vii–viii.

5. *DBFP*, IX, No. 20, No. 23. Meanwhile Chiang was arguing that Britain should include the Far East in any agreement she made with Russia.

6. *FRUS 1939*, III, 528–30.

7. *DBFP*, IX, No. 38, No. 93; *FRUS 1939*, III, 534.

8. Wright to Maze, 1 Aug. 1939, Maze Papers, I.G.'s Personal Correspondence, Non-Resident Secretary, Jan.–Sept. 1939, No. 55. Wright, who later became the biographer of Sir Robert Hart, was then the Non-Resident Secretary in the Customs' London office.

9. *FRUS 1939*, III, 746–49.

10. *Ibid.*, pp. 753–55.

11. Chang, *Inflationary Spiral*, p. 21; George E. Taylor, *The Struggle for North China* (New York, 1940), p. 25; Young, *Helping Hand*, pp. 154–55; *China's Wartime Finance*, pp. 166–71; *Economist, Commercial History and Review of 1938*, Feb. 1939, p. 64.

12. *DBFP*, VIII, No. 397, No. 409, No. 442, No. 456; *FRUS 1939*, III, 643–45.

13. Chungking pointed out that Japan had detained all the revenues collected in occupied China, save for a single remittance from Shanghai in June 1938, and that in order to make up the deficit, China had advanced about Ch $175,000,000. See *DBFP*, VIII, No. 423; Friedman, *British Relations with China*, p. 185; Young, *Helping Hand*, pp. 101–6; *China's Wartime Finance*, pp. 89–92; Clifford, 'Sir Frederick Maze', pp. 27–28.

14. *DBFP*, VIII, No. 426, No. 428, Nos. 436–38, No. 472.

15. *Ibid.*, No. 505.

16. *Ibid.*, No. 528. The most complete account of the various programmes to stabilize China's currency before Pearl Harbor is in Young, *China's Wartime Finance*, pp. 206–246.

17. *Ibid.*, No. 546; 344 *H.C.Deb.*, col. 2147; see also Great Britain, Accounts and Papers, Session 1938–1939, XVI, *Chinese Currency: Arrangements proposed in regard to the Chinese Currency Stabilization Fund*, Cmd. 5963.

18. *DBFP*, VIII, No. 565.

19. *The Times*, 9 March 1939; *NCH*, 15 March, p. 440.

20. *DBFP*, IX, No. 131.

21. *The Times*, 7 March, 1939.

22. *DBFP*, IX, No. 27; *Finance and Commerce*, 10 May 1939, pp. 388–89.

23. *FRUS 1939*, III, 401–2, 409.

24. Chang, *Inflationary Spiral*, pp. 293–94; Chou, *Chinese Inflation*, pp. 120–22; Young, *Helping Hand*, pp. 162–66; *Economist*, 10 June, p. 607; *DBFP*, IX, No. 110, No. 168, No. 289, Nos. 341–42, No. 602. Among the reasons for the British failure to contribute more to the Fund was the belief that the Chinese were mismanaging it. There was also considerable friction between Finance Minister Kung on the one hand, and Clark Kerr and T. V. Soong on the other. Soong and the British ambassador both wanted to implement the Customs agreement, going over Kung's head to Chiang if necessary, but despite the opposition to Kung, his closeness to Chiang seems to have saved him (*DBFP*, IX, No. 321; *FRUS 1939*, III, 702–3). For the credits of 1940, and the agreements of April 1941 which followed, see Young, *China's Wartime Finance*, pp. 232–44.

25. In a letter to *The Times*, 2 March 1939; see *FRUS 1939*, III, 781–83 for further evidence of Japanese trade discrimination.

26. *DBFP*, IX, No. 58, No. 172.

27. 345 *H.C.Deb.*, 3 April 1939, cols. 2422–23; China Association, *Annual Report, 1939–1940* (London, 1940), p. 18, Gull; *British Economic Interests*, p. 190.

28. China, Maritime Customs, *The Trade of China, 1939*, I, 23.

29. *FRUS 1939*, III, 402–3. Nothing in the Maze Papers clearly confirms that the puppets were directly benefiting from the revenues.

30. Clifford, 'Sir Frederick Maze', pp. 31–32.

CHAPTER XI

1. *DBFP*, VIII, Nos. 107–8, No. 111, No. 113, No. 118, No. 127.

2. *Ibid.*, No. 398; 347 *H.C.Deb.*, 15 May 1939, col. 967.

3. *FRUS 1938*, IV, 139–43.

4. *DBFP*, VIII, No. 496, No. 498.

5. *Ibid.*, No. 497; see No. 518 for a similar American move.

6. *NCH*, 1 March 1939, pp. 365–66, 368; *DBFP*, VIII, No. 495.

7. *DBFP*, VIII, No. 496, No. 507, No. 509, No. 515, No. 522, No. 532, No. 561; *FRUS 1939*, IV, 11–13; *NCH*, 8 March p. 411.

8. *DBFP*, IX, No. 9; *FRUS 1939*, IV, 24–29; *Oriental Affairs*, June 1939, pp. 318–19; *NCH*, 26 April, p. 148; 3 May, p. 191.

9. *DBFP*, IX, No. 44. Similar representations were made in Shanghai to Phillips, the S.M.C., and the French authorities (*Ibid.*, No. 46; *NCH*, 10 May, p. 234).

10. *DBFP*, IX, No. 9; *FRUS 1939*, IV, 36–40. The Voting List showed that on 1 April 1939, out of 3941 votes, the Japanese had 1301, the British 1198, and the Americans 397. No other nation had over 300. At this rate Phillips estimated that Japan should be able to win control of the Council by the time of the elections of April 1940 (*DBFP*, IX, 136n; No. 151).

11. *FRUS 1939*, IV, 61.

12. *DBFP*, IX, No. 151.

13. *FRUS 1939*, IV, 44–45.

14. *DBFP*, IX, No. 101.

15. *DBFP*, IX, No. 234; *Oriental Affairs*, March 1940, pp. 138–39; *FRUS 1939*, IV, 71–72, 74–75, 78, 83–84.

16. *FRUS 1939*, IV, 108–9; *DBFP*, IX, No. 63, No. 69, Nos. 78–79.

17. *DBFP*, IX, No. 79, Nos. 82–83.

18. *Ibid.*, No. 432, No. 501; *FRUS 1939*, IV, 160–62.

19. Taylor, *Struggle for North China*, pp. 125–33.

20. For an expression of this view, see K. E. Jordan to Sir F. Maze, 31 Dec.–5 Jan. 1938, in the Maze Papers, I.G.'s Personal Correspondence, Jan.–June 1938; Clifford 'Sir Frederick Maze', p. 29.

21. *DBFP*, VIII, No. 129, No. 244, No. 273, No. 345, No. 469.

22. *Ibid.*, No. 408.

23. *Ibid.*, Appendix II, Nos. iii–iv.

24. *Ibid.*, Appendix II, No. vi, No. ix, No. xi, No. xvi. The Council's Legal Authority doubted if there was sufficient evidence to warrant Ssu's surrender (*ibid.*, No. 443).

25. *Ibid.*, p. 557n.

26. *Ibid.*, No. 136, No. 226, No. 375.

27. *Ibid.*, No. 247, No. 317, No. 334, No. 336, No. 346.

28. *Ibid.*, Nos. 356–57. The Italian consul-general (whose personal sympathies seem to have been with his Western colleagues) joined in warning against the restrictions (*ibid.*, No. 340).

29. *Ibid.*, No. 358, No. 392, No. 401. Meanwhile Grew was instructed to point out that America's interests were also involved (*FRUS 1938*, IV, 163–64).

30. *DBFP*, VIII, No. 405.

31. *Ibid.*, No. 448.

32. *Ibid.*, No. 454; Piggott, *Broken Thread*, p. 314.

33. *DBFP*, VIII, No. 477, 482; Jones, *Shanghai and Tientsin*, p. 173.

34. *DBFP*, VIII, Nos. 489–90. At this point the Italian consul-general told his French colleague that his policy of support had been overruled, and Rome had decided to allow the Japanese the use of the Italian Concession (*ibid.*, No. 503).

35. *Ibid.*, No. 533, No. 537, No. 544, No. 554, No. 579; *DBFP*, IX, No. 2; Piggott, *Broken Thread*, pp. 314–16.

36. *DBFP*, IX, No. 2, No. 5, No. 15, No. 26.

37. *Ibid.*, No. 2; Jamieson to Tashiro, 11 April 1939, IMT 459, IPS Doc. 2383, pp. 507–8; in the microfilms of the Library of Congress archives from the Japanese Foreign Ministry, Reel WT 60. (This collection hereafter cited as Jap. Archives.)

38. See the reconstruction of events made by F. C. Jones, for the RIIA, *Eve of the War*, pp. 640–41.

39. *DBFP*, IX, No. 249.

40. RIIA, *Eve of the War*, p. 641.

41. *DBFP*, IX, No. 64, No. 180.

42. *Ibid.*, No. 64.

43. *Ibid.*, No. 86, No. 96. There were at the time some fourteen held by the British including the four involved in the Cheng case.

44. *Ibid,*, No. 89, No. 102, No. 113, No. 134, No. 137, No. 143, Nos. 148–49, No. 161, No. 169. Peking ordered all its employees out of the British and French Concessions, and the Yokohama Specie Bank was told to leave by the 14th (*ibid.*, No. 173). Homma was himself coming under fire from his superiors for his leniency towards the British, and his own chief of staff was urging action against the Concession (Piggott, *Broken Thread*, p. 139; Storry, *Double Patriots*, pp. 253–54).

45. *DBFP*, IX, Nos. 175–76, No. 181, Nos. 194–95; *FRUS 1939*, IV, 176–78.

46. *DBFP*, IX, No. 180, No. 191, No. 205, No. 243, No. 249.

47. *Ibid.*, No. 197, No. 203. To Dooman, Craigie made the rather bitter comment that Britain had picked poor ground on which to make a stand, and added that had it not been for Clark Kerr's opposition, the matter could have been settled 'without violence to British concepts of terminology' (*FRUS 1939*, IV, 181–82).

48. *DBFP*, IX, No. 180; p. 180n; 113 *H.L.Deb.*, cols. 549–52.

49. *DBFP*, IX, No. 242; *NCH*, 21 June, p. 492. The blockade of the French Concession was partly due to the demands of geography, as it was impossible to cut off the British Concession alone.

50. *DBFP*, IX, No. 198.

51. 348 *H.C.Deb.*, 13 June, cols. 1109–11; 15 June, cols. 1508–9; 113 *H.L.Deb.*, 20 June, 549–52; *The Times*, 17 June.

52. 348 *H.C.Deb.*, 14 June, col. 1279; 15 June, cols. 1508–9; 21 June, col. 2202.

53. *DBFP*, IX, No. 210, No. 218, Nos. 221–23; *FRUS 1939*, IV, 185, 213–17, 220–21; William L. Langer and S. Everett Gleason, *The Challenge to Isolation, 1937–1940* (New York, 1952), pp. 151–52.

54. *DBFP*, IX, No. 227. Clark Kerr generally agreed, as long as the talks were restricted to issues at Tientsin alone, and took place after Britain had threatened retaliation (*ibid.*, No. 231).

55. *DBFP*, IX, No. 248, No. 250, No. 276, No. 279.

56. *Ibid.*, Nos. 239–40, Nos. 254–55, No. 257, No. 266, No. 269; 349 *H.C.Deb.*, col. 386; 113 *H.L.Deb.*, cols. 760–62. Once again the useful General Piggott acted as intermediary, this time between Craigie and Hiranuma (IMTFE Record, Affidavit of Gen. Piggott, pp. 29233–34, Exhibit 3226).

57. *DBFP*, IX, No. 259.

58. *DGFP*, VI, No. 548; Ott to Berlin, 20 June 1939 and Boltze to Weizsäcker, 22 July 1939, IMT I, IPS Doc. 4050, p. 4549. Jap. Archives, Reel WT 5. On 5 July Craigie wrote Vice-Minister Renzo Sawada, objecting to Japanese press reports that he would discuss general questions of British policy, and insisting that he was only authorized to deal with the questions at Tientsin; IMT 459, IPS Doc. 2383, p. 226, Jap. Archives, Reel WT 60.

59. *DBFP*, IX, Nos. 325–26, No. 328.

60. *Ibid.*, No. 279, No. 350.

61. *Ibid.*, No. 365; 350 H.C.Deb., 24 July, col. 944.

62. *The Times*, 22 July, 25 July; *NCH*, 2 Aug., p. 178; *Japan Weekly Chronicle*, 27 July, p. 103; 3 Aug., p. 124.

63. *Daily Herald* (London), 25 July; *New Statesman and Nation*, 29 July, pp. 168–69.

64. *Oriental Affairs*, Aug. 1939, p. 60.

65. *NCH*, 2 Aug., p. 178; but both the *NCH* (2 Aug., p. 181) and *Finance and Commerce* (2 Aug., pp. 95–96) criticized the protest.

66. Craigie, *Behind the Japanese Mask*, p. 75; see also his comments at the time in *FRUS 1939*, IV, 231. For Hiranuma's statement, see *The Times*, 12 July; *DBFP*, IX, No. 372, No. 375. Ambassador Shigemitsu also told the Italian chargé in London that the formula represented a substantial modification of British policy (Italy, Ministero degli Affari Esteri, *I Documenti Diplomatici Italiani*, ottava serie, ed. Mario Toscano [Rome, 1952–], XIII, No. 651).

67. *DBFP*, IX, No. 389; *NCH*, 2 Aug., p. 178; *The Times*, 25 July.

68. *DBFP*, IX, No. 297, No. 306, Nos. 329–30.

69. For the background of the American move, see Langer and Gleason, *Challenge to Isolation*, pp. 157–58. On 27 July Lindsay saw Hull and asked him about the denunciation. 'I never before in my life drew such a complete blank', he reported. 'He spoke as if it were a purely commercial step with no political implications and all in the tone of a very anodyne note in which [the decision] was conveyed to [the] Japanese Government' (*DBFP*, IX, No. 405).

70. *DBFP*, IX, No. 376, Nos. 380–81, No. 392, Nos. 402–3.

71. *Ibid.*, No. 438.

72. *Ibid.*, Nos. 419–20.

73. *Ibid.*, No. 364, No. 433, No. 457, No. 485, No. 516, No. 541.

74. *Ibid.*, Nos. 491–92, No. 527, No. 537, No. 545; *DGFP*, VI, No. 762. From Tientsin the German consul wired that despite official denials of any connection with anti-British riots in the city, the Japanese army was doing all it could to wreck the negotiations (Stoller to Berlin, 6 Aug. 1939, IMT 1, IPS Doc. 4047, p. 4531, Jap. Archives, Reel WT 5).

75. *DBFP*, IX, No. 545, No. 549; *The Times*, 21 Aug. The Japanese statement is translated in IMT 459, IPS Doc. 2383, pp. 357–65, Jap. Archives, Reel WT 60.

76. *FRUS 1939*, IV, 260.

77. Craigie, *Behind the Japanese Mask*, p. 77.

78. See F. C. Jones's comments in RIIA, *Eve of the War*, pp. 649–50.

CHAPTER XII

1. *DBFP*, IX, No. 227. For the Spear case, see Piggott, *Broken Thread*, pp. 325–30.

2. *DBFP*, IX, No. 231.

3. *Ibid.*, No. 307.

4. *Ibid.*, Appendix I, pp. 528–32.

5. *Ibid.*, No. 116, No. 118, No. 150; the Hiranuma letter is in *FRUS Japan*, II, 1.

6. *DBFP*, IX, No. 473, No. 497, No. 509.

7. *Ibid.*, pp. 353n, 368n; No. 412, No. 453; Friedman, *British Relations with China*, p. 193; Young, *Helping Hand*, pp. 137–38; see also China, Ministry of Information, *China Handbook, 1937–1945*, revised edition (New York, 1947), pp. 164, 209.

8. Storry, *Double Patriots*, pp. 254–55.

9. See the comment of the Kwantung Army spokesman in *I Documenti Diplomatici Italiani*, ottava serie, XIII, No. 180.

10. *Idem*; United States, Department of State, *Nazi–Soviet Relations, 1939–1941*: *Documents from the Archives of the German Foreign Office*, ed. R. J. Sontag and J. S. Beddie (Washington, 1948), pp. 70–71.

11. *The Times*, 26 August.

12. *DBFP*, IX, No. 584.

13. *Ibid.*, Nos. 599–600.

14. *Ibid.*, No. 611.

15. *Ibid.*, No. 597; *FRUS 1939*, III, 217–20.

16. 337 *H.C.Deb.*, 27 June 1938, col. 1500.

17. Kirby, *War Against Japan*, I, 24.

18. Hector C. Bywater, 'Britain on the Seas', *Foreign Affairs* (New York), XVI, No. 2 (January 1938), pp. 215–16.

19. *DBFP*, VIII, No. 338, No. 487; Appendix I, No. i.

20. *Ibid.*, Appendix I, No. ii.

21. Kittredge, 'United States–British Naval Cooperation', Section I, Notes and Appendices, p. 26; G. Hermon Gill, *Royal Australian Navy, 1939–1942* (Canberra, 1957) (*Australia in the War of 1939–1945*, Series 2 [Navy] vol. I), pp. 41–43; Kirby, *War Against Japan*, I, 20; F. L. W. Wood, *The New Zealand People at War: Political and External Affairs* (Wellington, 1958) (*Official History of New Zealand in the Second World War, 1939–1945*), pp. 67, 76.

22. Butler, *Grand Strategy*, II, 13; Jean Decoux, *A la Barre de l'Indochine: Histoire de mon Gouvernement-Général (1940–1945)* (Paris, 1949), pp. 17–25.

23. Kirby, *War Against Japan*, I, 21; *DBFP*, IX, No. 322.

24. *DBFP*, IX, No. 6, No. 54, No. 434, No. 554; *FRUS 1939*, III, 525.

25. Bismarck to Tokyo, 9 Sept. 1939, IMT 1, IPS Doc. 4050, p. 4553, Jap. Archives, Reel WT 5.

26. *DBFP*, IX, Nos. 618–19.

27. *FRUS 1939*, III, 229, 237–38, 242–45, 247, 252–53, 255–59, 266–71; *FRUS Japan*, II, 15–19.

28. Kirby, *War Against Japan*, I, 23; *The Times*, 3 Oct., 14 Dec.; 352 *H.C.Deb.*, 25 Oct., col. 1438.

29. *The Times*, 14 Nov.; *FRUS 1939*, III, 294.

30. *FRUS 1939*, III, 169; 351 *H.C.Deb.*, 7 Sept., cols. 570–71. Nomura was an American expert, who had served as naval attaché in Washington; his chief job seems to have been to try to negotiate a commercial agreement with America, to replace the expiring treaty of commerce.

31. *DBFP*, IX, No. 441; *FRUS 1939*, III, 299–300, 323–25. On Wang, see RIIA, *Survey of International Affairs, 1939–1946: The Initial Triumph of the Axis*, ed. Arnold J. and Veronica M. Toynbee (London, 1958), pp. 549–52.

32. The following discussion of trade problems owes much to Medlicott, *Economic Blockade*, I, 338ff.

33. *NCH*, 29 Nov., p. 364. The pledge had in fact been made by the Ministry of Economic Warfare on 22 September, but was not publicized (Medlicott, I, 395–96). Japan was particularly concerned about her imports of German machinery for the extraction of oil from Manchurian coal (*The Times*, 1 Dec.).

34. RIIA, *Initial Triumph*, pp. 572–86.

35. *FRUS 1939*, III, 92–95, 98–99, 321–23.

CHAPTER XIII

1. RIIA, *Initial Triumph*, p. 566; Craigie, *Behind the Japanese Mask*, pp. 81–82. For Japanese-American relations in this period, see Herbert Feis, *The Road to Pearl Harbor: The Coming of the War Between the United States and Japan* (Princeton, 1950), pp. 38–75; RIIA, *Initial Triumph*, pp. 558–63; Langer and Gleason, *Challenge to Isolation*, pp. 298–311.

2. *The Times*, 26 Jan. 1940.

3. Great Britain, Accounts and Papers, Session 1939–1940, XII, *Japan No. 1: Correspondence between H.M. Government . . . and the Japanese Government regarding the . . . 'Asama Maru'*, January–February, *1940*, Cmd. 6166; see also Gill, *Royal Australian Navy*, p. 140; Craigie, *Behind the Japanese Mask*, pp. 82–84; RIIA, *Initial Triumph*, pp. 567–69.

4. Grew, Diary, 1940, III, 4252–53.

5. *FRUS 1940*, IV, 270–72.

6. Wang's promise was somewhat qualified by a simultaneous Japanese statement which claimed primacy for that country in the development and utilization of Chinese resources (*The Times*, 1 April.).

7. Clifford, 'Sir Frederick Maze', p. 32.

8. Shigemitsu to Arita, 23 March, IMTFE, Record, pp. 9675–77, Exhibit 1016.

9. *Japan Weekly Chronicle*, 4 April, p. 406. There was a striking contrast between this speech and one which Grew had delivered the previous October, when he had been outspoken on the subject of Japanese-American difficulties.

10. *NCH*, 3 April, p. 35; 359 *H.C.Deb.*, 3 April, cols. 164–65; *FRUS 1940*, IV, 10, 308–9; Craigie, *Behind the Japanese Mask*, p. 86.

11. *FRUS 1939*, IV, 250, 254–56; *FRUS 1940*, IV, 844–57; 362 *H.C.Deb.*, 19 June, cols. 140–41; Great Britain, Accounts and Papers, Session 1939–1940, XII, *China No. 1: (1940) Agreement between H.M. Government . . . and the Japanese Government relating to local issues at Tientsin, June 19, 1940*, Cmd. 6212.

12. 362 *H.C.Deb.*, 10 July, col. 1139; *FRUS 1940*, IV, 856–57.

13. Shigemitsu to Arita, 13 May 1940, IMTFE, Record, pp. 9683–86, Exhibit 1017.

14. *The Times*, 15 April; *FRUS 1940*, IV, 14–15.

15. *FRUS 1940*, IV, 13–16, 18.

16. *Ibid.*, pp. 17–20. Since early February Japan had been trying to induce the Dutch, both in The Hague and Batavia, to enter into trade talks with them. For the history of Japanese relations with the East Indies in this period, see Hubertus J. van Mook, *The Netherlands East Indies and Japan: Battle on Paper, 1940–1941* (New York, 1944).

17. *FRUS 1940*, IV, 20.

18. Winston S. Churchill, *Their Finest Hour* (Boston, 1949), p. 25. Lothian also argued for the stationing of the American fleet in mid-Pacific (*FRUS 1940*, III, 4).

19. Butler, *Grand Strategy*, II, 328.

20. *FRUS 1940*, IV, 25–26, 29; RIIA, *Initial Triumph*, p. 583.

21. *FRUS 1940*, IV, 26–27.

22. *Ibid.*, pp. 28–29. Three weeks earlier Arita had already hinted to Craigie that some such demands were under consideration (Grew Papers, Conversations, 1939–1940, pp. 135–36).

23. *Oriental Affairs*, July 1940, p. 7; *FRUS 1940*, IV, 36–37.

24. Kirby, *War Against Japan*, I, 45; *FRUS 1939*, IV, 359–60.

25. *FRUS 1940*, IV, 365–67; Wood, *New Zealand People at War*, p. 197.

26. *FRUS 1940*, IV, 367–72. Australia supported the British plans for a settlement, and was also naturally anxious for the American fleet to remain in the Pacific. This latter point became all the more important when on 28 June London informed

Canberra that after the loss of the French fleet, there was no longer any chance of sending a naval force to Singapore soon (Lionel Wigmore, *The Japanese Thrust* [Canberra, 1957] [*Australia in the War of 1939-1945.* Series I (Army) vol. IV], pp. 19-20).

27. *FRUS 1940*, IV, 374-76.

28. Kirby, *War Against Japan*, I, 45; *FRUS 1940*, IV, 40-41; 43-45, 395-96.

29. 363 *H.C.Deb.*, cols. 399-400.

30. *Manchester Guardian*, 15 July.

31. *The Times*, 18 July.

32. *The Times*, 17 July; *FRUS 1940*, IV, 49, 53; *FRUS Japan*, II, 101.

33. *FRUS 1940*, IV, 49-51.

34. Craigie, *Behind the Japanese Mask*, p. 88.

CHAPTER XIV

1. Winston S. Churchill, *The Grand Alliance* (Boston, 1950), pp. 600-1. On the eve of the war Roosevelt did in fact give Lord Halifax as firm a commitment as he could; but would it have stood if American territory had not been attacked? See Raymond Esthus, 'President Roosevelt's Commitment to Britain to Intervene in a Pacific War', *Mississippi Valley Historical Review*, L, No. 1 (June 1963), 28-38.

2. Decoux, *A la Barre de l'Indochine*, pp. 42-49.

3. Kirby, *War Against Japan*, I, 52; G. W. Stöve, 'Queen's Navy at War', *United States Naval Institute Proceedings*, LXXVI, No. 3 (March 1950), 289-301.

4. The agreement is in *Pearl Harbor Attack*, Part 15, pp. 1485-1550. See also Kirby, *War Against Japan*, I, 58; Butler, *Grand Strategy*, II, 425-26; Samuel Eliot Morison, *History of United States Naval Operations in World War II*, vol. I, *The Battle for the Atlantic, September 1939-May 1943* (Boston, 1947), pp. 38-49.

5. Kirby, *War Against Japan*, I, 62-63; the Singapore war plan (ADB-1) is in *Pearl Harbor Attack*, Part 15, pp. 1551-84.

6. Morison, *Rising Sun in the Pacific*, pp. 49-50; Kittredge, 'United States-British Naval Cooperation', Section IV, chap. xiv, pp. 342, 349-50; chap. xv, pp. 404-5, 430-32.

7. Kirby, *War Against Japan*, I, 75, 85; Churchill, *Their Finest Hour*, pp. 166-67, 187, 588-89, 854-59; S. W. Roskill, *The War at Sea, 1939-1943*, vol. I, *The Defensive* (London, 1954) (*History of the Second World War*, U.K. Military Series ed. J. R. M. Butler), pp. 554-59.

8. Kirby, *War Against Japan*, I, 81-82. Churchill had regarded the position at Hongkong as untenable, and earlier opposed this move as a useless diversion of forces.

9. *NCH*, 10 Jan. 1940, p. 48; *The Times*, 8 Jan., 11 Jan.

10. *FRUS 1940*, IV, 727–29, 734; *Oriental Affairs*, March 1940, pp. 139–40.

11. *Oriental Affairs*, Dec. 1940, p. 262; March 1941, pp. 140–46.

12. *NCH*, 3 April, pp. 6, 11; 10 April, p. 46; 17 April, pp. 87, 90–91, 95.

13. *FRUS 1940*, IV, 742–43, 749–52, 829–30.

14. For the correspondence on this, see *FRUS 1940*, IV, 762–83, *passim*.

15. *Oriental Affairs*, Feb. 1941, pp. 97–100; *NCH*, 29 Jan., pp. 166–67.

16. *FRUS 1941*, IV, 824–56, *passim*; *Oriental Affairs*, May 1941, pp. 244–46.

17. See Clifford, 'Sir Frederick Maze', pp. 32–33.

18. *FRUS 1940*, IV, 419–20.

19. 365 *H.C.Deb.*, cols. 301–2. At the same time Churchill asked for an American squadron, 'the bigger the better, to pay a friendly visit to Singapore' (*FRUS 1940*, IV, 163).

20. Sir Josiah Crosby, *Siam: The Crossroads* (London, 1945), p. 120; *FRUS 1940*, IV, 112. The British released seven training aircraft from Hongkong to Indochina, and asked that the United States sell some from Manila. On 16 September they proposed joint military aid to Indochina, but Hull refused, pointing out that this would only lessen the amount of supplies available for Britain (*ibid.*, pp. 116, 120–21).

21. *FRUS 1940*, IV, 177–98.

22. *Ibid.*, pp. 214–16, 222; *FRUS 1941*, V, 2–5.

23. Jones, *New Order*, p. 235.

24. *Ibid.*, p. 236; RIIA, *Initial Triumph*, pp. 621–22; *FRUS 1941*, V, 32–34, 39–41, 73–74.

25. *FRUS 1941*, V, 9–10, 22–23, 29, 57, 93, 99, 112.

26. *Ibid.*, pp. 93–94.

27. *Ibid.*, pp. 112–14, 117–18, 120–24.

28. *Ibid.*, pp. 170–380, *passim*. There is no adequate account of Thai relations with the West in this period. Crosby's book tells little, but there is a brief account of the American side in James V. Martin, 'Thai-American Relations in World War II', *Journal of Asian Studies*, XXII, no. 4 (August 1963), 451–67.

29. Earl of Avon, *The Memoirs of Anthony Eden, Earl of Avon: The Reckoning* (Boston, 1965), p. 354; *Pearl Harbor Attack*, Part 6, p. 2512; Part 4, p. 2014.

30. IMTFE, Record, pp. 9782–87, Exhibit 1039; Shigemitsu to Matsuoka, 8 Feb., *ibid.*, pp. 9789–93, Exhibit 1040; Matsuoka to Shigemitsu, 8 Feb., *ibid.*, pp. 9794–95, Exhibit 1041; *FRUS 1941*, V, 55, 61–62, 69; Avon, *Reckoning*, pp. 356–57.

31. *FRUS 1941*, v, 70, 74–77; *FRUS Japan*, ii, 137–43; William L. Langer and S. Everett Gleason, *The Undeclared War, 1940–1941* (New York, 1953), p. 325; Avon, *The Reckoning*, p. 359.

32. Matsuoka to Shigemitsu, 18 Feb., IMTFE Record, pp. 9811–13, Exhibit 1046; Churchill, *Grand Alliance*, pp. 178–79; *FRUS 1941*, v, 79–81.

33. *FRUS 1941*, iv, 48–49; *FRUS 1941*, v, 84–86, 96–99. The press, learning of this, took it as an offer to mediate in Europe, but Shigemitsu, when he saw Churchill on the 24th, denied that his country had any such intention (Churchill, *Grand Alliance*, 179–80; IMTFE Record, pp. 9818–32, Exhibits 1048–49, 1051).

34. *FRUS 1941*, v, 101, 106n.

35. Jones, *New Order*, pp. 250–52.

36. Langer and Gleason, *Undeclared War*, pp. 329–30.

37. Churchill, *Grand Alliance*, p. 179; *FRUS 1941*, v, 83; see also pp. 103–5.

38. Chauvel, the Vichy Foreign Minister, had also warned the United States of a Japanese move of this sort (*FRUS 1941*, v, 65).

39. *FRUS 1941*, iv, 912–13; Sir Llewellyn Woodward, *British Foreign Policy in the Second World War* (London, 1962), pp. 171–72. This volume is part of the official history of the war.

40. *FRUS 1941*, iv, 143–45. For the German efforts to have Japan attack Singapore, see Presseisen, *Germany and Japan*, pp. 283–92; the records of Matsuoka's conversations with the Germans may be found in *Nazi-Soviet Relations*, pp. 281–316, and *DGFP*, xii, No. 218, No. 222, No. 230, No. 233, No. 278. Singapore was an important subject in all these talks, but while Matsuoka made no secret of his own pro-German sympathies, he refused to be drawn into making any promises in the name of his government.

41. Churchill, *Grand Alliance*, pp. 189–90.

42. Because of his relations with the Japanese embassy Cripps was still unable to see Matsuoka officially, and accordingly the American ambassador engineered a 'casual' meeting between the two at the Moscow Art Theatre. Cripps gave Matsuoka the Churchill memorandum, and in return received the promise that Japan had no hostile intentions against British possessions (*FRUS 1941*, iv, 938–41, 967–68).

43. *FRUS 1941*, iv, 210–12, 234; Medlicott, *Economic Blockade*, ii, 99–100, 105; Woodward, *British Foreign Policy*, pp. 172–73.

44. Jones, *New Order*, pp. 263–64; Woodward, *British Diplomacy*, p. 174; *FRUS 1941*, v, 213–14. Matsuoka's ouster was due not only to his procrastination in the American negotiations, but also to his advocacy of a Japanese attack on Russia after Hitler's invasion of that country; both of these positions combined to isolate him more and more from his colleagues in the cabinet. See the Konoye Memoirs, IMT 3, IPS Doc. No. 570, pp. 230–50, Jap. Archives, Reel WT 6.

45. Avon, *Reckoning*, p. 361.

46. *FRUS 1941*, I, 345–54, 356–63; Churchill, *Grand Alliance*, pp. 439–40.

47. Churchill, *Grand Alliance*, p. 446.

48. Woodward, *British Foreign Policy*, pp. 175–76; for the American discussions on the warning, see *FRUS 1941*, IV, 370–76.

49. *Manchester Guardian*, 25 Aug.

50. *FRUS 1941*, IV, 563–64, 585–86; *Pearl Harbor Attack*, Part 12, pp. 91, 117–19; Grew, Diary, 5 Nov. 1941, pp. 5946–48; Woodward, *British Foreign Policy*, p. 178.

51. Jones, *New Order*, pp. 301–2; Churchill, *Grand Alliance*, p. 590.

52. Churchill, *Grand Alliance*, pp. 591–92.

53. *Ibid.*, p. 595.

54. *FRUS 1941*, IV, 642–47, 650–51, 654–56, 666–67; Churchill, *Grand Alliance*, pp. 596–97; Woodward, *British Foreign Policy*, pp. 179–84.

55. *FRUS Japan*, II, 766–80.

56. *Pearl Harbor Attack*, Part 2, p. 494; Part 3, p. 1341; *FRUS 1941*, V, 372.

CHAPTER XV

1. Winston S. Churchill, *India: Speeches and an Introduction* (London, 1931), p. 94.

2. Woodward, *British Foreign Policy*, p. 189n.

3. Churchill, *Grand Alliance*, pp. 606–8.

4. *Ibid.*, p. 597.

5. Hull, *Memoirs*, I, 533. Some of these conclusions have appeared in Nicholas R. Clifford, 'Britain, America, and the Far East, 1937–1940: a Failure in Cooperation', *Journal of British Studies*, III, no. 1 (November 1963), 137–54.

6. *FRUS 1937*, III, 792–94.

7. *Ibid.*, pp. 575–76.

8. *DBFP*, VIII, No. 99.

9. *FRUS 1938*, IV, 71–72.

10. *DBFP*, IX, No. 460; *FRUS 1939*, III, 564–68.

11. For an official expression of this view, see the *Tokyo Gazette*, No. 15 (September 1938), pp. 10–11.

12. As Sir Norman Angell and Lord Cecil (among others) did; *The Times*, 8 Oct., 13 Oct. 1937.

13. *The Times*, 31 Dec. 1937; the M.P. was Lieutenant-Commander Fletcher.

14. Feiling, *Neville Chamberlain*, p. 325, and v. *supra*, p. 33. Typical of one aspect of Hull's outlook was his complaint in September 1937 that foreign countries were

not paying enough attention to his statements of principle of 16 July and 23 August 1937. 'It is a pity', he wrote to the American minister in Bern, 'that other nations have not more generally realized how such public utterances and the public reiteration of these principles would strengthen the principle of validity of treaties and foster the growth of a world-wide determination to resolve differences by peaceful means only' (FRUS 1937, IV, 13–14).

Bibliography

A. OFFICIAL PUBLICATIONS

1. *Official Documents*

China. The Maritime Customs. *The Trade of China*. Shanghai, annual, 1936–1941.

China. Ministry of Information. *China Handbook, 1937–1945: A Comprehensive Survey of Major Developments in China in Eight Years of War. Revised and Enlarged with 1946 Supplement.* New York: Macmillan, 1947.

Great Britain. Accounts and Papers.
Session 1936–1937, vol. XII. *Imperial Conference, 1937. Summary of Proceedings.* Cmd. 5482.
Session 1938–1939, vol. XVI. *Chinese Currency, Arrangements proposed in regard to the Chinese Currency Stabilization Fund.* Cmd. 5963.
Session 1939–1940, vol. XII. *Japan No. 1 (1940). Correspondence between His Majesty's Government in the United Kingdom and the Japanese Government regarding the Removal of German Citizens from the Japanese Ship 'Asama Maru'. January–February 1940.* Cmd. 6166.
Session 1939–1940, vol. XII. *Thailand No. 1 (1940). Treaty of Non-Aggression between His Majesty in respect of the United Kingdom and the King of Thailand (12 June 1940).* Cmd. 6211.
Session 1939–1940, vol. XII. *China No. 1 (1940). Arrangement between His Majesty's Government in the United Kingdom and the Japanese Government relating to Local Issues at Tientsin. June 19, 1940.* Cmd. 6212.
Parliamentary Debates, House of Commons, Official Report, Fifth Series. 1936–1941.
Parliamentary Debates, House of Lords, Official Report, Fifth Series. 1936–1941.
Trade and Navigation Accounts, 1936–1941.

Great Britain. Admiralty. *Navy List*. London, annual, 1936–1941.

Great Britain. Board of Trade. *Accounts Relating to the Import Trade and the Re-export Trade of the United Kingdom for each of the Years 1938–1944.* London, no date.

Great Britain. Department of Overseas Trade. *Report on Economic and Commercial Conditions in China, April 1935–March 1937.* London, 1937.

Great Britain. Foreign Office. *Foreign Office List and Diplomatic and Consular Yearbook.* London, annual, 1931–1941.
Documents on British Foreign Policy, 1919–1939. Second Series, ed. Rohan Butler and J. P. T. Bury. Vols. VIII–IX. London, 1960–1965.

Documents on British Foreign Policy, 1919–1939. Third Series, ed. E. L. Woodward and Rohan Butler. Vols. I–IX. London, 1949–1955.

Italy. Ministero degli Affari Esteri. *I Documenti Diplomatici Italiani*, Ottava Serie (1935–1939), ed. Mario Toscano. Vols. XII–XIII. Rome, 1952–1953.
I Documenti Diplomatici Italiani, Nona Serie (1939–1943), ed. Mario Toscano. Vols. II–III. Rome, 1957–1959.

Japan. Cabinet Information Bureau. *Tokyo Gazette.* Tokyo, monthly, 1937–1941.

League of Nations. *Official Journal.* Geneva, 1937–1939.

Shanghai. Municipal Council. *Annual Report and Budget.* Shanghai, 1937–1941.

United States. Congress. *Hearings before the Joint Committee on the Investigation of the Pearl Harbor Attack.* 79th Congress, 1st Session. 39 parts. Washington, 1946.

United States. Department of State. *The Conference of Brussels, November 3–24, 1937.* Washington, 1938.
Documents on German Foreign Policy, 1918–1945. Series D (1937–1945). Vols. I, IV–XIII. Washington, 1949–1964.
Foreign Relations of the United States, Diplomatic Papers. 1935–1941. Washington, 1952–1958.
Nazi-Soviet Relations, 1939–1941. Documents from the Archives of the German Foreign Ministry, ed. R. J. Sontag and J. S. Beddie. Washington, 1948.
Papers Relating to the Foreign Relations of the United States, Japan: 1931–1941. 2 vols. Washington, 1943.

2. *Official Histories*

Brooke-Popham, Robert. 'Operations in the Far East from 17 October, 1940–27 December, 1941.' Supplement to the *London Gazette*, 20 January 1948, 535–76.

Butler, J. R. M. *Grand Strategy*, vol. II: *September, 1939–June, 1941.* London, 1957. *History of the Second World War, U.K. Military Series*, ed. J. R. M. Butler.

Gill, G. Hermon. *Royal Australian Navy, 1939–1942.* Canberra, 1957. *Australia in the War of 1939–1945, Series 2: Navy:* vol. I.

Hasluck, Paul. *The Government and the People, 1939–1941.* Canberra, 1952. *Australia in the War of 1939–1945, Series 4: Civil:* vol. I.

Kirby, S. Woodburn, et al. *The War Against Japan*, vol. I: *The Loss of Singapore.* London, 1957. *History of the Second World War, U.K. Military Series*, ed. J. R. M. Butler.

Maltby, C. M. 'Operations in Hongkong from 8–25 December, 1941.' Supplement to the *London Gazette*, 27 January 1948, 699–725.

Maltby, Paul. 'Report on the Air Operations During the Campaigns in Malaya and the Netherlands East Indies from 8th December 1941 to 12th March 1942.' Supplement to the *London Gazette*, 20 February 1948, 1347–1415.

Medlicott, W. N. *The Economic Blockade*. 2 vols. London, 1952, 1959. *History of the Second World War, U.K. Civil Series*, ed. W. K. Hancock.

Morison, Samuel Eliot. *History of United States Naval Operations in World War II*. Vol. I *The Battle of the Atlantic, September 1939 to May, 1943*. Boston: Little, Brown, 1947. Vol. III. *The Rising Sun in the Pacific, 1931 to April, 1942*. Boston: Little, Brown, 1948.

Percival, A. E., 'Operations of Malaya Command from 8th December 1941 to 15th February 1942.' Supplement to the *London Gazette*, 20 February 1948, 1245–1346.

Roskill, S. W. *The War at Sea, 1939–1945*, vol. I: *The Defensive*, London, 1954. *History of the Second World War, U.K. Military Series*, ed. J. R. M. Butler.

Watson, Mark Skinner. *Chief of Staff: Prewar Plans and Preparations*. Washington, 1950. *The United States Army in World War II: The War Department*.

Wigmore, Lionel. *The Japanese Thrust*. Canberra, 1957. *Australia in the War of 1939–1945*, Series I: *Army*, vol. IV.

Wood, F. L. W. *The New Zealand People at War: Political and External Affairs*. Wellington, 1958. *Official History of New Zealand in the Second World War, 1939–1945*.

Woodward, Llewellyn. *British Foreign Policy in the Second World War*. London, 1962.

B. PUBLISHED WORKS

1. *Books*

Ahlers, John. *Japan Closing the 'Open Door' in China*. Shanghai: Kelly and Walsh 1940.

Angell, Norman, *The Defence of the Empire*. New York: Appleton, 1937.

Auden, W. H. and Isherwood, Christopher. *Journey to a War*. New York: Random House, 1939.

Avon, Earl of (Anthony Eden). *The Memoirs of Anthony Eden, Earl of Avon: Facing the Dictators, 1923–1938*. London: Cassell; Boston: Houghton, Mifflin, 1962.

—— *The Memoirs of Anthony Eden, Earl of Avon: The Reckoning*. London: Cassell; Boston: Houghton, Mifflin, 1965.

Barnett, Robert W. *Economic Shanghai: Hostage to Politics, 1937–1941*. New York: International Secretariat, Institute of Pacific Relations, 1941.

Bassett, Reginald. *Democracy and Foreign Policy: A Case History, the Sino-Japanese Dispute, 1931–1933*. London: Longmans, 1952.

Bertram, James. *First Act in China: The Story of the Sian Mutiny*. New York: Viking, 1938.

Bertram James. *Unconquered: Journal of a Year's Adventures Among the Fighting Peasants of North China.* New York: John Day, 1939.

Birkenhead, Earl of. *Halifax: The Life of Lord Halifax.* London: Hamish Hamilton, 1965.

Bloch, Kurt. *German Interests and Policies in the Far East.* New York: International Secretariat, Institute of Pacific Relations, 1940.

Blum, John M. *From the Morgenthau Diaries: Years of Crisis, 1928-1938.* Boston: Houghton, Mifflin, 1959.

Borg, Dorothy. *The United States and the Far Eastern Crisis of 1933-1938.* Cambridge, Mass: Harvard University Press, 1964.

Borton, Hugh. *Japan's Modern Century.* New York: Ronald, 1955.

Butler, J. R. M. *Lord Lothian.* London: Macmillan, 1960.

Butow, Robert J. C. *Tojo and the Coming of the War.* Princeton: Princeton University Press, 1961.

Byas, Hugh. *Government by Assassination.* New York: Knopf, 1942.

Carter, Gwendolen. *The British Commonwealth and International Security: The Role of the Dominions, 1919-1939.* Toronto: Ryerson, 1947.

Casey, Lord (Richard Casey). *Personal Experience: 1939-1946.* New York: McKay, 1962.

Chang Chung-fu. *The Anglo-Japanese Alliance.* Baltimore: Johns Hopkins University Press, 1931.

Chang Kia-ngau. *China's Struggle for Railway Development.* New York: John Day, 1943.

—— *The Inflationary Spiral: The Experience in China, 1939-1950.* Cambridge, Mass: Technology Press, 1958.

Chou Shun-hsin. *The Chinese Inflation, 1937-1949.* New York: Columbia University Press, 1963.

Churchill, Winston S. *The Second World War.*

—— *The Gathering Storm.* London: Cassell; Boston: Houghton, Mifflin, 1948.

—— *Their Finest Hour.* London: Cassell; Boston: Houghton, Mifflin, 1949.

—— *The Grand Alliance.* London: Cassell; Boston: Houghton, Mifflin, 1950.

Cooper, Alfred Duff. *Old Men Forget: The Autobiography of Duff Cooper.* London: Hart-Davis, 1953.

Craig, Gordon A., and Gilbert, Felix, eds. *The Diplomats, 1919-1939.* Princeton: Princeton University Press, 1953.

Craigie, Robert L. *Behind the Japanese Mask.* London: Hutchinson, 1946.

Crosby, Josiah. *Siam: The Crossroads.* London: Hollis and Carter, 1945.

Dallin, David J. *Soviet Russia and the Far East.* New Haven: Yale University Press, 1948.

Dalton, Hugh. *The Fateful Years: Memoirs, 1931–1945.* London: Muller, 1957.

Decoux, Jean. *A la Barre de l'Indochine: Histoire de mon Gouvernement-Général, 1940–1945.* Paris: Plon, 1949.

Dirksen, Herbert von. *Moscow, Tokyo, London.* Norman: Oklahoma University Press, 1952.

Eden, Anthony. See Avon.

Etherton, P. T. and Tiltman, H. Hessell. *Japan: Mistress of the Pacific?* 2nd edn. London: Jarrolds, 1934.

Feiling, Keith. *The Life of Neville Chamberlain.* London: Macmillan, 1946.

Feis, Herbert. *The Road to Pearl Harbor: The Coming of the War Between the United States and Japan.* Princeton: Princeton University Press, 1950.

Fitzgerald, C. P. *Revolution in China.* New York: Praeger, 1952.

Friedman, Irving S. *British Relations with China, 1931–1939.* New York: International Secretariat, Institute of Pacific Relations, 1940.

Grenfell, Russell. *Main Fleet to Singapore.* London: Faber and Faber, 1951.

Grew, Joseph C. *Ten Years in Japan.* New York: Simon and Schuster, 1941.

Gull, E. M. *British Economic Interests in the Far East.* New York: International Secretariat, Institute of Pacific Relations, 1943.

Halifax, Earl of. *The American Speeches of the Earl of Halifax.* New York: Oxford University Press, 1947.

—— *The Fulness of Days.* London: Collins, 1957.

Harcourt-Smith, Simon. *Japanese Frenzy.* London: Hamish Hamilton, 1942.

Hodson, H. V., ed. *The British Commonwealth and the Future: Proceedings of the Second Unofficial Conference on British Commonwealth Relations, Sydney, 3rd to 17th September, 1938.* London: Oxford University Press, 1939.

Holland, William L., and Mitchell, Kate, eds. *Problems of the Pacific, 1936. Proceedings of the Sixth Conference of the Institute of Pacific Relations . . . 15–29 August, 1936.* Chicago: Chicago University Press, no date.

—— *Problems of the Pacific, 1939. Proceedings of the Study Meeting of the Institute of Pacific Relations . . . November 18–December 2, 1939.* New York: Institute of Pacific Relations, 1940.

Hsia Chin-lin. *British Far Eastern Policy, 1937–1940.* Chungking: China Information Publishing Co., 1940.

Hubbard, G. E. *British Far Eastern Policy.* New York: International Secretariat, Institute of Pacific Relations, 1943.

Hull, Cordell. *The Memoirs of Cordell Hull.* 2 vols. New York: Macmillan, 1948.

Iklé, Frank. *German Japanese Relations, 1936–1940.* New York: Bookman, 1956.

Ishimaru Tota. *Japan Must Fight Britain*, trans. G. V. Rayment. New York: Telegraph Press, 1936.

Japan in East Asia. 'Printed for Private Distribution.' Bristol: Western Printing Services, 1939.

Jones, F. C. *Japan's New Order in East Asia: Its Rise and Fall.* London: Oxford University Press, 1954.

—— *Manchuria since 1939.* London: Oxford University Press, 1949.

—— *Shanghai and Tientsin, with Special Reference to Foreign Interests.* London: Oxford University Press, 1940.

Kawakami, Kiyoshi Karl. *Japan in China: Her Motives and Aims.* London: John Murray, 1938.

Knatchbull-Hugessen, Hughe. *Diplomat in Peace and War.* London: John Murray, 1949.

Langer, William L. and Gleason, S. Everett. *The Challenge to Isolation, 1937–1940.* New York: Harper, 1952.

—— *The Undeclared War, 1940–1941.* New York: Harper, 1953.

Levi, Werner. *Modern China's Foreign Policy.* Minneapolis: University of Minnesota Press, 1953.

Levy, Roger, Lacam, Guy, and Roth, Andrew. *French Interests and Policies in the Far East.* New York: International Secretariat, Institute of Pacific Relations, 1941.

Liu, F. F. *A Military History of Modern China, 1924–1949.* Princeton: Princeton University Press, 1956.

Lu, David J. *From the Marco Polo Bridge to Pearl Harbor: Japan's Entry into World War II.* Washington: Public Affairs Press, 1961.

Mansergh, Nicholas. *Survey of British Commonwealth Affairs: Problems of External Policy, 1931–1939.* London: Oxford University Press, 1952.

Miller, Eugene H. *Strategy at Singapore.* New York: Macmillan, 1942.

Moffat, Jay Pierrepont. *The Moffat Papers: Selections from the Diplomatic Journals of Jay Pierrepont Moffat,* ed. Nancy H. Hooker. Cambridge, Mass: Harvard University Press, 1956.

Mook, Hubertus J. van. *The Netherlands East Indies and Japan: Battle on Paper, 1940–1941.* New York: Norton, 1944.

Mowat, Charles L. *Britain Between the Wars, 1918–1940.* London: Methuen, 1955.

Murphey, Rhoads. *Shanghai: Key to Modern China.* Cambridge, Mass: Harvard University Press, 1953.

Percival, A. E. *The War in Malaya.* London: Eyre, 1949.

Piggott, F. S. G. *Broken Thread: An Autobiography.* Aldershot: Gale and Polden, 1950.

Pratt, John T. *War and Politics in China.* London: Jonathan Cape, 1943.

Pratt, Julius M. *Cordell Hull, 1933-1944*. New York: Cooper Square, 1964.

Presseisen, Ernst L. *Germany and Japan: A Study in Totalitarian Diplomacy, 1933-1941*. The Hague: Martinus Nijhoff, 1958.

Quigley, Harold. *Far Eastern War, 1937-1941*. Boston: World Peace Foundation, 1942.

Rappaport, Armin. *Henry L. Stimson and Japan*. Chicago: University of Chicago Press, 1963.

Remer, C. F. *Foreign Investments in China*. New York: Macmillan, 1933.

Reynolds, Philip A. *British Foreign Policy in the Inter-war Years*. London: Longmans, 1954.

Rosinger, Lawrence K. *China's Wartime Politics, 1937-1944*. Princeton: Princeton University Press, 1944.

Rowse, A. L. *Appeasement*. New York: Norton, 1961.

Royal Institute of International Affairs. *Documents on International Affairs, 1931-1938*. ed. J. W. Wheeler-Bennett, S. Heald and M. Curtis. London: Oxford University Press, 1932-1942.

—— *Political and Strategic Interests of the United Kingdom*. London: Oxford University Press, 1939.

—— *Survey of International Affairs, 1931-1938*, ed. A. J. Toynbee and V. M. Boulter. London: Oxford University Press, 1932-1941.

—— *Survey of International Affairs, 1939-1946: The World in March 1939*, ed. A. J. Toynbee and F. T. Ashton-Gwatkin. London: Oxford University Press, 1952.

—— *Survey of International Affairs, 1939-1946: The Eve of the War*, ed. A. J. and V. M. Toynbee. London: Oxford University Press, 1958.

—— *Survey of International Affairs, 1939-1946: The Initial Triumph of the Axis*, ed. A. J. and V. M. Toynbee. London: Oxford University Press, 1958.

Sherwood, Robert E. *Roosevelt and Hopkins: An Intimate History*. New York: Harper, 1948.

Shigemitsu Mamoru. *Japan and Her Destiny: My Struggle for Peace*, ed. F. S. G. Piggott, and trans. O. White. London: Hutchinson, 1958.

Simon, Viscount (Sir John Simon). *Retrospect: The Memoirs of the Rt. Hon. Viscount Simon*. London: Hutchinson, 1958.

Smith, Sara. *The Manchurian Crisis*. New York: Columbia University Press, 1948.

Stimson, H. *The Far Eastern Crisis*. New York: Harper, 1936.

Storry, Richard. *The Double Patriots: A Study in Japanese Nationalism*. Boston: Houghton, Mifflin, 1957.

Strabolgi, Baron (Joseph Montague Kensworthy). *Singapore and After: A Study of the Pacific Campaign*. London: Hutchinson, 1942.

Tamagna, Frank. *Banking and Finance in China.* New York: International Secretariat, Institute of Pacific Relations, 1942.

—— *Italy's Interests and Policies in the Far East.* New York: International Secretariat, Institute of Pacific Relations, 1941.

Taylor, A. J. P. *The Origins of the Second World War.* London: Hamish Hamilton, 1961.

Taylor, George E. *The Struggle for North China.* New York: International Secretariat, Institute of Pacific Relations, 1940.

Teichman, Eric. *Affairs of China: A Survey of Recent History and Present Circumstances in the Republic of China.* London: Methuen, 1938.

Templewood, Viscount (Sir Samuel Hoare). *Nine Troubled Years.* London: Collins, 1954.

Thomas, A. F. *I Speak for Japan.* Tokyo (?), 1938 (?).

Thornton, A. P. *The Imperial Idea and its Enemies: A Study in British Power.* London: Macmillan, 1963.

Toynbee, Arnold J., ed. *British Commonwealth Relations: Proceedings of the First Unofficial Conference at Toronto, 11–21 September, 1933.* London: Oxford University Press, 1934.

Tsien Tai. *China and the Nine Power Conference at Brussels in 1937.* New York: St. John's University Press, 1964.

Ugaki Kazushige. *Ugaki Nikki (Ugaki Diary).* Tokyo, 1954.

Utley, Freda. *China at War.* London: Faber and Faber, 1939.

—— *Japan's Feet of Clay.* London: Faber and Faber, 1936.

—— *Japan's Gamble in China.* London: Secker and Warburg, 1938.

Walters, F. P. *A History of the League of Nations.* 2 vols. London: Oxford University Press, 1952.

Wei, Henry. *China and Soviet Russia.* Princeton: Van Nostrand, 1956.

Welles, Sumner. *The Time for Decision.* New York: Harper, 1944.

Wohlstetter, Roberta. *Pearl Harbor: Warning and Decision.* Stanford: Stanford University Press, 1962.

Wu, Aitchen K. *China and the Soviet Union: A Study of Sino-Soviet Relations.* London: John Day, 1950.

Yanaga Chitoshi. *Japan Since Perry.* New York: McGraw, 1949.

Yoshida Shigeru. *The Yoshida Memoirs: The Story of Japan in Crisis,* trans. K. Yoshida. Boston: Houghton, Mifflin, 1962.

Young, Arthur N. *China and the Helping Hand, 1937–1945.* Cambridge, Mass: Harvard University Press, 1963.

—— *China's Wartime Finance and Inflation, 1937–1945*. Cambridge, Mass: Harvard University Press, 1965.

2. *Articles*

'Anglo-Japanese Relations', *Round Table*, XXIX (1939), 676–88.

Arima Seiho. 'The Anglo-American Naval Program', *Contemporary Japan*, VII (1938), 58–67.

Barrett, R. T. 'British Responsibilities in South China', *Asiatic Review*, XXIV (1938), 147–56.

Boorman, Harold L. 'Wang Ching-wei: China's Romantic Radical', *Political Science Quarterly*, LXXIX (1964), 504–25.

'British Shipping in the Orient', *Round Table*, XXIX (1939), 531–46.

Bryan, J. Ingram. 'Japan's Foreign Policy', *Empire Review and Magazine*, LXV (1937), 301–8.

Bywater, Hector C. 'Britain on the Seas', *Foreign Affairs*, XVI (1938), 210–21.

Ch.-Walden, E. A. 'The Sino-Japanese War and the Open Door', *International Affairs* (London), XVI (1938), 629–54.

Chamberlain, William H. 'Naval Bases in the Pacific', *Foreign Affairs*, XII (1937) 484–94.

Clifford, Nicholas R. 'Britain, America and the Far East, 1937–1940: A Failure in Cooperation', *Journal of British Studies*, III (1963), 137–54.

—— 'Sir Frederick Maze and the Chinese Maritime Customs, 1937–1941', *Journal of Modern History*, XXXVII (1965), 18–34.

Crowley, James B. 'A Reconsideration of the Marco Polo Bridge Incident', *Journal of Asian Studies*, XXII (1963), 277–91.

Esthus, Raymond A. 'President Roosevelt's Commitment to Britain to Intervene in a Pacific War', *Mississippi Valley Historical Review*, L (1963), 28–38.

'The Future in China', *Round Table*, XXIX (1939), 309–22.

Green, O. M. 'An Anglo-Japanese Entente?' *Empire Review and Magazine*, LXV (1937), 365–69.

—— 'Great Britain's Chance in the Far East', *Empire Review and Magazine*, LXV (1937), 12–18.

Hauser, E. O. 'The Challenge to British Sea Routes', *Amerasia*, I (1937), 215–18.

—— 'Singapore, an American Problem', *Atlantic Monthly* CLXVII (1941), 133–38.

Inouye, Viscount. 'Anglo-Japanese Relations', *Empire Review and Magazine*, LXVI (1937), 90–95.

'Japan's Challenge to the West', *Round Table*, XXVIII (1938), 230–45.

'Japan's New Order', *Round Table*, XXXII (1941), 65–81.

Jaffe, Philip J. 'Britain and the Far East', *Amerasia*, I (1937), 183–86.

Kawakami, Kiyoshi K. 'Japan at Shanghai', *Empire Review and Magazine*, LXVI (1937), 342–47.

Kennedy, Malcolm D. 'The Future of Anglo-Japanese Relations', *Asiatic Review*, XXXV (1939), 777–85.

Kerr, Mark. 'Japan, China and the Far East', *Empire Review and Magazine*, LXV (1937), 85–89.

Kindersley, R. 'British Overseas Investments in 1935 and 1936', *Economic Journal*, XLVII (1937), 642–62.

—— 'British Overseas Investments, 1937', *Economic Journal*, XLVIII (1938), 609–34.

Martin, James V. 'Thai-American Relations in World War II', *Journal of Asian Studies*, XXII (1963), 451–67.

Masatake Okumiya. 'How the Panay was Sunk', *United States Naval Institute Proceedings*, XLIX (1953), 587–96.

Matsuoka Yosuke. 'The New Order in East Asia', *Contemporary Japan*, VIII (1939), 1–9.

Mitchell, Kate. 'Revitalizing British Interests in China', *Far Eastern Survey*, VI (1937), 139–45.

Onishi Hauki. 'Anglo-Japanese Relations and China, II. Japan Expects . . . !' *Contemporary Japan*, VII (1938), 402–13.

Paauw, Douglas S. 'Chinese National Expenditure during the Nanking Period', *Far Eastern Quarterly*, XII (1952), 3–26.

—— 'The Kuomintang and Economic Stagnation, 1928–1937', *Journal of Asian Studies*, XVI (1957), 213–20.

Pratt, John T. 'America, Britain and China', *Contemporary Review*, CLVIII (1940), 47–55.

'Sea Power in the Eastern War', *Brassey's Naval Annual*, 1942, 150–60.

Shibata Yuji. 'Britain's Choice: Japan or Red China', *Contemporary Japan*, VI (1937), 454–63.

Smallwood, H. St. Clair. 'Japan and Aggression', *Empire Review and Magazine*, LXVI (1937), 286–90.

—— 'Japan's International Relations', *Empire Review and Magazine*, LXV (1937), 218–22.

'Smoke and Fire Ruin the Far East', *Round Table*, XXVII (1937), 725–39.

Storry, Richard. 'Konoye Fumimaro, the Last of the Fujiwara', *St Antony's Papers, No. VII: Far Eastern Affairs, No. II*, ed. G. F. Hudson. London: Oxford University Press, 1960, 9–33.

Stöve, G. W. 'Queen's Navy at War', *United States Naval Institute Proceedings*, LXXVI (1950), 289–301.

Ugaki Kazushige. 'Sino-Japanese Peace Talks, June–September, 1938', trans. E. H. M. Colegrave, *St Antony's Papers, No. II: Far Eastern Affairs, No. I,* ed. G. F. Hudson. London: Oxford University Press, 1957, 94–104.

Wheeler, Gerald E. 'Isolated Japan: Anglo-American Diplomatic Cooperation, 1927–1936', *Pacific Historical Review,* xxx (1961), 163–78.

Wilds, Thomas. 'How the Japanese Fortified the Mandated Islands', *United States Naval Institute Proceedings,* LI (1955), 401–7.

Woodhead, H. G. W. 'Anglo-Japanese Relations and China, I. England Expects.. !' *Contemporary Japan,* VII (1938), 395–402.

—— 'Sino-Japanese Hostilities: A Frank British Opinion', *Contemporary Japan,* VI (1937), 411–18.

3. *Periodicals and Reports*

British Chamber of Commerce, Shanghai. *Journal.* 1936–1941. Monthly.

China Association, London. *Annual Report.* 1937–1941.

Daily Herald. 1938–1941.

The Economist. 1936–1941.

Finance and Commerce. 1937–1941.

Japan Weekly Chronicle. 1937–1941.

Manchester Guardian. 1937–1941.

New Statesman and Nation. 1937–1941.

New York Times. 1937–1941.

North China Herald. 1936–1941.

Oriental Affairs. 1936–1941.

The Spectator. 1937–1941.

The Times. 1937–1941.

Time and Tide. 1937–1941.

C. UNPUBLISHED SOURCES

Donnithorne, A. G. 'Economic Developments Since 1937 in Eastern and South-eastern Asia and their Effects on the United Kingdom.' Mimeographed; prepared for the 11th Conference of the Institute of Pacific Relations, Lucknow, 1950.

Grew, Joseph C. Papers, 1937–1941, Houghton Library, Harvard University.

International Military Tribunal, Far East. Records of Proceedings. Mimeographed, Tokyo, 1946–1948.

Moffat, Jay Pierrepont. Papers, 1937–1938, Houghton Library, Harvard University.

Japan. Archives of the Ministry of Foreign Affairs, Library of Congress (microfilm). (English sections used.)

   IMT 1. Analysis of Documentary Evidence. Reel WT 5.

   IMT 2. Kido Diary. Reel WT 5.

   IMT 3. Konoye Memoirs. Reel Wt 6.

   IMT 74. Summary of Outstanding Anglo-Japanese Cases in China. Reel WT 19.

   IMT 75. Interchange between the Ministry of Foreign Affairs and the British Government . . . February 7–April 25, 1941. Reel WT 19.

   IMT 261. Negotiations between Japan and Great Britain, 1940–1941. Reels WT 37–38.

   IMT 350. Outline of Guiding Principles for the Central Political Conference . . . November 1, 1939. Reel WT 46.

   IMT 417. Documents relating to Great Britain from 1940 to the outbreak of World War II. Reel WT 55.

   IMT 429. Documents Relating to Great Britain . . . November 1940–August 1941. Reel WT 56.

   IMT 459. Telegrams . . . concerning the Tientsin Incident, 1939–1940. Reels 59–60.

Kim, Chonghan. 'Konoye Fumimaro and Japanese Foreign Policy: 1937–1941.' Unpub. Ph.D. dissertation, 1956, Indiana University. University Microfilms, Ann Arbor, Michigan., pub. no. 17,964.

Kittredge, Tracy S. 'United States-British Naval Cooperation, 1939–1942,' MS in the custody of the Director of Naval History, Washington, D.C.

Maze, Frederick. Papers, 1931–1941, Library of the School of Oriental and African Studies, London University.

Tai Erh-ching. 'British Opinion of the Sino-Japanese War, 1937–1941.' Unpub. Ph.D. dissertation, 1952, London University.

Index

Peking: British predominance, 5; British troops, 14, 134; Legation Quarter, 16; name changed, 53; Chinese silver in, 61–2, 75
Peking and Tientsin Times, 115
Peking–Mukden Railway, 63
Peking Provisional Government: established, 53; economic policies, 58, 75, 102; and Customs, 58; other puppets, 86; foreign views on, 113–14; Foreign Minister killed, 116. *See also* Puppet governments
Peking–Tientsin Silver Committee, 75
Phillips, G. Godfrey, 148
Phillips, Sir Herbert, 72
Phillips, Adm. Sir Tom, 50, 148
Piggott, Gen. F. S. G., 116, 124, 127
Plymouth, Earl of, 39
Poland, 98, 129, 136
Popular Front, 3, 34
Prince of Wales, HMS, 148, 151
Pukow–Siangyang railway, 63
Puppet governments: before Lukouchiao, 8; in occupied China, 53, 86, 106, 134–5, 138–9; and Customs, 57–8, 105–6, 180; economic policies of, 61, 101–5; in Shanghai, 73, 148–9; foreign views on, 113–14. *See also* Wang Ching-wei; Peking Provisional Government; Nanking Reformed Government; Trade and Exchange Controls

Quarantine speech, 32–5 *passim*, 163
Quo Tai-chi, 18, 36, 59, 82, 96

Railways: loans, 10, 63, 82, 170; British investments in, 56, 62–3; Japanese occupation, 62–3
Rangoon, 101
Reprisals Order, 135
Repulse, HMS, 148
Ribbentrop, Joachim von, 28, 153
Roosevelt, Franklin D.: 'parallel' and 'joint' action, 19; quarantine speech, 32–3, 39, 163; U.S. isolationism, 35; Yangtse attacks, 49–50; approach to

Britain, 76–7; abrogation of Japanese treaty, 123–4; and Netherlands Indies, 141; and Churchill, 141, 155; and U.S.-Japanese talks, 152, 155, 156, 157
Rowse, A. L., 4
Rumania, 98
Russo-Japanese war, 5

Sanctions: and U.S.A., 26, 32–3, 49–50, 100–1, 123–4; pressure for, in Britain, 31–2, 67, 83, 120–1, 186; British consideration of, 34–5, 55, 77–8, 80–1, 93–5, 100–1, 128; and League, 36, 87; Brussels Conference, 38–43; Craigie's views, 50–1, 62, 84, 93–5, 121, Japanese views, 92–7; Chinese requests, 133; funds frozen, 154–5; possible effects on Japan, 166
Sansom, Sir George, 127–8
Sato Naotake, 11
Sawada Renzo, 102–3, 110, 134
Seeckt, Gen. Hans von, 8
Shanghai: fighting, 1932, 7–10; general situation, 15–16, 22–3, 68–9; British interests, 16, 69–70; outbreak of fighting, 22–6, 30, 173; defence plans, 25, 149; fall of, 26, 45, 69; economic effects of war, 30, 61, 63, 64, 69, 111; under occupation, 56, 70–4, 99, 107–11; and Customs, 60, 73, 106, 150; N. and E. districts, 69–70, 73, 103; terrorism in, 72, 74, 108, 109–11, 148–9; courts problem, 73–4, 85, 108, 109, 149; western extra-Settlement area, 73, 108–9, 111; British views on, 79; Craigie-Ugaki talks, 83–5; British troop withdrawal, 142, 149; in 1941, 148–50; Japanese enter, 157. *See also* Shanghai, Land Records: Shanghai Municipal Council; Shanghai Municipal Police; Shanghai Volunteer Corps
Shanghai–Hanchow–Ningpo railway, 63
Shanghai Inland Navigation Co., 64
Shanghai, Land Records, 69, 109, 110